the BINGE WATCHER'S guide to *The Golden Girls*

AN UNOFFICIAL COMPANION

Marissa DeAngelis

For more information contact:
Riverdale Avenue Books
5676 Riverdale Avenue
Riverdale, NY 10471.

www.riverdaleavebooks.com
Design by www.formatting4U.com
Cover by Scott Carpenter

Digital ISBN: 9781626016149

Trade Paperback ISBN: 9781626016156
First Edition, January 2022

Dedication

Though I wish I could have one of those one-word dedications, I do feel that I owe many people thanks for this book. I guess that since it's a *Golden Girls* book, it's fitting that I've been collecting Golden Girls my whole life — that is, groups of strong, supportive women to help and guide me through the world. So, this book is dedicated to:

- First, my mother, Camille, who is all the *Golden Girls* wrapped in one woman. Wise sage, voice of reason, sexy knockout, and earth mother. And my dad, Ernie, the best man in the world, who's been surrounded by *Golden Girls* his whole life and hasn't complained — much. I'm lucky to have these two as parents.
- My sisters. I'm the youngest of four daughters, so it's not a surprise that I was destined to visualize, and write about, women in groups of four. So, cheers to the fabulous Tracy, Liza, and Danielle.
- My twin Danielle, who should get a separate line in this dedication for all the hours of *Golden Girls* she watched and studied, knowing somehow, this day would come.
- My grandmothers, Mary and Theresa, the first real-life examples of women over 60 that were funny and strong, and tough as nails.
- My Aunt Marilyn. Oh, I can't tell you how supportive she's been during the 18 months of writing this book. I literally CANNOT write it in this book.
- My original *Golden-Girl* gang: Dani, Jolie, Adina, Lindsey, and Chelsey. You can fight over which *Golden Girl* you are, and which one of you is Stan.
- My Aunt Donna, who always gave me my favorite books to read when I was little and knew I was a writer before I did.
- Holly, my biggest fan, who always told me I was a genius, even when there was no indication at all. What would I do without you?

- Pamela Des Barres, my fairy godmother in LA and New York. Inspiring as a writer, and a friend, and after all, it was in your writing workshop that this opportunity came my way!
- Lori Perkins, my publisher, for making me an author, not just a writer!
- Gwynne, Roger, and Lori K., who housed me in Los Angeles, and gave me a place to write when I needed it the most. Thank you!
- My nieces and nephews: Luke, Sunny, Serena, Leo, and Vivi
- My summer-camp *Golden Girls*: Rachie and Jenny
- My text-therapy group: Buffy, Zina, Lauren, Faithe, and JoAnn
- Susan Harris, a true icon, feminist, everything. So underrated in my opinion, I wish she had written 1,000 more sitcoms.
- *The Golden Girls* themselves — Bea Arthur, Estelle Getty, Rue McClanahan, and Betty White. Amazing actresses and performers, who did not disappoint me when I learned what kind of women they were.

This book was written before and during the pandemic, and in that time, I moved across the country and had some strange adventures and life experiences, and learned some tough lessons, much like *The Golden Girls* themselves. I hope you, the reader, use this book as a handy guide to enjoy the show and gain some insights into why the show is relevant today.

Table of Contents

Introduction

"I had to write 'Golden Girls'... I've never gotten excited about a network idea before, but this was compelling. I could write grown-ups."
—Susan Harris, September 1985

I was eight years old in 1985—the kind of kid that was pretty open to watching anything on television. But when my 73-year old grandmother suggested *The Golden Girls*, I was most definitely *not* enthusiastic. A show about four old women living in Miami? There's hardly any difference between 50 and 80 when you're eight, but I had nothing better to do, so I watched.

And I was an immediate fan.

It was just funny. The jokes were relatable, even the jokes I didn't get. What seemed like *just* a show about women over 50 worked on so many other levels. It had heart, but wasn't overly sentimental. It was progressive, without being liberal. Actually, it was progressive while being hardly political at all.

I guess that's a big part of why, 30 years later, *The Golden Girls* is one of the most popular shows in syndication and available to stream. It's a comfort food. And per my television-watching expertise, it's one of the best shows to have on while sick—or perhaps during a pandemic. It's, of course, endlessly quotable and I'd say it compares nicely to *Steel Magnolias* in that regard. But it's more than that.

First of all, it must be said that my grandmother Mimi, who introduced me to the show, was 100% a Sophia. No quiz needed. She was a petite, red-headed Italian woman, who on a first impression seemed really sweet until she gave you a quick, Don Rickles-esque insult. Come to think about it, Estelle Getty might have stolen her act.

My other grandmother Nana was probably more of a Blanche. Though she was a New York City lady instead of a southern belle, she often wore hoop earrings and red lipstick well into her 70s, and had a love for Jack Nicholson and John Forsythe. Actually, there was a little Sophia in her as well, because you wouldn't want to mess with her. That's for sure.

My love for *The Golden Girls* became widely known amongst my friends over the years, and we often recited our favorite lines. And of course, which *Golden Girl* we were. Though it's common now to find similar quizzes online, as a kid it felt like a coming out event. It's no shocker that I identified as a Sophia, since I'm 4'9, Italian, with no filter and an endless supply of sarcastic remarks. At summer camp, I was disciplined more than a few times by the camp director for sneaking into the Main House to watch episodes. How I wish I could have told her, "Hey, listen, I'm writing a book!"

By 1995, when the show was on in syndication and I was in high school, I began feverishly taping episodes from the Lifetime network. This was hard work back then—and it sounds archaic—but I actually sat there, starting and stopping at the exact right time to make sure the commercials stayed out. This actually gave me a horrific, *Golden Girls*-related injury when trying to record. How many people can say that? My mother had called me downstairs for dinner, and as I turned around too quickly, my foot hit the wall. The toe popped right out of its socket, while I screamed and sobbed to my chocolate labrador, Bailey, who thought I was absolutely nuts. Few can say that they suffered for their love of *The Golden Girls*, but I assure you that this was one of my top three most painful childhood moments. My left foot turned more colors that night than Bea Arthur's entire *Golden Girls* wardrobe.

The Golden Girls was also the perfect vehicle to get my cousin Jolie, and friend Adina, drunk for the first time. I had them play a simple game of shots where each of us were assigned a *Golden Girl*, and each time that character's name was said, that person had to do a shot. I highly recommend this if you don't want to do something more complex, like a quiz, trivia game, or a more elaborate binge party. Jolie and Adina, by the way, were blitzed in about four episodes, but still showed up for work the next day. I did not. True story.

My love for the show persevered into college, and since I didn't have access to a DVR, I had to view episodes like a cavewoman—on VHS tapes, before I went to sleep. My roommates found this unnerving, until the nightly hypnosis worked, and they too became fans (thank you Bari, Kim, and Meg).

So, here I am now in 2022, and *The Golden Girls* is always on. In many ways, it's more popular than ever. But *why* is a popular question. And I guess there are a lot of reasons. Firstly, it was just plain funny. You know something is well written when an eight-year-old and 73-year-old can both watch it and laugh together. And often for different reasons. That's kind of how it is.

The Golden Girls ages with you because it's about so many inevitable life experiences: divorce, death, heartbreak, unemployment, aging, and friendships both good and bad. Your viewpoint on all of these issues may evolve through the decades, yet the show always has a smart, humorous perspective that gives you a fresh way to look at them.

A crucial part of the writing was that from the very first episode, all four women were complex, full characters with elaborate backstories. After a few episodes, you knew who they were as children and the worlds they grew up in. You couldn't put them in a box as just "the wise-old grandmother" as other shows often did with senior-aged actresses. They embodied their teenage selves, their married selves, and their childhood selves. They were still falling in love and starting careers. They found their children annoying. They had crushes on celebrities. They could be insecure and silly, and somehow, they were always trying new things. These characters didn't retreat into their old age—they were having fun. They were women fulfilling life goals.

If the term #squadgoals had been a thing back then, well, this show is your squad goal.

But still, why write a book? Why *read* a book? Reading is so last century. It takes a certain amount of ego to ask you to read my words. I'm not Donald Trump, who clearly had all the words and wisdom to write almost 20 books. This is my first. So why this book? Why now?

At this time in American history, with the #MeToo movement, political fragmentation at its worst, a recovery from a worldwide pandemic, and an international wave of genuine ennui, it feels like this is just a good time to laugh. And an even better time to watch a show that demonstrates a progressive life goal for older women, and young people, of all genders and sexualities. Maybe the life goal *isn't* marriage and children. Sure, *you can do that.* But how nice to think that no matter how that all turns out, you can have a post-age-of-50 end game of moving in with your friends in a warm city, dating, doing some charity work, and finding a career.

The Golden Girls represented a downsized fantasy life of sorts, where both joy and happiness were the true finish line, with all the former pressures left behind. They lived like college kids and dated like they were on *Friends*. They talked about dreams they still had to fulfill, indulged in hobbies, and slept around. They learned from their earlier mistakes. Relived and worked through earlier traumas. They were bullied. And sometimes they were bullies. They got stood up by men and stood up men in return. They acted like schoolgirls with crushes. I only wish I could see these women on dating apps now.

This is a show for any and every generation, from Millennials to Baby Boomers and everything in between.

What's the big deal though?

What I'd really love to point out to the readers of this book is how *The Golden Girls* portrayed progressive issues. This was a show with a genuinely forward-thinking perspective, that I couldn't fully appreciate at the time. It was easy to miss how radical all of it was behind the humor; it certainly flew over my head when I was a kid. When you're young, you think all the battles have been fought and won. I didn't think gay marriage was a big deal, or that showing middle-aged women dating and having sex was something being fought over in writing rooms. But it was. Susan Harris—the show's creator—had to defend story lines just because they were happening to women. At the time, middle-aged people on television were having all kinds of sex, *but they were men* (John Forsythe on *Dynasty* was in his 60s and no one blinked an eye).

I've perused a few books, a few websites, re-watched episodes that I had already watched at least 30 times, and the conclusion I've come to is that the brains behind this show were some real woke-peeps. And it goes beyond politics. Though the actresses fought for many liberal causes, Estelle Getty was actually a Republican. Betty White normally kept her political views private, but the show's voice was clear—gay rights, animal rights, and women's rights for equal pay and sexual freedoms were the *golden way*.

Also, this was a show that not only made you love and appreciate women, it made you look at older women a little differently. Most people enjoyed the show (and still do) because the actresses reminded them of their mothers, aunts, and grandmothers. And that's still the case. As for me… I like compelling writing, and I've adored this show for over 30 years. And if you haven't watched, or someone you know loves it, or you just want to delve a little deeper into this phenomenon, then enjoy my guide.

And thank you for being a friend.
Marissa DeAngelis
Winter 2022

The Zeitgeist

"They had each other... they didn't have to see themselves at a certain age, winding up lonely and alone. Being alone, you can create your own family."—Susan Harris

The idea for *The Golden Girls* came to creator, Susan Harris, from her husband Paul Junger Witt (who would become one of the powerhouse producers) who worked for NBC at the time. The original concept was that it would be a show about women in their 40's living in Miami, as they were eager to capitalize on *Miami Vice's* popularity. They wanted to call it *Miami Nice*.

Susan Harris was more than well-respected by then and her husband was part of the Witt/Thomas/Harris production company, so when Susan Harris decided to go ahead with the concept of *The Golden Girls,* NBC took it seriously. Harris had initially felt she was done with television after a remarkably successful run as a writer on *Maude,* and as the creator of the groundbreaking show *Soap*. But perhaps most notably, she wrote *Maude's* infamous abortion episode called *Maude's Dilemma*, which aired in 1972.

What pushed Harris to take on this new show was that the idea of creating something about older women appealed to her. Though, Harris was thinking older, maybe 60s and 70s. I suppose people take it for granted now, but this whole show was revolutionary in that there hadn't been a show that had four female leads of *any* age. A few months after Witt and Tony Thomas poked their head into one fateful NBC meeting, where the idea was being circulated, the pilot script from Susan Harris arrived, with four characters in mind:

Dorothy Zbornak: Recently divorced from a cheating husband of 38 years, Dorothy was a cynical, sarcastic New Yorker, and written mostly from Susan Harris's own voice. Dorothy was the brainiac, and the one who was often thought of as serious and no fun. The name Zbornak came from Susan's assistant, Kent Zbornak.

Rose Nylund: A widow from the insane, small town of St. Olaf, Minnesota, Rose was the ditz of the group. But she was more than that. She was naive, innocent, childlike, and often didn't get sarcasm, which was thrown at her often.

Blanche Devereaux: A hypersexual, Southern belle (though not Southern from the inception) from Georgia, Blanche was the owner of the house and also a widow. She was also the one most likely to be vain, overconfident, and shallow. Her sexual escapades became more and more notorious throughout the seasons.

Sophia Petrillo: An even-more blunt, sarcastic version of Dorothy, Sophia was Dorothy's own mother. Having escaped from a burning nursing home, she never leaves—mostly because she is so popular with audiences. She was also the wise-old sage who spiced up her advice with stories from Sicily, and sometimes Brooklyn.

The Golden Getty

Estelle Getty was first to be cast, as Harris and producers had thought the part of Sophia would be the most difficult. Initially, they had in mind a fat Italian mama with a bun. Boy, did things go the other way! Estelle Getty had been a virtual unknown at the time, with her biggest role having been as Harvey Fierstein's mother in the play, *Torch Song Trilogy*. Beyond that, she had just done little bits of TV and movie parts.

When Estelle auditioned for Sophia, it's said that she just nailed it. Even though she was asked to keep coming back for a month, what she didn't know was that she was the only one in contention. Paul Witt said to one of the producers, "Don't let her out of the room till you're satisfied, because she's the one." It was also Estelle who came up with the iconic straw, top-clasping purse. She had felt that Sophia needed a prop, and old ladies carry everything they own in their little bags.

(For more about Estelle Getty, check out her autobiography, *If I Knew Then What I Knew Now... So What?*)

The Golden Switcher-Rue

The casting of Betty White and Rue McClanahan is somewhat infamous as it involved a switcheroo, as they say. The pilot script was getting plenty of attention and it was obvious that it had tremendous potential. So, it was no surprise that they were looking at Hollywood heavyweight and TV darling, Betty White. She was already a familiar television face, known mostly as Sue Ann Nivens from *The Mary Tyler Moore Show,* but also guest-star stints on *All in the Family* and many other shows.

Rue McClanahan meanwhile had started blossoming as an actress in her late 30s, starting out as Vivian Harmon on *Maude*. She was still working on *Mama's Family* as Aunt Fran, where she was absolutely miserable playing a mousy character. She and Betty White were both excited about *The Golden Girls* script, but slightly reluctant about the parts they were given. According to McClanahan, she couldn't believe she was offered Rose, but went in anyway. Jay Sandrich, one of the directors, must have felt the same, because after Rue read, he had her switch parts saying, "I don't believe for one second you're innocent." This made Rue ecstatic.

But Betty on the other hand, was truly surprised. After the producers spoke with her, she really understood the character of Rose, and also, that perhaps the audience would be bored with her playing another nymphomaniac like Sue Ann Nivens. The way Jay explained the character to Betty was that Rose takes everything literally. No nuance.

(Read more about Betty White's iconic years on television, in just one of her autobiographies, *Here We Go Again: My Life in Television*)

(And for even more about Rue McClanahan, her autobiography is obviously named, *My First Five Husbands... and the Ones Who Got Away*)

The Last Piece of the Golden Puzzle

So, with one Girl left to go, the word around town was that the show was looking for a Bea Arthur-type. The producers initially didn't know that Harris had written it entirely with Bea Arthur in mind, but there were numerous problems with this. It didn't seem like Bea was interested, and it didn't seem like NBC was all that keen on casting her either. They were worried about some of the fallout from *Maude*'s controversial abortion episode, so they had Elaine Stritch audition, which went terribly. (Elaine Stritch admitted as much in her one-woman show, years later.)

So, they returned to what they called Plan A, which was trying again for Bea. According to Rue McClanahan, she called Bea Arthur and Bea was reluctant at the idea of doing a show where "Maude and Vivian meet Sue Ann Nivens." But when Rue explained that she and Betty had switched parts, Bea seemed to like this and came in. The rest as they say... is *Golden Girls* history.

Coco—The Lost *Golden Girl*

Many people forget that the *Golden Girls* pilot had included another character—a gay houseboy named Coco, played by Charles Levin. This character played well in the first episode, and the studio audience loved him, but after much deliberation from the powers that be, they ended up cutting the character, never to be mentioned again. There are different theories as to the decision, but most agree that there were just too many characters to fit in 23 minutes.

Also, as Paul Witt and Susan Harris pointed out, if the women had a houseboy and weren't doing their own housework, what would they be doing in their scenes? It would look rather privileged, and they wanted them to look relatable. Some people speculated that having an overtly gay character was problematic, but that wasn't the case. That could've been another reason to not include him, but not primarily. Ultimately, his scenes were eliminated from as many places as possible, and he was never referred to again, which is weird. Then again, plot points and characters are *often* never mentioned again.

Since its release, you can readily name all the sitcoms that took the outlined approach of four women of different, opposite backgrounds, that become friends. In fact, right after *The Golden Girls* aired, *Designing Women* started with four, Southern women, of a slightly younger demographic. The show *227*, about four black women, was also released at the same time, and in the decade following the template just seemed to work. Shows like *Living Single (1993)*, *Sex and the City*, (1998) and *Girlfriends (2000)* would continue the trend.

I often make the statement that *Sex and the City* is clearly the heir apparent to *The Golden Girls*, with Carrie's Manhattan brunch events replacing the Miami kitchen table in Blanche's house. Like Carrie, Bea is the level-headed lead character with the ex-boyfriend that keeps reemerging like Stan. Miranda, is perhaps, Sophia, the wise-old cynical sage. Charlotte, like Rose, is the naive, innocent one who believes in fairy tales. And Samantha is Blanche taken to the 10th level, about 10 years younger, and far raunchier. And on *Sex and The City*, the audience had front row seats to Samantha's sexual escapades. Of course, I'm not the first person to make this connection. At the TV Land Awards in 2004, Bea Arthur did a parody of *Sex and The City*, where she played Carrie.

Casting note from an expert

I asked Felicia Fasano, a real-life casting director—whose credits include *Better Things*, *Kevin Can Go F**K Himself*, and *Californication*—about the casting process, and she did confirm that: "The casting was brilliant. I think it has a lot to do with the script. It starts with the script. That draws the talent." I was also compelled to ask her how she would cast the show today, to which she replied: Rita Moreno (Sophia), Sharon Stone (Dorothy), Sally Field (Rose), and Jennifer Lewis (Blanche).

The reception

During the 1985 NBC upfronts, the screening of *The Golden Girls* got a standing ovation, then received a full order of 12 episodes. Twenty-five million people tuned in for the pilot episode, and *The Golden Girls* was in the Nielsen Top 10 for most of its seven seasons (six of the seven seasons to be exact).

The location

Blanche Devereaux's fictitious home address was 6151 Richmond Street in Miami, Florida, but the exterior shots of Season One were of a Brentwood, Los Angeles home at 245 North Saltair Avenue. In 2020, the house sold for four million dollars—you can view the outside of the house, but not the inside, as it's a private residence. When the show became successful, a replica of the house was created at MGM Studios Theme Park in Orlando, Florida. In 2003, the house was demolished. Like many sitcoms, the show was filmed on a soundstage at Ren Mar Studios, now Red Studios (846 N. Cahuenga Blvd in Los Angeles).

The costumes

Judy Evans, the costume designer, wanted the four women to have four, unique looks to reflect their personalities. According to Evans, "I wanted a sexy, soft, and flowing look for Rue, a tailored, pulled-together look for Bea, a down-home look for Betty, and comfort for Estelle." She also allowed the women to wear outfits that they generally favored. Bea Arthur liked loose-fitting clothing, like long sweaters, along with sandals, because she didn't enjoy wearing shoes. While playing *Maude*, she had formed this signature look, and Evans continued it in her designs. Much of Dorothy's wardrobe was custom-made because finding flattering clothing for taller women was often challenging.

The format

The Golden Girls was shot live in front of a studio audience on videotape. Most episodes followed a similar format: one or more of the women would have a problem, often involving other family members or the man they were dating. Usually around mid-episode, they would gather around in the kitchen and chat about the problem, while eating and telling anecdotes about their own lives (though Rose's tales were often nonsensical and off-topic, while Sophia's were made-up). Some episodes featured flashbacks to previous episodes, while others were flashbacks to events never shown, or events that occurred before the series timeline began.

The song

The Golden Girls theme song is as beloved as the show. It's hard to believe that it wasn't the first choice. That honor was supposed to be bestowed on Bette Midler's famous 1973 tune, "Friends" which alas, was too expensive. So, the powers-that-be hunted for a new theme, and music coordinator, Scott Gale, thinks it was Paul Witt that remembered, "Thank You for Being a Friend," a modest, Andrew Gold hit from 1978. They wanted a female vocal and chose in-demand session singer, Cindy Fee, who sang it in one take. Fee says she had done so many jingles and theme songs that she had no idea how popular this one would be, but that she could make a pretty good living on just that song, for which she still receives fan mail.

The Awards

The Golden Girls was one of the most successful and iconic television shows of all time, being both a critical and ratings success. The series received a variety of awards, including 11 Emmy Awards (with 68 nominations), four Golden Globe Awards (with 21 nominations), five American Comedy Awards (all wins), two Directors Guild of America Awards (with three nominations), and one Writers Guild of America Awards (with five nominations). The lead actresses all won Emmy Awards; Arthur, McClanahan and White won the award for Outstanding Lead Actress in a Comedy Series, and Estelle Getty won for Outstanding Supporting Actress in a Comedy Series. *The Golden Girls* is only one of four comedy series in which all the lead and supporting actors were recognized with an Emmy. The other three are *Schitt's Creek*, *All in the Family*, and *Will & Grace*. The cast was also named Disney Legends in 2009.

The LGBTQ Following

The Golden Girls was an immediate hit among the LGBTQ community for a myriad of reasons. First off, the Girls dealt with storylines regarding gay friends and relatives in real, and sometimes surprising ways. The plots ran the gamut, from a brother coming out of the closet, a lesbian friend getting a crush on one of the Girls, Blanche dating a man who ultimately enjoys dressing up as a woman, and finally, Dorothy's cross-dressing brother, Phil. There were well-thought-out portrayals of the prejudices during that era, but often it was shown that a person's lifestyle or sexuality choices were just not that big a deal to these women. And *that* was a big deal. The show's message was often something Sophia would say with a quick, "This is life. Deal with it."

As for the straight boys, I believe there are a number of them that secretly watched (and still watch) *The Golden Girls*... Dare I say that I know a few that crushed on Blanche growing up, and can name a few of her outfits that they found particularly sexy. Her black and white negligee is a particularly fond memory of theirs.

Michael Musto, writer of *Out Magazine*, declared in 2014, that he was addicted to *The Golden Girls* and it was the gayest show on TV. That was a bold statement for 2014. He loves it for all the obvious reasons, but he does have an intriguing theory, that perhaps he is not alone in: That *The Golden Girls* are basically gay men in dresses. He has them profiled as The Bitchy Queen, The Slutty Gay, The Ditzy Twink, and The Old Gay in the Corner. And I don't have to tell you which characters are which. He doubles down on this theory by admitting that even their activities get gayer and gayer, by putting on shows, dabbling in the art world, and of course, dressing as Sonny and Cher. He notes that many gay references (beyond the gay plots and supporting gay characters), were written by Marc Cherry, who went on to create the juggernaut *Desperate Housewives* (another offshoot of four different women living near each other). You can even find gay references in Rose's St. Olaf stories, like the fable of Hansel & Hansel, or that the town's best hairdresser was the fabulous Mr. Ingrid. (https://www.out.com/entertainment/michael-musto/2014/07/14/ why-golden-girls-still-gayest-show-tv)

But I found an even better explanation of The Golden Girls/LGBTQ phenomenon, on a deeper level here: "The transgressive power of *The Golden Girls* is that it's a show about the construction of a chosen family rather than a biological family, a very queer conceit." (https://www.buzzfeed.com/louispeitzman/why-gay-men-still-love-the-golden-girls)

The Legacy

Everyone loves an outlier. And *Golden Girls* is a show that although it never had to crawl back from low ratings, it represented four ultimate underdogs: four women over 50. And in 2022, when no artist's legacy is sacred, and the attention span has dwindled down to nothing, this show remains popular. Sixty-eight Emmy nominations and 11 wins, and 35 years since its premiere. No flashy plot gimmicks, no surprise deaths. What gives?

It's inherently feminist, yet it drew every woman to be in its audience, and probably a good handful of them didn't think of themselves as such. Just being a woman who had made it to her middle age and then some; just being a woman who raised children; just being a woman trying to survive a divorce or get a job at that age... just showing these experiences was a feminist approach and yet, it was just portraying life experiences that were ignored in the media, but instantly relatable. And they were relatable to straight men, gay men, and gay women, and straight women, and everyone in between, because it turns out, life is just life in all its messiness: your mother drives you nuts with insults, your dating life disappoints you, you never reach your high school potential, and you're hiding secrets from your kids. Who doesn't get that? But the deeper issues came in episodes that were about gay writes, age discrimination in the work force, confronting race, and dating the disabled.

The writers and creators of *The Golden Girls* reached out to many groups that weren't seen or heard, and they did so in a playful way that wasn't condescending, and they never left the humor behind. And they showed family life to be complicated, surprising, and unpredictable. When Dorothy's son gets engaged to a black woman that's 20 years older than he is, Dorothy's more worried about the age difference, and his family's more concerned about the racial divide. When Blanche dates a man in a wheelchair, he turns out to be a jerk, just like a lot of Blanche's dates turn out to be. There's no sanctimonious nonsense making him a martyr. And when Rose mulls over getting engaged to a little person, he ends up breaking up with her because she's not Jewish. All of these episodes turned out to be fan favorites (though, don't get me started on Hulu removing one of them from their streaming lineup, I will discuss later).

How to watch *The Golden Girls* as of 2022

Right now, you can watch *The Golden Girls* with subscriptions to Hulu Plus and DIRECTV. You're able to stream *The Golden Girls* by renting or purchasing on Amazon Instant Video, Microsoft, Google Play, Vudu, and iTunes. In fact, with its addition to Disney Plus on July 2nd, 2021, you can now watch it on every major streaming platform.

The ultimate comfort show...

The pandemic seemed to provide a good reason to sit with The Girls. According to a Hulu spokesperson, during the 2020 quarantine, viewers watched nearly 11 million hours of the sitcom in April 2020.

Obviously...

You'll want to get this 21-disc DVD set, if you have a DVD player — it comes with a playing-card deck with each of Girls as a different suite.

Why the show ended

Most sources say that Bea Arthur began to grow tired of the show during the fifth season. Many actors on successful shows will stay on until the shows are canceled, with most sitcoms becoming less-than-stellar at around the sixth season. But *The Golden Girls* was still at its high point, both in quality and in ratings. Bea, apparently, was one of those rare performers that perhaps enjoyed a certain upper echelon of greatness, and maybe felt the jokes were getting too extreme. I also suspect that there were one too many jokes about her appearance. She, of course, did sign on through the seventh season, but according to Betty White:

"It's like four points on a compass. We were each so different from the other: It was east, west, north and south. I think that's why we fit together so well. And for the first five years, it was such a happy thing. And we'd sit round, between scenes, instead of going to our dressing rooms, we'd yak, and talk about you know, very intimate scenes, and then all of a sudden, we'd realize it was blocking day and you'd look up and there was a microphone over your head that we hadn't counted on. The last couple of years Bea just decided she didn't want to do situational comedy anymore, and she was not comfortable, and she was not happy, and some of the bloom rubbed off a little bit. And again, I think we ended just a clip too early. I think there was a lot of life. But there's no point if one isn't happy."

The finale

"One Flew Out of the Cuckoo's Nest," the series finale that aired in 1992, was watched by 27.2 million viewers, and as of 2017, was the 16th-most-watched TV series finale.

(https://www.goodhousekeeping.com/life/entertainment/g325 08766/the-golden-girls-facts/?slide=37)

Spinoffs

A continuation, *The Golden Palace*, aired in the 1992–1993 season, starring all the actresses except Bea Arthur (although she did guest star). Susan Harris later created *Empty Nest* and *Nurses* as spin-offs with some character crossovers.

Film

Forever Golden: A Celebration of The Golden Girls was released in select movie theaters across North America via Fathom Events on September 14, 2021. The film featured five episodes: "The Pilot," "Flu Attack," "The Way We Met," "Ladies of the Evening" and "Grab That Dough."

Rue la Rue

In 2017, a Golden Girls-themed restaurant called Rue la Rue Cafe was opened by Rue McClanahan's close friend Michael La Rue in Washington Heights, New York. Michael had inherited many of Rue's belongings and decorated with them. Unfortunately, the eatery closed after less than a year.

Golden Girls Day!

Official Golden Girls Day is July 30th, based on the day that it began streaming on Hulu. This is your day to binge the show and for the superfan, invite your friends over, and throw a full-on Binge-Watcher's Party. I am not Martha Stewart (no kidding is said in unison by those that know me) but here is where I outshine Miss Stewart (see the section, How to Binge).

Susan Harris, on older women's sexuality

"If it was a big deal, and I don't know that it was, I think people could breathe a sigh of relief if they had never heard that before, or other things before, that we were able to do that, with little or no opposition. And once we got the viewers, they stayed with us. We had young kids watching that were big fans and much older people that were big fans; it really spanned generations."—Susan Harris

Susan Harris, on writing for risky topics

"Comedy is much more tolerable to hear something that you wouldn't be receptive to hear straight. I think we were political a lot of the time. And sometimes it was very unpopular, but we didn't care. Our main object was to entertain, but if entertaining, we could place some ideas, and thoughts so much the better. As long as we had the audience, the few that were offended could shut the TV off. That's the Sophia and Dorothy in me."—Susan Harris

20 Golden Facts about *The Golden Girls*

Susan Harris, who wrote the famous *Maude* abortion episode, was also the creator of the revolutionary television show, *Soap*.

Bea Arthur heard about the show because they were casting Dorothy as a "Bea Arthur-type" but people were saying that she wasn't interested in doing TV again.

It was Betty White's Hollywood connections that got them Burt Reynolds and Bob Hope to guest star on the show.

Bob Hope asked for the writers to give him jokes for a golf event in exchange for appearing on the show.

The Golden Girls is only one of four live-action television shows where all the main actors won Emmys. The others are *All in the Family*, *Will & Grace*, and Sc*hitt's Creek.*

Despite her character, Estelle Getty was one year younger than Bea Arthur, while Betty White was the oldest cast member.

Betty White was also the oldest member on her previous sitcom, *The Mary Tyler Moore Show.*

Estelle Getty suffered from almost debilitating stage fright, and the writers often had to cut her scenes, or film them without the studio audience. Years later, it was suspected that this was the early-onset of Lewy Body Dementia, which she would suffer from later on.

In 1988, the four women performed for The Queen of England who had invited the stars to perform live at the Royal Variety Performance in London. They performed two of their best kitchen scenes, with a bit of censoring.

Rue McClanahan had it in her contract that she could keep Blanche's wardrobe. All those amazing negligees did not go to waste!

The two-part episode "Sick and Tired" was autobiographical for Susan Harris, who had a real-life struggle with chronic fatigue syndrome and used her frustration with being dismissed by doctors as a plotline for Dorothy.

Bea Arthur hated cheesecake, and rarely puts it in her mouth during the famous cheesecake-eating, kitchen scenes.

Estelle Getty got a facelift after the first season was picked up for more episodes, making the makeup department's job all the more difficult as she was already about 20 years younger than the 80+ year-old Sophia.

The theme song was almost Bette Midler's "Friends," but it was deemed too expensive. I have to admit that though I love Bette, that tune depresses me a little, and I'm so glad they went with "Thank You for Being a Friend."

The Golden Girls was one of the first shows to tackle LGBTQ issues, like with Blanche's brother not only coming out as gay but returning and wanting to marry his partner. They were also often recognized for doing a good job in writing about issues like AIDS awareness, and people with disabilities.

Desperate Housewives creator Marc Cherry began his penchant for writing wild women over 40 on *The Golden Girls*. He said that he got death threats—which he considered a badge of honor—for the episodes about Blanche's brother.

In 2019, on *The Kelly Clarkson Show*, *The Property Brothers* (Drew and Jonathon Scott) revealed they want to do a renovation of *The Golden Girls'* house.

Estelle Getty had lines she wouldn't cross as far as making gay-bashing jokes or jokes about death, even though her character, Sophia seemed to have no filter and would insult anyone or anything.

Quentin Tarantino had a small non-speaking role as an Elvis impersonator, which paid him about $3,000 dollars and helped him stay afloat while making *Reservoir Dogs*.

According to Bea Arthur's son, she used to get annoyed that Betty White would interact with the live studio audience, much to their absolute joy. Sorry Bea, but the love for Betty has only gotten more intense since her passing.

The Golden Girls

GOLDEN GIRL BIOS

Bea Arthur

Born May 13th, 1922, Bea Arthur's entertainment career spanned seven decades. She was most well known for her television roles as Maude Findlay on the 1970s sitcom *Maude*, and as Dorothy Zbornak on the 1980's sitcom *The Golden Girls,* both of which won her Emmys. She also won the Tony Award for Best Featured Actress in a Musical for her performance as Vera Charles in the original cast of *Mame* (1966). Bea passed away on April 25, 2009 of lung cancer at the age of 86.

Her early life

Born Bernice Frankel, Bea was the second of three daughters born to Rebecca and Philip Frankel, in Brooklyn, New York, and was raised in a Jewish home. At 16, Bea developed an illness called coagulopathy, in which her blood would not clot, causing her parents to send her to an all-girls' boarding school. Afterwards, she went to Blackstone College for Girls in Virginia.

In 1943, during World War II, she enlisted as one of the first members of the United States Marine Corps Women's Reserve. After basic training, she served as a typist at Marine headquarters and then transferred to a Motor Transport School in North Carolina. She also worked as a truck driver and dispatcher between 1944 and 1945 and was honorably discharged with the rank of staff sergeant.

After serving, Bea studied for a year at the Franklin School of Science and Arts in Philadelphia, becoming a licensed medical technician. In 1947, after interning at a local hospital, she decided against working as a lab technician to leave for New York and enroll in the School of Drama at The New School. That same year, she married fellow Marine, Robert Alan Aurthur. While they divorced three years later, she kept his surname, changing it to "Arthur."

And off to the theater

Bea spent almost 20 years in the New York theater earning a respectable reputation with roles in off-Broadway productions like Lucy Brown in Marc Blitzstein's English-language adaptation of Kurt Weill's *The Threepenny Opera* in 1957. She also took Broadway parts like Yente the Matchmaker in the 1964 premiere of *Fiddler on the Roof.* In 1966, Bea lost the titular role of *Mame* to Angela Lansbury, instead taking the supporting role of Vera Charles which won her a Tony Award for Best Featured Actress in a Musical.

The big break

Bea's turning point came in 1971 when Norman Lear cast her as Maude on *All in the Family—as* Edith Bunker's outspoken, liberal feminist cousin and the obvious opposite of Archie.

That casting would give "Maude" her own series, which debuted in 1972 and garnered Bea several Emmy and Golden Globe nominations, including her first Emmy win in 1977 for Outstanding Lead Actress in a Comedy Series. *Maude* would also have a significant place in the history of the feminist movement by addressing controversial political topics of the era such as the Vietnam War, menopause, nervous breakdowns, gay rights and spousal abuse.

The most famous *Maude* episode, "Maude's Dilemma," centers around Maude considering getting an abortion. Dozens of affiliates refused to broadcast the episode, substituting either a repeat from earlier in the season or a TV special in its place. But by the time all the flak had died down, and the stations had reinstated it the following summer, a reported 65 million viewers watched the two-episode arc. The series was a continued success, but ended after six seasons in 1978, by Bea Arthur's choice.

And another golden break

TV success came again with *The Golden Girls*, as the show was being cast without her, but with the role of Dorothy being conceived by Susan Harris as a "Bea Arthur type." Everyone seemed to have the idea that Bea Arthur didn't want the role, though Arthur claims she hadn't seen or heard about this till much later.

She would play Dorothy Zbornak, a divorced substitute teacher living in a Miami house owned by Blanche Devereaux (Rue

McClanahan). Her performance led to several Emmy nominations over the course of the series, and an eventual Emmy win in 1988. She decided to leave the show after seven years, resulting in it being moved from NBC to CBS and retooled as *The Golden Palace,* in which the other three actresses reprised their roles. Bea made a guest appearance in a two-part episode of *The Golden Palace.*

After the gold

After Bea left *The Golden Girls*, she made several memorable guest appearances on television shows, including the cartoon *Futurama* in the Emmy-nominated 2001 episode "Amazon Women in the Mood," as the voice of a Femputer who ruled the giant Amazonian women. She was also nominated for an Emmy for Outstanding Guest Actress in a Comedy Series for her performance in an episode of *Malcolm in the Middle* as Mrs. White, Dewey's babysitter. She also appeared as Larry David's mother on one episode of *Curb Your Enthusiasm.*

In 2001, Bea toured in her one-woman show, alternately titled *An Evening with Bea Arthur* and *And Then There's Bea.* She returned to Broadway in 2002 to star in *Bea Arthur on Broadway: Just Between Friends,* based on her life and career. The show was nominated for a Tony Award for Best Special Theatrical Event. On March 7, 2004, Bea Arthur taped a parody of *Sex and the City* playing Sarah Jessica Parker's character Carrie Bradshaw. Then in 2005, she participated in the Comedy Central roast of Pamela Anderson, where she recited sexually explicit passages from Anderson's book *Star Struck* in her usual deadpan fashion. This is on YouTube and truly hysterical!

Personal life and causes

Bea was married twice. Her first marriage lasted from 1944 to 1950, to Robert Aurthur. Soon afterwards, she married director Gene Saks and adopted two sons, Matthew and Daniel. She and Saks remained married until 1978.

She was a known supporter of the LGBTQ community, later taking on the cause of youth homelessness and animal rights as well. Regarding politics, she considered herself a liberal Democrat and close politically to her character Maude. She was a champion of equal rights for women and an active advocate of the elderly and Jewish communities. Contrary to her Maude character however, she was initially skeptical of the women's rights movement.

Bea Arthur died of cancer on April 25th, 2009 at the age of 86, and donated $300,000 to the Ali Forney Center, a New York City organization that houses homeless LGBTQ youths.

A little extra about Bea

Much can be found online about whether the actresses got along and there are articles that quote Betty White as saying Bea didn't like her very much, or quote Rue as claiming that Bea had been a little distant or inconsistent with her over the years. But if you listen and read all the stories, like I did, you can surmise that they did get along *fairly* well.

It appears to me that Bea was professional and sometimes standoffish, but not a mean or unkind person. And I believe she genuinely liked and respected the other women, as they liked and respected her. But their personalities were as different as their characters. She was, by all accounts, an introvert and her way of working was entirely different from say, Betty White. As you will see from the episode recaps, I suspect that the writing on *The Golden Girls*—which frequently insulted her appearance—was rather grating on her ego.

I have to add my utmost respect that she pulled the plug on both *Maude* and *The Golden Girls* at their high points, demonstrating that she chose art over money. As a fan, I think she made the right choice. With *The Golden Girls*, it was right at the point where the jokes were becoming repetitive and the plots were becoming silly, but the quality had not noticeably dipped. I see Bea Arthur as a real class act, and like the rest of the women, I think that she was an A-plus performer with a heart of GOLD.

Estelle Getty

Born July 23rd, 1923, Estelle Getty was best known for her role as Sophia Petrillo, mother of Dorothy Zbornak on *The Golden Girls* and its spinoff, *The Golden Palace.* She also played the character on *Empty Nest* and *Nurses.* She won an Emmy in 1988 and Golden Globe in 1985 for her role as Sophia Petrillo. After retiring from acting in her later years, she battled with Lewy Body Dementia which ultimately took her life at 84 years old, on July 22, 2008.

Her early life:

Born Estelle Scher to Charles and Sara Scher in 1923, she was raised in a Jewish home in the Lower East Side of New York City. Her father installed glass windows into automobiles and trucks and her mother was a homemaker. Estelle developed an interest in becoming an actress when her father would take the family to the Academy of Music to watch live vaudeville performers. After graduating high school, she worked as a secretary while going on auditions, as her father didn't think she'd be able to make a living as an actress. In 1947, she married Arthur Gettleman—a man she met at a party with theater friends and she would later use his last name for her stage name. They had two sons, Carl and Barry.

The big break

For decades, Getty won roles in the New York City theater circuit while working for her family's glass business. But her big breakout came in 1982, as Mrs. Beckoff in the play *Torch Song Trilogy*, a role that Harvey Fierstein wrote specifically for her. It was this role that put her in the minds of *The Golden Girls'* creators.

The golden ticket

Estelle was an immediate sensation as Sophia Petrillo on *The Golden Girls*—so beloved even in the pilot episode that the role was extended for her, cutting the part of Coco the Houseboy. She auditioned many times, thinking that she had competition, but in reality, it was just her coming back for rereads. She was a year younger than Bea Arthur but relied on the makeup department and a wig to make her look as if she was in her 80s.

After the gold

Estelle Getty reprised her role as Sophia Petrillo on three other television shows: *The Golden Palace, Empty Nest*, and *Nurses***.** She was also heavily involved in HIV/AIDs activism. She had lost many friends and family members to the disease, like her nephew Steven Scher in 1992, and her *Torch Song Trilogy* co-star Court Miller in 1986. In 1988, Getty wrote an autobiography named, *If I Knew Then, What I Know Now... So What?* with the help of Steve Delsohn, published by Contemporary Books. She also released an exercise video in 1993 for senior citizens called *Young at Heart: Body Conditioning*.

On July 22, 2008, Estelle Getty died in Los Angeles at the age of 84, as a result of dementia with Lewy Bodies. She's buried in Hollywood Forever Cemetery, with a headstone that reads "With Love and Laughter" and adorned with a Star of David. According to her *Golden Girls* co-stars, she was not able to converse with them because of the disease, and they had seen signs when she began to struggle with cue cards on *The Golden Girls*. She had initially been thought to have been suffering from Parkinson's disease.

A little extra about Estelle

The most frustrating and endearing thing I learned about Estelle was how she suffered through stage fright during the filming of *The Golden Girls*, which was likely due to the early onset of her illness. She is said to be the only actor who ever asked writers to cut her lines during performances. New writers on *The Golden Girls* were told that Getty would break their heart, because she would be able to do long monologues in rehearsal, but then the stage fright would get her, and they would often cut or film scenes without the audience. I wish she had been a little younger when the world discovered her talent or that there had been a diagnosis and cure for what she was going through. Her timing and talent leapt off the television screen.

Rue McClanahan

Born February 21st, 1934, Rue McClanahan was a television and Broadway performer who became most famous for her role as Blanche Devereaux on *The Golden Girls*. Blanche was the owner of their Miami home where the Girls lived, and also the man-crazy sexpot with a narcissistic streak. In 1987, she won an Emmy for Outstanding Lead Actress in a Comedy Series for her role as Blanche.

Her early life

Eddi-Rue McClanahan was born in Healdton, Oklahoma, to Dreda Rheua-Nell and William Edwin McClanahan. She was raised Methodist and was of Irish and Choctaw ancestry—according to her autobiography, her great-grandfather, was named Running Hawk. Growing up, she acted in school plays and won the gold medal in oration. She was quite the student—a National Honor Society member—and later earned a Bachelor of Arts degree, cum laude, at the University of Tulsa, where she majored in German and Theatre.

The beginning of her career

As a member of the Actors Studio in 1957, McClanahan made her professional stage debut in the play *Inherit the Wind* at Pennsylvania's Erie Playhouse. It wasn't until 1969 that she won a role on Broadway, portraying Sally Weber in the original production of John Sebastian and Murray Schisgal's musical, *Jimmy Shine*. She also found small parts on soap operas like *Another World* in 1970 as Caroline Johnson and *Where the Heart Is*, as Margaret Jardin. Then, much like Bea Arthur, her fortune changed because of Norman Lear. She was cast as part of a swinging couple trying to seduce the unsuspecting Bunkers on *All in the Family*, and then got a permanent role on *Maude* as Maude's best friend Vivian Cavender. This was where she would not only meet and work with Bea Arthur but come under the purview of future *Golden Girls* creator Susan Harris.

The golden break

Rue McClanahan's big breakthrough came, of course, as Blanche Devereaux, the sex-crazed southern belle that owns a house in Miami. For that role, she received four Emmy nominations and one win in 1987 for Outstanding Lead Actress in a Comedy Series. She also received three Golden Globe nominations for Best Performance by an Actress in a TV Series.

After the gold

Rue continued working on multiple television series after *The Golden Girls*, including *Law & Order, Touched by an Angel*, and *King of the Hill*. In 2003, she appeared in the musical romantic comedy film *The Fighting Temptations* as Nancy Stringer, with Cuba Gooding, Jr., Beyoncé Knowles, Mike Epps, and Steve Harvey. In 2005, she replaced Carole Shelley as Madame Morrible in the musical *Wicked* on Broadway. Her final role was in *Sordid Lives* on the Logo channel.

The marrying kind

Rue McClanahan was married six times, and the details and tribulations of those marriages is in much better detail in her autobiography, *My First Five Husbands ... and the Ones Who Got Away*. But here is a list of them:

Tom Bish (1958 - 1959) (divorced) (1 child, Mark Bish)
Norman Hartweg (1959-1961) (divorced)
Peter DeMaio (1964-1971) (divorced)
Gussie Sam Fisher (1976-1979) (divorced)
Tom Keel (1984-1985) (divorced)
Morrow Wilson (1997-2010) (her death)

Her later years

Like the rest of the Girls, McClanahan was a supporter of gay rights and an advocate for same-sex marriage. In 2009, she appeared in the star-studded *Defying Inequality: The Broadway Concert—A Celebrity Benefit for Equal Rights*. McClanahan also spent her time helping organizations that fought cancer, AIDS, and cruelty against animals. She died on June 3, 2010 after a stroke at 76.

A little extra about Rue

Rue followed in the footsteps of Bea Arthur and did a solo act based on her life story and autobiography. The show dished a lot about her career, but by her own admission never trash-talked. She discussed having an abortion, her failed marriages, and mentioned that Bea Arthur was annoyed by her. I think what occurs to me most is that in her real life, she kept marrying men hoping that the next one would be the right one. But as Blanche, she got to be quite particular and not settle for less-than perfect. It must have been liberating to act not only as sexually free, but financially and even emotionally independent.

Betty White

Betty Marion White was born on January 17th, 1922 and was perhaps one of the greatest and most beloved entertainers of all time. White is the only woman to have received an Emmy in all comedic categories, and also holds the record for longest span between Emmy nominations—her first was in 1951 and her last in 2011. Her Emmy wins were as a Guest Actress on *Saturday Night Live* in 2015 and *The John Larroquette Show* in 1996; Lead Actress on a Comedy Series for *The Golden Girls* in 1986; and Outstanding Continuing Performance by a Supporting Actress in a Comedy Series for *The Mary Tyler Moore Show* in 1975 and 1976. She's also one of the first women to produce a television show—*Life with Elizabeth*, a series she starred in in the 1950s.

Her early life

Betty was born in Oak Park, Illinois, to Christine Tess and Horace Logan, but moved to Alhambra when she was just a toddler. She was an only child, and at only eight years old made her radio programming debut. Her grandfathers were Greek and Danish, and her grandmothers were both Canadian, with English and Welsh roots. She went to Beverly Hills High School and had originally wanted to become a forest ranger (inspired by trips to Sierra, Nevada) but women were not allowed to be rangers at that time. She became interested in writing and performing in school plays, and the rest is entertainment history.

On the radio and then TV

In the 1930s and 1940s, Betty began modeling and making rounds on the radio, before auditioning at studios where she was often turned down for "not being photogenic."

In 1945, while volunteering with the American Women's Voluntary Services, White met her first husband Dick Barker, a United States Air Force pilot. They divorced within a year and White returned to Los Angeles. Then in 1947, she married Lane Allen, a Hollywood talent agent—a marriage which also ended in divorce, in 1949, after Allen pressured White to give up her career to become a homemaker. Whoa, bad call Mr. Allen. Do you all see how misogyny and chauvinism could potentially rob the world of greatness, entertainment, and smiles?

During this time, Betty was offered her own radio show called *The Betty White Show*. She had also began appearing as co-host with Al Jarvis on *Hollywood on Television*, on KLAC in Los Angeles. In 1951, Betty was nominated for her first Emmy Award as "Best Actress." This was the very first award and category in the new Emmy history designated for women on television. Betty then began hosting the show by herself in 1952, filling five and a half hours, six days a week of live ad-lib television for four years.

Also in 1952, she co-produced and starred in her own series, *Life with Elizabeth*, which was nationally syndicated from 1952-1955. The show was derived from the KLAC show and was one of the few produced by a woman, let alone a woman as young as 28! While *Life with Elizabeth* aired, she started *another* talk show called *The Betty White Show (the second version)*. Throughout the 50s and 60s, White also began a 19-year stint as commentator on the annual Rose Parade broadcast on NBC (co-hosting with Roy Neal and later Lorne Greene), and appeared on a number of late-night talk shows, including *The Tonight Show,* where she was a favorite guest of Johnny Carson's.

Let the game shows begin

Betty White starred in an *unsuccessful* sitcom called *Dream Girl,* where even she has said, "that was the only time I have ever wanted to get out of a show." *The Betty White Show* was rebooted for a third time, while she began a new successful venture—game shows. During the 1960s and 1970s, Betty became a game-show darling on such staples as *Password, Super Password, What's My Line*, *Match Game*, and *To Tell the Truth.*

In 1963, she married Allen Ludden—the host of *Password*—who would become the love of her life, and they would remain married until his death from stomach cancer in 1981. Ludden had proposed to White at least twice before she accepted. They did not have any children together, but she was the stepmother to three of his children. When asked by Larry King if she would marry again, she replied, "Once you've had the best, who needs the rest?"

Moore of Betty

In the 70s, Betty White became famous for her portrayal of the man-hungry Sue Ann Nivens on *The Mary Tyler Moore Show* (1970-1977), who started as a guest star in the fourth season, before becoming a regular cast member. A running joke on the show was how Sue Ann displayed a sunny public persona but was really cynical and sardonic. She was allegedly cast because they were looking for someone who could play "sickeningly sweet, like Betty White." She won two Emmys for this role, and when the show ended was offered an opportunity to star in the fourth version of *The Betty White Show*. Like Rue McClanahan, White also appeared on the sitcom *Mama's Family,* playing Ellen Harper Jackson, from 1983-1984.

And then the Gold

Betty White's tenure on *The Golden Girls* began in 1985 as Rose Nylund. As the story has been told over and over, she was originally thought of for the part of Blanche because of her indelible portrayal of Sue Ann Nivens. But the director of the pilot, Jay Sandrich, was considering switching her and Rue, as Rue wasn't keen on the part of Rose. And the rest is magic. All the parts on the show were iconic and nominated multiple times for Emmys and Golden Globes. (Sidenote: On both *The Mary Tyler Moore Show* and *The Golden Girls*, White was the oldest cast member, and the last surviving cast member.)

After *The Golden Girls*

Betty repeated her role as Rose Nylund on *The Golden Girls'* spinoffs *The Golden Palace, Empty Nest,* and *Nurses*. And her career barely slowed down in the following decades. She appeared on many sitcoms and dramas like *Suddenly Susan*, *The Practice, Yes, Dear,* and *Boston Legal.* Also worth noting was her Emmy-winning, guest-starring role on *The John Larroquette Show*, where Estelle Getty and Rue McClanahan returned for a *Golden Girls* parody.

But Betty's reach extended further into film and commercials. In 2009, she starred with Sandra Bullock and Ryan Reynolds in the film *The*

Proposal and participated in a Mars Bars commercial that won the top spot in the Super Bowl Ad Meter for that year. That was a big year as she was also the recipient of the Screen Actors Guild Life-Achievement Award. Then in 2010, she became the oldest host of *Saturday Night Live*, at 88 years old and won her seventh Emmy Award as Outstanding Guest Actress in a Comedy Series. She won her first Grammy Award in 2012 for a spoken word recording of her bestseller *If You Ask Me*, won the UCLA Jack Benny Award for Comedy for her contribution to comedy in television, and was roasted at the New York Friars Club. In 2018, PBS celebrated her as The First Lady of Television.

Betty White passed away on December 31st, 2021, in Los Angeles just shy of her 100th birthday. A documentary was shown in select movie theaters on her birthday, January 17th, 2022 called *Betty White: A Celebration.*

A little extra about Betty

Many people might not know this, but Betty White took an early stance on civil rights. When *The Betty White Show* (the second version in 1954) faced criticism for inclusion of an African American tap dancer, Arthur Duncan, White's response was, "I'm sorry. Live with it," and gave him even more airtime. Duncan didn't know about this at the time, and went on to have a popular run on *The Lawrence Welk Show*, and other television appearances.

I don't think people today realize what a bold move that was, and it speaks not just to her character, but also her strength. It's popular now for all of us to publicly make stances supporting causes, but these were times when people's jobs and finances were truly on the table. Often people's lives, along with their livelihoods, were at risk as well. We are all so quick to pat ourselves on the back for being woke enough and are so sure that we would be the one making these brave choices 60 years ago. I hope I would have been one of them. But the truth is not that many people were on the right side of history when their paychecks and safety were threatened.

And what I like about this story is that I just learned about it while writing the book. There are a thousand reasons to love Betty White. So many celebrities and artists have disappointed me over the last few years, but Betty, and honestly all of the *Golden Girls*, did not, in writing and researching this book.

Books Authored by Betty White:

*If You Ask Me And Of Course You Won't (*2011)
Betty & Friends: My Life at the Zoo (2011)
Here We Go Again: My Life in Television (1995)
Betty White in Person (1987)

Charities Betty White Supported

American Heart Association
American Humane Association
American Stroke Association
Autism Speaks
Desmond Tutu Peace Centre
Elton John AIDS Foundation
Everyone Matters
Farm Sanctuary
Friars Foundation
GLAAD
Helen Woodward Animal Center
Human Rights Campaign
Los Angeles Police Memorial Foundation
Morris Animal Foundation
NAACP
Onyx and Breezy Foundation
PAWS/LA
Petco Foundation
Red Cross
Screen Actors Guild Foundation
spcaLA
Special Olympics
St. Francis Food Pantries and Shelters
St. Jude Children's Research Hospital
The Trevor Project
USC Shoah Foundation Institute

Before You Watch

So, you're probably reading this book as a fan, for which I thank you. Or you're reading this book as someone who has never watched the show. I'm still thanking you. Those are two extremely different groups of people and I have to guide you both, somehow simultaneously. What I'll tell you is this: I want you to be able to flip through the Episode Guide, learn a bit about each episode and where it fits in the lexicon of show. The truth is, in this day and age you can get a lot of information on Google, IMDb and Wikipedia. But I want you to know my rating system, plus gather a few tidbits along the way.

Some things to think about

Just a heads up on the spinoff, *Golden Palace*, that I won't be delving into. I totally get that Betty, Rue, and Estelle were trying to keep their hustle going, but I just did not care for it. That's hard for me to say, and tough to admit, but there you have it. I also won't be chatting about *Empty Nest* and *Nurses,* because the focus here is just the seven-season arc of *The Golden Girls*.

Also, this show and its lack of fact checking will drive a modern viewer absolutely nuts. In the current era, where a character's history is usually carefully and methodically outlined, you won't believe how often simple continuity mistakes were made, like how many children the women have, what year they graduated high school, or how many years they were married.

For *The Golden Girls*, freelance writers were often hired and a lot of dialogue and plots were seemingly not checked. I'm surprised the actresses didn't simply intervene and say, "Hey, my character has [this many] children."

Oh, the Children

You're going to notice that I have some issues with some of the plotlines regarding the Girls' children. I felt the casting really suffered there, as it did with plots about young children in general. As strong as the show was about relating to older people, the writing was not strong in examining the lives and dialogues of younger people during the 80's and 90's.

The Shaming

Some of the show might get criticized for the slut or fat shaming that the Girls engage in. I don't have a problem with it, mostly because friends do tease each other about such things. But I have to say, the relentless insults regarding Bea Arthur's appearance did rub me the wrong way as I binged the series. They mostly come from Sophia, but a lot of them come from Blanche, and some even come from Rose. I think they were too much and too unkind, and I did read that Bea Arthur once cried during a script reading. So, it might be my biggest problem with the show. I don't even think she's an unattractive woman, and as a short girl, I wish I was 5'9, so the tall jokes are a little lost on me.

Perfectly progressive

This show either gets praise for being progressive and ahead of its time or condemned for not being woke enough. I personally think that it's so woke that you'll need a nap after you watch it. And I think the actresses, the writers, producers, and Susan Harris did more for woke causes than a whole lot of people ranting and raving about stuff on social media. In other words, don't come at me with your criticism of *The Golden Girls*. In my eyes, they are golden.

Golden Girls products to play with or purchase for your Binge party: Get your gold on!

These toys and games will add a real wow factor to a Golden-Girls theme party!

Girls gotta have Funko!

Funko wouldn't be complete as a company of pop-culture collectibles without adding The Golden Girls to the mix — I just had to buy them for myself. Adorable!

The board game that's "a cheesecake" cut above

Reviews indicate The Official Golden Girls Board Game: Who Ate the Last Piece of Cheesecake? is the golden standard for Golden Girls board games.

Four women, four stories

Learn more about the characters, in their own words. Whether it's Sicily, Brooklyn, Georgia, or back in St. Olaf. Just Google Golden Girls biographies!

Chi-chi-Sophia!

Another prized possession of mine. For the fan that is a Sophia superfan, you can't go wrong here. Especially if you consider Sophia wiser than Buddha, look to this Chia Sophia instead of a Buddha statue.

Take your golden shot

How you drink your drink is your choice. One for every St. Olaf or Sicily tale? A shot for every time Stan comes to the door? Or maybe a deeper cut of when Blanche says, "I am stunned?"

Worth monopolizing your time

A fun way to add gizmos and fun facts to the classic Monopoly game.

I see this tarot card deck in your future

This does a really splendid job of connecting the characters and plots of the show in with an authentic tarot deck. I highly recommend, especially if you know someone that reads Tarot cards.

Tips on the Binge

You can do a classic binge

Nothing wrong with this. Start with Season One and keep going. This show doesn't have one particularly weak season—they're all strong.

Watch my favorites or the fan favorites

You can scan my guide for the four-heart episodes, but the three-heart episodes are arguably a lot of fan favorites.

Visit IMDb.com for an entire ranked episode list

Again, not entirely identical to my tastes, but solid crowdsourcing here. However, they rank the finale as #1, which I think is a little strange.

Hulu makes it easy

Hulu, as of 2022, has a few Binge sections that make the choice for you: Quick Binge, the Stanley Chronicles, and Sing it, Sister.

The Best Binge for plots that include all the Girls!

The Competition (Season 1, Episode 7)
Flu Attack (Season 1, Episode 21)
Ladies of the Evening (Season 2, Episode 2)
The Actor (Season 2, Episode 14)
The Artist (Season 3, Episode 13)
The Auction (Season 4, Episode 11)
The Mangiacavallo Curse Makes a Lousy Wedding Present (Season 5, Episode 23)
Henny Penny... Straight, No Chaser (Season 6, Episode 26)
A Midwinter's Night's Dream, Parts 1 & 2 (Season 7, Episodes 20/21)

Dorothy dramas and dalliances:

That Was No Lady (Season 1, Episode 14)
Till Death Do We Volley (Season 4, Episode 19)
Foreign Exchange (Season 4, Episode 24)
Sick and Tired, Parts 1 & 2 (Season 5, Episode 1/2)
One Flew Out of the Cuckoo's Nest, Parts 1 & 2 (Season 7)

Rose's ridiculous escapades:

Rose the Prude (Season 1, Episode 3)
In a Bed of Rose's (Season 1, Episode 15)
A Little Romance (Season 1, Episode 13)

It's a Miserable Life (Season 2, Episode 5)
You Gotta Have Hope (Season 4, Episode 17)
Witness (Season 6, Episode 21)
Old Boyfriends (Season 7, Episode 14)

Blanche spells B.E.D. episodes:
End of the Curse (Season 2, Episode 1)
Diamond in the Rough (Season 2, Episode 22)
Yes, We Have No Havanas (Season 4, Episode 1)
The One That Got Away (Season 4, Episode 3)
Mrs. George Devereaux (Season 6, Episode 9)
Melodrama (Season 6, Episode 19)
The Case of the Libertine Bell (Season 7, Episode 1)
Journey to the Center of Attention (Season 7, Episode 19)

Spicy Sophia's saucy slices of life:
Heart Attack (Season 1, Episode 10)
Old Friends (Season 3, Episode 1)
Larceny and Old Lacy (Season 3, Episode 3)
Sophia's Wedding, Parts 1 & 2 (Season 4, Episodes 6/7)
Not Another Monday (Season 5, Episode 7)
The Days and Nights of Sophia Petrillo (Season 4, Episode 2)
How Do You Solve a Problem Like Sophia (Season 6, Episode 8)
Girls Just Wanna Have Fun... Before they Die (Season 6, Episode 10)

Dysfunctional Family Affairs
The Sisters (Season 2, Episode 12)
My Brother, My Father (Season 3, Episode 17)
Once in St. Olaf (Season 6, Episode 2)
Wham Bam, Thank You Mammy (Season 6, Episode 5)
Mother Load (Season 7, Episode 6)
The Monkey Show, Parts 1 & 2 (Season 7, Episodes 8/9)

Your Golden Binge Party

Whether you're having superfans or newbies—or ideally a mix of both—there are definitely some must-have components to a *Golden Girls* binge party. You can add more of course, but I recommend these.

Depending on how crafty you are, you can Google how to create *Golden Girls* themed decor, but certainly think Miami. Think pastels, wicker furniture, and shoulder pads. My Aunt Marilyn had a special appreciation for the kitchen tablecloths as well, which were usually of bright-colored floral or tropical motifs. Maybe even think of Rose's favorite show, *Miami Vice*. But damnit, if you're going to have anything written outside your door, or have a sign for your guests, it better say, "Thank you for being a friend!"

You should have a *Which Golden Girl Are You? (*there's one in this book*)* quiz of sorts for all attendees to take, to determine which character they are most like. Don't you wanna know if you're dealing with a room full of Dorothys or a room full of Blanches? Of course, you can give them badges with their character name if you'd like.

The Menus

At its most basic, there are three types of food items that must be served at a *Golden Girls* party: Italian food (just pizza works wonderfully), alcoholic or non-alcoholic beverages, and cheesecake (chocolate is the one that they first ate together, by the way). The point of a *Golden Girls* party, at its heart, is to laugh and enjoy your friends. So, if you're stressing about food and decor, you're kind-of missing the point. I suggest, as Dorothy would say, "Pizza dammit, I want pizza." Below is a list of more clever concoctions inspired by the show.

A Wedding Meal for Marrying a Polygamist: (from The Pilot)

Enchiladas
Cucumbers
Stone crabs
Oysters
Tea
Gin with beer back

Sophia's "Eat a Little of This & That" Italian Non-Meal: (from The Heart Attack)

Scungilli
Sausage & peppers
Fettuccine Alfredo
Fried mozzarella

Mushrooms with gorgonzola
Cannelloni
Milk Duds

Rose's "Nothing out-of-the-ordinary" Before-Bed Snack (From The Auction)

Handful of snowcaps
Couple of devil dogs
Some Oreos
A ho-ho chopped up in a bowl of fruit cocktail with heavy syrup

Customized *Golden Girls* Cuisine for the Superfans

Bacon, lettuce, and potato sandwiches
A "Naughty" Ice Cream Sundae inspired by Neals Fielander
Maple syrup honey brown sugar molasses Rice Krispies log!
"Pilfered" cheeseballs
Linguine with ear-salve (pesto) sauce

If you're ordering pizza, might I suggest calling it:

Dorothy's "Dammit, I Want Pizza"
Sophia's "Picture It, Sicilian"
"Back in Brooklyn"-Style

The Music

Obviously, as these women were born between 1900-1930s, you would want to play some old-school jazz. Tony Bennett is mentioned more than once, but let's not forget that Dorothy has a known love for both Sinatra and The Beatles. If you really want to mix things up, the superfan would remember that the Girls attended a Madonna concert in the first season and Sophia listens to Prince on her Walkman (so you can sprinkle some 80's tunes in). And my god, Sonny and Cher are an absolute must for a *Golden Girls* Playlist. And for some Dorothy & Stan nostalgia, don't forget Cole Porter & Gershwin.

Here's a *Golden Girls* playlist based on music and performers they mentioned.

Begin the Beguine by Julio Iglesias
Georgia On My Mind by Ray Charles
Girls Just Wanna Have Fun by Cyndi Lauper
Holiday by Madonna

I Get a Kick Out of You by Nat King Cole
I Got You Babe by Sonny and Cher
I Left My Heart in San Francisco by Tony Bennett
In the Mood by the Glenn Miller Band
Miami Vice Theme Song by Jan Hammer
New York, New York by Frank Sinatra
Purple Rain by Prince
She Loves You by The Beatles
Someone to Watch Over Me by Ella Fitzgerald
Strangers in the Night by Frank Sinatra
Tennessee Waltz by Patsy Cline
Thank You for Being a Friend by Cindy Fee

Binge-Watching Party: My Signature Golden Girls Cocktails

Depending on how rowdy you want your guests to get—and whether you're serving alcohol or non-alcoholic beverages—you can try the shot game I mentioned earlier. It's simple and you can have everyone use the character they were matched with on the quiz. For a more relaxed evening, you can choose wine instead (Sangria for Blanche, a Cabernet Sauvignon for Sophia, White Wine/Chardonnay for Dorothy, and a Dessert Wine for Rose).

The Dorothy or The Brooklyn Substitute Teacher

It's like a Manhattan (except for a kinky vermouth swap, but "who are you to judge"), with a more cynical attitude. She's all business, unless you take her to the Rusty Anchor or Beatlemania.

2 oz. rye whiskey
.75 oz dry vermouth (replace the sweet vermouth of a Manhattan, because she ain't sweet)
2 dashes of Angostura bitters (any bitters will do, it's Dorothy after all)
1 orange twist for garnish (she's in Florida, after all)
*May cause you to answer all the *Jeopardy* answers correctly, but still not get picked as a contestant.

The Blanche or The Southern Bellhop

For the restless bad girl and The Scarlett O'Hara-wannabes that want to drink and watch dirty movies on a rainy day, I combined the famous Scarlett O'Hara cocktail with an Alabama Slammer, and added even more sweetness, sourness, and spiciness. Because our Blanche is a complicated woman.

2 oz. Southern Comfort
1/2 oz. peach schnapps
2 ounces cranberry
1 jalapeno slice
Dash of agave or a splash of grenadine
Lime wedge for garnish
Shake drink before serving
*May cause you to French kiss the pillows and get arrested in Chattanooga.

The Rose or The Minnesota Mudslide

Every good girl has a dark side that wants to ride off on a motorcycle and drink something sweet, with marshmallows in front of a fireplace. If you're a real *Golden Girls* fan, you know that Rose has a twisted competitive side. But she has the biggest sweet tooth, so if you want to throw M&Ms or Skittles at the bottom of this drink, I assure you, it would be on-brand.

1 cup milk
1 cup ice cubes
1 oz. vodka
½ oz. coffee liquor
½ ounce Irish cream liquor
3 tablespoons coffee creamer (recommended flavors: French vanilla or hazelnut)
Chocolate syrup and toasted marshmallows, not for garnish, but to devour like a child.
*St. Olaf story not included.

Pour the vodka into the blender first. Then add the coffee liquor, Irish cream liquor, coffee creamer, and the milk. Lastly, pour the ice into the blender.

Put the lid on the blender and pulse to crush the ice or use the blender's ice setting. Pour into your glass and add garnish. You can toast the marshmallows if you'd like.

The Sophia or The Godmother's Negroni

Marlon Brando was the Godfather, and his favorite drink was a Negroni. But on this show, Sophia's the Sicilian boss with all the answers. But don't get her angry—she's got a few curses up her sleeve, and no one would suspect her of a crime. I've combined three versions of the Negroni to fit her personality: the Classic Italian mixed with the Americano version, mixed of course with the Half-sized Negroni, because our Sophia, much like myself, is pint-sized fun.

½ oz. Campari
½ oz. vermouth
¾ oz. tequila or gin (whichever you prefer)
1 oz. soda water
A slice of lemon for garnish, and a smart answer for everything

The Golden Girls Quiz: Which Golden Girl Are You?

The point of the quiz, and ultimately, the whole show, is that though you may identify much more with one character, you will find that over your entire lifetime, there's a touch of each Golden lady inside all of us. We are each the fun & sexy one; the smart & serious one; the innocent & nurturing one; and the wise and cynical one.

1. **Your sleepwear most likely consists of...**
   A. Something sexy, made of silk or lace, or half naked... or let's face it, naked.
   B. Sophisticated, matching pajama set, or a long T.
   C. Cotton or flannel, pajama set or nightgown, all for comfort, not style.
   D. A snuggly robe with a nightgown.
   E. None of the above

2. **When you tell a story...**
   A. It's usually dramatic, making yourself the star of your own epic miniseries.
   B. It's a well-timed, sentimental story, with only a recently discovered perspective.
   C. It's a long, tedious, nonsensical story that makes your friends want to murder you.
   D. It's an allegory: with a lesson, a historical context, and a little bit of humor.

E. None of the above

3. **Your sex life has always been...**
   A. Racy, plentiful, and you may have a book of all your escapades. Or you should.
   B. Full of mostly unsatisfactory lovers, so when a good one comes along, you can really lose your pride.
   C. Kind of a mystery. You come off like a prude, yet many lovers have been impressed with your skills. Also, you've had more lovers than anyone would guess.
   D. More about quality than quantity, but you have been described as a spicy lover, with many tricks up your sleeve. Also, you've learned some tricks from self-described sluts.
   E. None of your goddamn business.

4. **Your cooking style...**
   A. Almost non-existent, though you simmer enough in the bedroom to make up for the lack of simmering in the kitchen.
   B. You see cooking more as a chore. You'll get it done, but your heart's not in it.
   C. You get a real joy out of cooking—unfortunately, no one else does.
   D. Your cooking is so good that men have proposed to you after you've cooked for them.
   E. None of the above.

5. 5. **Your number of lovers...**
   A. Possibly over 150 (but who's counting?)
   B. Close to 50 (but ask me how many were good?)
   C. Around 30 (solid number for a goody goody)
   D. 25 or less (but you racked up most of those numbers later on in life)
   E. A lady never tells...

6. **A romantic evening for you would be...**
   A. A fancy restaurant, then dancing, then sex on the beach, sex at a motel, or a hotel, or a Holiday Inn... you get the point.
   B. Something culturally stimulating like the theater, then an engaging conversation over dinner, then a high-class evening somewhere you'll be seen by important people.

C. Something out of the ordinary, maybe even quirky like a dance contest, then watching the sunrise over steaming cups of hot cocoa…
D. You're young at heart, so you like a man to whip up some silly shenanigans. You don't need a lot of money spent on you, and can have a lot of fun playing games right at home.
E. None of the above

7. **Your type of guy…**
A. Rich, charming, and you're always in danger of someone sleazy.
B. Smart, kind, whimsical, and respectful of you in a way that your ex wasn't.
C. The opposite of you. The kind of guy that knows what you don't know and finds all your quirks totally charming.
D. He's got to be old-school, funny, a little bit tough, but a little bit cuddly.
E. None of the above

8. **Your choices of favorite books are:**
A. Romantic sagas, Danielle-Steele romances, and let's face it, anything trashy.
B. You're a bit of a book snob about the Classics (Hollywood tell-alls may have snuck in).
C. Fairy tales, allegories, cookbooks, and simple, popular reads. You really have not read the Classics or much of anything and get confused when someone even brings up authors.
D. You don't really have any. You're well-versed in literature, even though you haven't read the books. You can fake it and you know the references.
E. None of the above.

9. **Your feelings towards animals:**
A. No, thank you. They are filthy beasts, and the only filthy beasts you allow are the men in your bed.
B. You act a little hostile towards them, but that can be traced to a traumatic pet experience you had as a child.
C. You love animals more than people and would sleep in a zoo if you could.
D. You don't bother them if they don't bother you. You'd consider living with a pet because you do get along with them.

E. None of the above.

10. Your feelings toward children:

A. They don't seem to like you or relate to you.
B. They are afraid of you.
C. They don't respect you and usually take advantage of you.
D. They do relate to you and think you are one of them.
E. None of the above

11. Your ideal career path would probably be...

A. Something involving the arts and social events.
B. A teacher or a lawyer.
C. Something involving helping people.
D. Almost anything because you're versatile; you can serve people or be comfortable being totally in charge.
E. None of the above

12. You'd most enjoy living in...

A. Small, wealthy towns, where there's a sense of old-fashioned values.
B. Metropolitan cities, where there is a lot of hustling, bustling and cultural events to stimulate your thirst for knowledge.
C. Rural areas and farm towns. Ideally, you want to know everyone's name and see animals everywhere you go.
D. Villages and areas with old-school values, whether it's a close-knit neighborhood or a European town.
E. None of the above

13. Your friends might criticize you for...

A. Being a bit self-centered, vain, and egotistical.
B. Being a buzzkill and a perfectionist.
C. Being a bit naive, and ditzy, and not understanding what anyone's talking about.
D. Being a bit sneaky, always breaking the rules and getting into trouble.
E. None of the above

14. In high school, you were known to be...

A. The belle of the ball, but a boyfriend stealer.
B. A bookworm, and sometimes taken advantage of by cooler kids.
C. Popular and active, though a bit of a prude.
D. Exactly the same as you are now—spicy and sarcastic, taking no bull from anyone, even teachers.
E. None of the above

15. Your wardrobe might be criticized for...

A. Dressing too young for your age.
B. Being boring and never sexy.
C. Not keeping up with the styles.
D. Wearing the same thing all the time.
E. None of the above

16. **Your closest friends and family might describe you as...**

A. A tramp, but a fun one.
B. A buzzkill, but someone who will give rational advice.
C. A goody goody, but someone who will never say no to a favor.
D. A little too blunt, but someone who will break the rules to get you out of a jam.
E. None of the above

17. Your views on religion:

A. You say you follow a religion, but you would call yourself lapsed. Every now and then, you bargain with God.
B. You follow the basics of the religion you were born into.
C. You don't take your own religion so seriously, as you think of it as just one way to absorb nature and life, and you wish you could just sit in one inclusive church with all religions.
D. You don't really practice your religion; you just save it for the superstitions, putting curses on people, and emergency prayers when you need a favor.
E. None of the above.

18. What would happen if you kissed another woman's man at a party...

A. When *haven't* I kissed another woman's man at a party?
B. I wish my life was that exciting.

C. There was that time it was a full moon and I was stressed out, but I would *never*.
D. What am I a tramp? Okay, one time I was accused of that, but it wasn't me.
E. None of the above

Odds are you favored one of these more than the other., but the point of the show—and certainly the point of the book—is that we have a bit of each of the Girls hiding within us. So, inevitably, you received a mix of all four answers.

If you received mostly As, you are most like Blanche.

You are a bit of sexpot, a vixen; you are a romantic, addicted to love and passion, and you will find a date, not just on a Saturday night, but on a Tuesday morning. Your appearance is important to you, and you can be vain and self-centered, but in the end, you are a good friend and loyal to the people you love. Your youth was full of drama and excitement, and you've collected many lovers that still cheer your name. But more importantly, you are fun at a bar and will be adding to your Book of Trysts till you are 110 years old.

If you received mostly Bs, you are the most like Dorothy.

You are a bit of a teacher and a buzzkill; you are pragmatic, serious, and responsible. You have always played life by the book and done the responsible thing, though life hasn't always rewarded you for it. In your older years, you have come to show your wilder, more care-free side and finally make some of your wilder dreams come true. When you were younger, you let friends and lovers take advantage of you, but your self-confidence has finally emerged. You will cut somebody down pretty quickly if they mess with you or somebody you care about.

If you received mostly Cs, you are the most like Rose.

You're an earthmother, a salt-of-the-earth genuine soul; you're often naive, and though people mistake you for being ditzy, you have stronger instincts about people than most of your friends. Because you always come from a place of honesty, you can sense when someone else isn't giving you a straight story. You're hopelessly old-fashioned, love animals and nature, and you love people that appreciate those qualities in you. Jerks and city slickers have no appeal to you, and you don't give your heart away easily. You can't help but take care of people in need, are often relentlessly optimistic, and are the type of person that still sleeps with her childhood teddy bear.

If you received mostly Ds, you are most likely a Sophia.

You are quick-witted, sarcastic, and often say shockingly insulting things to people, and yet, you get away with it. Let's just say you have a certain kind of charm. You're romantic and spicy, but you don't fall in love frequently, and when you do, you're still the boss. You're always up to something, whether it's for your amusement or getting a good deal. You're quick to help out friends, but you're no pushover, and you need your nap time. You value family and friends more than anything, even when they drive you nuts. But when someone wrongs you, you will put a curse on them.

The Golden Girls

SEASON ONE

The Pilot

"This is the perfect pilot."
—Bruce Paltrow, St. Elsewhere *executive producer*

"Normally with new shows, they take only a few minutes' worth of clips to show the advertisers. But with The Golden Girls, they decided to show the whole pilot. And from what I've been told, the audience in the grand ballroom at the Waldorf Astoria hotel laughed so loud that they ended up missing some of the lines. Five minutes after it finished, my phone rang, and it was my friend, Grant Tinker, who was then at NBC. He said, 'Betty, don't make any plans for the next couple of years. I think you're going to be very busy.'"—Betty White

"Everyone there, from the performers to the craft guy to the network to us, knew it was a home run."—Paul Witt

The pilot was recorded on April 17th, 1985, requiring two tapings in front of a live audience. One was the "dress show" to work out kinks and rewrite lines that didn't work, with the other "live show" later in the evening. The big surprise for the producers wasn't that the show got so many laughs, but that Estelle Getty—who they already knew was capable of getting plenty of big laughs—was immediately such an audience favorite, leading to the decision to cut the character of Coco, the gay houseboy.

Coco (Charles Levin) was well-liked by the live audience, who hadn't seen an obviously flamboyant character as part of a main cast, let alone being perfectly accepted by the other characters, but with only 23 minutes of show to film, Coco was eliminated. I do wish he had come back with an update, but only a few characters returned in this show—that just wasn't the writers' style.

1-1 "The Pilot/The Engagement"

Written by: Susan Harris
Aired: September 14, 1985
Director: Jay Sandrich
Guest Cast: Coco (Charles Levin), Harry (Frank Aletter), the policeman (Meshach Taylor), the minister (F. William Parker)
Summary: Sophia moves in after her nursing home burns down and Blanche accepts a wedding proposal.
Rating: ❤❤❤

"Oh, it is wonderful dating in Miami. All the single men under 80 are cocaine smugglers." —Dorothy

Pilots are rarely good; it's almost possible for them to be great. But every fan of this show knows that *The Golden Girls* pilot delivered magnificently. The truth is a lot of pilots have casts that the audience likes. After all, networks look for chemistry between actors, run audience tests, and do exhaustive research just to make sure. But it's always a crapshoot. That's where the script comes in. Sometimes networks try too hard to cast a certain actor in a role, or something about the context of the script just doesn't ring true. Or the lines just seem contrived. For *The Golden Girls*, the actresses and the lines were perfect.

Most of the actresses weren't exactly playing against their type. Sure, Betty White wasn't a ditz, but she was a genuinely optimistic person—so Rose fit her well. Bea Arthur as Dorothy worked because it wasn't too far from her Maude character. Bea couldn't play a weak wallflower. She was strong and said what she meant, so when she walked into the house with lines about how she's a substitute teacher and that she told the class to leave because they were too ugly, the audience was on board.

But then Dorothy has this amazing monologue about aging, and how she wishes she was still 40, that makes the audience just fall in love with her. Or at least, I think they did. It's that magical acting and writing, because in that moment Bea Arthur is so real and vulnerable, yet not overdramatic. It hits all the right notes.

Then Rose entering, complaining about how she dealt with too many sad people, even though she works as a grief counselor, speaks to her obliviousness and quest for joy above all else. Blanche at this point is not quite the Blanche we will come to know. She's slightly younger and clearly the most man-crazy, but the southern accent hasn't emerged yet, and her charming egocentrism is just bubbling over the surface when she insults Rose's thighs.

We meet Coco, the houseboy that was not meant to be. I wish he had returned at some point for continuity, or "whatever happened to that houseboy we had?" sort of thing, but we'll soon learn that continuity is this show's weakest spot!

Dorothy, Rose and Coco discuss Blanche's new man Harry, and what Blanche likes about him. Apparently, she likes that he's a gentleman and is still interested in sex. She'll get pickier in later seasons. But the big news is that he proposed! They get a surprise visit from Sophia—the eternal scene-stealer—who's even more blunt than Dorothy. She tells Blanche that she looks like a prostitute, and calls Coco "the fancy man." Blanche provides some backstory, telling Rose that Sophia had a stroke and lost the part of her brain that censors what she says.

This becomes particularly rich, because throughout the series the more we learn about Sophia, the more we understand that she was born like this and it's not due to a stroke. Honestly, as an Italian girl from New York myself, I'm estimating that 85% of this behavior is due to the New Yorker/Italian part. The rest has only been slightly exacerbated by age and the stroke.

Sophia complains about her nursing home burning down and how they had bells going off like crazy, scaring the residents with heart problems, but the best part is how quickly she sees through Harry. She exclaims, "The man is a scuzzball" which gets a huge laugh from the audience. But then, just as the show did previously with Dorothy, we get a poignant monologue from Rose about how lucky they were to find each other—how lonely life can be at that age and how sad it'll be to separate again. I mean, this was a lot of sadness to unwrap, but I think it nabbed an audience right away. Nobody was writing stuff like this at the time.

Dorothy and Rose wait up with Coco to find out whether Blanche said yes to Harry, which she does, but not without letting the girls know that they can live there until they find a place. Dorothy and Rose talk about their husbands, and Dorothy reveals that her ex ran off with a stewardess on his way to Hawaii and hopes that he falls into a volcano.

Sophia enters and gives her first speech about having incontinence issues, which again, the audience adores.

The wedding day arrives, and Rose corners Dorothy about being suspicious of Harry and how she wants to warn Blanche. She claims to have a hunch and that her hunches are never wrong. She also claims that Indira Gandhi would still be alive if she'd taken her call. Dorothy restrains Rose, throwing her into the bedroom closet. Meanwhile, Blanche waits for Harry who's 30 minutes late, only to have a policeman come to the door to tell her that he's been arrested for bigamy.

He gives her a crappy note from Harry mentioning how he "really liked her" and doesn't even use the word "love." Boo, Harry. McClanahan plays this scene really well, both heartbroken and shocked. Again, spectacular acting and solid writing.

The episode ends with Rose and Dorothy on the lanai (though they don't use that word yet) discussing Blanche's recent depression, while Sophia pretends to be sleeping. Dorothy gives a speech comparing how Irish people, Jewish people, and Italians grieve—which is actually quite original—when Sophia butts in with a crack about how she wants to be left when she dies. Then Blanche comes out, suddenly chipper, and says she's feeling better thanks to the Girls, who are like her family. They have clearly done a lot of bonding in the few months they've lived together, but again, the acting pulls it off. It's a common feeling I have with this show, that it goes right up to the line of cornball, but they rarely cross it. It's cute, funny and comforting.

Golden Nuggets

There are lots of goofs that would come become commonplace concerning character's ages, how long the Girls had been married, and how long their husbands have been dead. Rose says Charlie's been dead for 15 years, but in a later episode he dies right before she moves to Miami. Also, Dorothy describes Stan as a 65-year-old man, but he's her age. Based on them being married for 38 years, and getting married at about 18, that would put him in his late 50s.

The monologue that Dorothy gives in the kitchen about feeling old after talking to 20-somethings, and how she looked in the mirror is powerful. And you get it just a few minutes into the episode. Even when I was a kid in the 80s, that scene kind of popped because it didn't sound like other sitcom dialogue. It sounded real and genuine.

Rose explains to Dorothy that Blanche needed a date to George's funeral, because she needs a man. But she emphasizes needs a man.

Dorothy seamlessly comes in from work and starts the very first mini-kitchen confession, as she delves into feeling so much older than the 20-something teachers at work and how she wishes she was 40 again.

Maybe I was born cynical, or I just watched too much TV as a kid, but quick proposals were always obvious red flags. I knew this by the time I was nine years old.

A scene had to be cut where Coco commiserates with Sophia about his dating life, as the network decided that the gay character would be okay so long he didn't discuss dating men. This was a long time before Will & Grace.

The original "scuzzball" line was actually, "the man is a douchebag."

You'll hear Blanche's first "I'm stunned" at the end when she hears the news about Harry.

This episode has the first known instance of the word "pee" heard on network television.

I know television writing has changed so much in over three decades, but I would argue that this is a pilot to analyze for how to do it right. The Girls' backstories are defined, their character flaws exposed, and even their sense of humor, strengths, weaknesses and sensibilities are outlined in just under 25 minutes.

For instance, Dorothy's tough enough to handle her job, and a marriage falling apart, but she's vulnerable and we soften towards her immediately as she complains about feeling old. And Rose has a lot of funny lines where she comes off as dumb, but she's the one with the correct instincts about Harry. She may not understand sarcasm or nuance, but she has what they call emotional intelligence. Blanche is man-crazy, but also values friendship. And Sophia, probably the least developed in the pilot, is a truth teller and the audience suspects that it was no stroke that got her to start insulting people. She was born doing that.

1-2 "Guess Who's Coming to the Wedding?"

Written by: Paul Bogart, Winifred Hervey
Aired: September 21, 1985
Director: Paul Bogart
Guest Cast: Stanley Zbornak (Herb Edelman), Kate (Lisa Jane Persky), Dennis (Dennis Drake)
Summary: Dorothy's daughter gets married and she has to confront her ex-husband, Stanley, about the end of their 38-year marriage.
Rating: ♥♥♥

"Have you ever met a man who knew how to push all your buttons?" —Dorothy
"Just once. He was a cabana boy in Pensacola."—Blanche

Bea Arthur slays this episode with her scene at the end, but it's also the first time we meet her ex-husband, Stanley Zbornak. Their relationship is so well-written, and so familiar to people who have gone through divorce. At this point, they're bickering and passive-aggressive, but it will evolve and devolve with a lot of humor and sincerity. Dorothy is the type of woman who says exactly what you'd want to say, right in the moment. Her speech at the end to Stanley is probably what many women wish they had said to their exes.

Golden Nuggets

Dorothy's speech at the end. Classic Dorothy diatribe.

Blanche's mention of the sorority gossip about Miss MacGyver is one of the first examples of same-sex coupling on the show, and they do it in a rather offhand, casual way, which was pretty progressive at the time.

A rare episode where no one has sex. Also rare, no St. Olaf story!

Sophia reveals her notable issues with priests. She's a devoted, yet rebellious Catholic.

You're out of order! Obviously, Stan is, but also this episode was filmed fourth. The producers however thought it was so strong that they pushed it up, as it established Dorothy's strength and vulnerability so well.

Kate and Dennis are so blah and so boring, that as a viewer you'll kind of be waiting for the Girls to be back in focus (especially if you're viewing for the first time).

Having the second episode delve into the reality of what happens when a middle-aged woman is pushed aside by her husband, demonstrates the strong, feminist viewpoint of the show. But it keeps Stan likable and Bea Arthur doesn't play this shrill. You see the hurt in her eyes.

1-3 Rose the Prude

Writers: Susan Harris, Barry Fanaro, Mort Nathan
Aired: September 28, 1985
Director: Jim Drake
Guest Cast: Harold Gould (Arnie)
Summary: Rose considers having sex with a new boyfriend even though she has never slept with any other man since her late husband.
Rating: ❤❤❤

"Now when you lean over, it looks like someone let the air out of your face. Honey, lean over a mirror some time and take a look at yourself. I think you better take a sedative before you look." —Dorothy

The first season does a good job making us fall in love with each character. This episode is for Rose, and Betty White shows all her tenderness and sweetness in more than one scene. It also has the first sex talk around the kitchen table and it's fantastic. Years later, I realize this concept was revolutionary not just because it was women talking about sex in a real way, but because they were women over 50. Hearing Sophia, an 80+ grandmother talk about sex with such delight was so refreshing. Then hearing Blanche's straight and to-the-point revelation of the first time she had sex after her husband dies is what made the show barrier-breaking. This is, in my opinion, the precursor to the *Sex and the City* brunch scenes.

The B story is light and playful, devoted to Sophia and Dorothy's card playing.

Golden Nuggets

The first discussion about sex around the kitchen table (though Rose is not present) is a must-watch. Also, Rose tells the Girls that she hasn't been with a man since Charlie died, but she will repeat this story in a later episode, regarding the fact that Charlie died while having sex with her. Continuity regarding marriages and the number of children the Girls have, is definitely not the show's strong point.

First sex talk around the kitchen table is the most notable, but an honorary mention goes to an earlier scene where Blanche recalls a sexual episode with adhesive tape.

Susan Harris is the GOAT (Genius of All Time). Enough can't be said of her writing talents, and I think it's because she's a woman. Apparently, Terry Hughes says she phoned in that scene from an airplane, because the episode wasn't funny enough and it killed. Later on, it was used in a performance for the Queen of England.

Some hints at the idiocy of St. Olaf are here, where Rose hasn't even heard of a prostate. But the true insanity of the town has yet to come.

As in the last episode, Sophia and Dorothy's relationship is close in a real way, as evidenced by their teasing and card playing.

Betty White won her first Emmy for the show for this episode.

We meet the actor Harold Gould, one of the most beloved guest stars, who will later play Rose's permanent boyfriend Miles in Season Five.

Besides Arnie revealing that he "patted a few bottoms," this episode is pretty sex-positive for a show in the 1980s. It shows older women still interested in sex, and Arnie is respectful of Rose's boundaries.

1-4 Transplant

Aired: October 5, 1985
Director: Paul Bogart
Writer: Susan Harris
Guest Cast: Sheree North (Virginia Hollingsworth)
Summary: Blanche's estranged, younger sister Virginia, comes to visit to ask for her kidney.
Rating: ❤❤

"And I had to wear that green dress. Which you knew was my worst awful color. Made me look just like a swamp frog."—Blanche

The writers very consciously wrote episodes to show off each actress' talent, and this one is no different. And why not? First Bea, then Betty, and now Rue. And Rue plays it wonderfully, toeing the line between hatefulness towards her sister, yet remaining lovable and amusing. She plays the vain, southern vixen for all its worth, but when it comes down to it, when her sister wants the kidney, she comes through. But she's not above bitching about it.

Blanche's family dynamics will run through a few episodes, and her sisters' fighting make for entertaining fodder worthy of a soap opera. Still, it's not a favorite episode of mine, with a weak B story about the Girls watching a baby. Hold tight, there will be much better Blanche episodes coming.

For serious fans, you should note that this episode has a different directing style than most, in that it's directed by Paul Bogart and not Terry Hughes, who used a much more dramatic style utilizing close-ups. McClanahan worked well with him and Terry Hughes, but Betty White seemed to prefer Hughes' lightness. I prefer Hughes by a long shot.

Golden Nuggets

Sophia's insistence that there is no choice here is heavy. You give up your kidney because it's family. Blanche's explanation of Sophia to her sister is, "She's Italian." It's a quick explanation of how Sophia sees the world.

Rose says she never heard of hating one's sister, but in a later episode it's revealed that she does in fact, hate one of her sisters. Also, Blanche states that Virginia is the only family she has, yet in later episodes, we meet her brother, her other sister, and her father.

The sexual interplay is fun and pragmatic between Blanche and her sister, hearing about how they fought over boys, and how Blanche claimed to love them after just two dates. “I was fast.”

No sex in this episode, which might be why it’s not a particularly top one on my list.

Another reason this episode is kind of weak is a lack of Sicily stories, St. Olaf stories, and great South stories.

First mention of Dorothy’s brother Phil.

Most women on this show will reveal they were the victim of a cheating husband, and in this case, the cheater was Virginia’s husband.

1-5 The Triangle

Aired: October 19, 1985
Director: Jim Drake
Writer: Susan Harris, Winifred Hervey
Guest Cast: Elliot Clayton (Peter Hansen)
Summary: Dorothy's boyfriend causes a rift between the girls when he makes a pass at Blanche, but Dorothy doesn't believe her.
Rating: ❤❤❤

"I know I look square, but I'm like my father's tractor. I take a while to warm up but once I do, I can turn your topsoil till the cows come home."—Rose

This is an episode that, upon re-watching, demonstrates so much that it's written by women and couldn't have been written the same way by men. We see that Blanche might be sexually free, but she still has rules. Or at least has definitive lines when it comes to her friends. Though she's initially interested in Dorothy's guy, Elliot, Blanche won't go behind Dorothy's back. And then, as intelligent as Dorothy is, we see that she does have a blind spot when it comes to Blanche.

But just because Blanche is seemingly oversexed, is she any less trustworthy? Is she targeted by Elliot because he knows her friend will choose him over her? In the #MeToo era, where believing women is so much at the forefront, these questions take on more significance. In other words, your friend *is* probably telling the truth, rather than the other way around. Also, it's interesting that Rose, who is painted as naïve and simpleminded, believes Blanche just on her instincts. There are a few episodes where Rose actually comes out as the smartest.

Golden Nuggets

For Betty White fans, she's clearly conjuring Sue Ann Nivens from *The Mary Tyler Moore Show* with Rose's attempt at acting sexy.

Not a lot of talk about sex, but this is the first one we see Dorothy in a relationship.

We also get Sophia's first Sicily story and it's a great one about her and Mama Celeste. Sophia's stories will often follow this format, where there is a reveal at the end that one of the characters in her past is in fact, famous. And it always works as a laugh line.

This was also the first *Golden Girls* episode where Bea Arthur received an Emmy nomination, though she lost to Betty White. Personally, I think they should've nominated her for "Guess Who's Coming to the Wedding?"

1-6 On Golden Girls

Aired: October 26, 1985
Director: Jim Drake
Writer: Susan Harris, Liz Sage
Guest Cast: David (Billy Jacoby)
Summary: Blanche's 15-year-old grandson comes to visit, and the Girls have trouble disciplining him.
Rating: ❤❤

"Is that all you Italians know how to do? Scream and hit?"—Blanche
"No. We also know how to make love and sing opera."—Sophia

This episode is a good example of the show's biggest weakness—that as good as it is about writing about older people, it's not quite as adept at writing the younger generation. These writers are definitely not mimicking John Hughes. Everything about this episode seemed antiquated, even when I was only eight years old.

David is portrayed almost as if the writers never met teenagers. He brings home friends who blast music and wake up a house of older women, as if that's what teenage boys thought was a good time in 1985.

Then, in a quick attempt at some sort of resolution, there's a fight, a runaway attempt, Sophia slaps him, they make him do chores, and by the end of it all they're all happy together. I don't know who bought into this. I couldn't help but think that someone on the writing staff had a mean grandson. You almost think someone actually was going to write the words "It's that damn rock & roll music!" Either way, what saves the episode is the scene in bed between Dorothy and Sophia, and the scene between Dorothy and David.

Golden Nuggets

The first scene of Dorothy and Sophia sharing a bed, where Dorothy shares "the bear dream" is precious. Those two were always so cute and the fact that Estelle was a little younger than Bea makes it all the more amazing that they pulled off the mother/daughter chemistry.

Punishment in Rose's childhood meant milking a cow that was sitting on a stool. Now that's brutal.

The guy playing Billy is the son of the guy who plays Michael, Dorothy's son.

This is the first episode where Sophia calls Dorothy "pussycat."

We get our first reference to Blanche's parenting and how she regrets not being the most present mother to her children, as she let nannies do most of the work.

I don't know how to feel about this one because I'm Italian, and my own personal experience is that kids that were hit as children were never better behaved than the kids that weren't. Hitting all the time doesn't seem to work, but there were children growing up (and you know who they are) that every parent would just look at during birthday parties and think, "I wish their parents would smack them just once."

1-7 The Competition

Aired: November 2, 1985
Director: Jim Drake
Writer: Susan Harris, Barry Fanaro, Mort Nathan
Guest Cast: Augustine Bagatelli (Ralph Manza)
Summary: The Girls get competitive when stakes are raised during a bowling tournament.
Rating: 

"Anyone who has ever competed understands what you're going through. So, listen sweetheart. If you don't feel like bowling, you don't have to. You just hold on to the bowl, and I'll throw you down there."—Dorothy

This episode has it all. All four Girls have funny moments and it shows them as multi-faceted. Sophia wins out as the most adorable and it's the first episode that showcases Estelle Getty's acting chops as broader than the wisecracking old lady. Little kids at the time saw themselves in her, and in this episode, she is literally trying to sneak away with her boyfriend on a trip.

Meanwhile Rose shows that she has a brutal, competitive streak. Though we'd imagine Blanche to be the competitive nightmare, she gets insane performance anxiety. Dorothy throws the game because, like us, she can't handle how cute Sophia and Auggie are trying to win for a nostalgic trip to Sicily. She may be tough and strict, but not made of stone. So, this episode mixes the A and B stories perfectly and is just a bunch of wins.

Golden Nuggets

Cute and satisfying ending. Sophia gives Dorothy the emerald earrings and Rose adds the names on the statue, telling you a lot about how seriously deranged Rose is, and how solid Sophia and Dorothy are.

Blanche mentions a story about being dumped for a girl named Rebecca. She probably wouldn't have named her daughter Rebecca had this been the case. Also, Blanche's stories about never being dumped are remarkably inconsistent throughout the series.

When Sophia says to her red sauce, "if this sauce was a person, I'd get naked and make love to it" is great. I kind of love that she says "person" and not man or woman. When it comes to that sauce, she's so turned on that she becomes pansexual.

We get our first mention of one of many of Sophia's previous fiancés.

No St. Olaf story. Boo. But the episode is so strong that it doesn't need one.

High marks for portrayals of older women dating. Sophia is supposedly about 81 in this episode and she's as smitten with her ex as a teenager.

1-8 Break-In

Aired: November 9, 1985
Director: Paul Bogart
Writer: Susan Harris
Guest Cast: Lester (Robert Rothwell), The Salesman (Christian Clemenson)
Summary: Rose freaks out and becomes afraid after the Girls' home is burglarized.
Rating: ♥♥

"Please, please, she did things on that stage I never did with my husband."—Dorothy

This episode is definitely overtly political. A lot of shows in the 1980s and 1990s have the perspective that it's a bad idea to purchase a gun for home protection. And though I am a huge proponent of safe gun legislation, I think this trope always reads a little forced. Granted, Rose is in a fragile mental state when she buys the gun, but still. What inevitably happens is that Rose almost kills someone.

Sure, she gets her gusto back after attacking an innocent person, and isn't afraid anymore, but the gun thing bothers me. A household of four women living alone, owning a gun, isn't a bad idea. Dare I say it's a decent idea, as long as everyone has their eyesight checked and learns how to use it. I just hate when shows write stories where someone buys a gun and suddenly becomes an irresponsible idiot.

However, there's still enough humor in this episode to save it: Sophia scaring the dog into submission, Lester and the vase, and of course Blanche's retelling of going to the police station and spraying mace when she thinks it's hairspray.

Golden Nuggets

The opening scene where the Girls discuss the Madonna concert is refreshing, and it's not because they're taking their grandkids. Sophia does call Madonna a slut, but hey, she's an unfiltered Italian lady. Love her or leave her.

Rose acts afraid of big dogs, but in later episodes certainly isn't. The vase that gets shot also makes an amazing recovery in later episodes.

Blanche's retelling of her waking George up in the middle of the night when she thought she heard an intruder, ends on a sexy note as most Blanche stories do.

Miami might be known for law-enforcement hiccups, but I don't think they'd return evidence to Blanche before a trial.

If they're going to live in Miami—beyond buying guns and getting dogs—Blanche needs to hide her jewelry better and Rose needs to get a better idea of what cocaine looks like.

1-9 Blanche and the Younger Man

Aired: November 16, 1985
Director: Jim Drake
Writer: Susan Harris, James Berg
Guest Cast: Alma Lindstrom (Jeanette Nolan), Dirk (Charles Hill)
Summary: Blanche attempts to date a younger man, while Rose smothers her visiting mother.
Rating: ❤❤❤

"This is strictly off the record, but Dirk's nearly five years younger than I am."—Blanche
"In what Blanche, dog years?"—Dorothy

This episode is confusing, because the main plot seems to be Rose smothering her visiting mother, yet the title is about Blanche and the younger man. Either way, both stories provide humor, though Blanche's provides more. She diets and exercises for a few days to look fabulous, all to realize that the guy just wants to take her out because she reminds him of his mother. I'm not sure who is guiltier of the mixed messages. A Saturday night dinner date isn't a friend request, but on the other hand, Blanche, 20-something year old guys aren't usually looking for a 50-something girlfriend—unless it's a sugar mama. So be skeptical.

Also, Blanche ordering almost no food is a kind-of-weak stereotype. If a younger man does go for an older woman, I don't think it's because she doesn't eat. Of course, the date is portrayed as a weak stereotype too. I don't buy that anyone is so dumb as to say they liked working at a museum because they enjoyed lifting the artwork. But the exchange about reading *Pumping Iron* and how the movie couldn't top the book cracks me up.

On the flip side, ageism is better addressed with how Rose treats her mother like she's incompetent and unable to do anything. The scenes are almost embarrassing for Betty White, because neither she nor Rose seem like they could ever be that unreasonable.

For insiders, it should be noted there's a lot of sentiment in this episode because both Betty and Bea's mothers were dying while this episode was being rehearsed, with Bea's passing away two days before. Also, the writers added the scene where Betty talks about her husband dying, which was reminiscent of Betty's husband who had died a few years before. On top of that, the actress playing Alma was having trouble with her lines all week. It seems like it was an emotional roller coaster kind of filming week.

Golden Nuggets

Turns out, Walt Disney was not cryogenically frozen. I know? He was cremated. So there, you learned something.

Alma for the winning sex story of the episode! This is combined with a St. Olaf story that apparently, when Rose's mom tells one, is kind of riveting and involves an ex-con.

It must be noted that in this episode, the makeup these women have on while in their pajamas is extraordinary—and heavy. Also, this show always had these women in A-game pajamas and nightgowns.

1-10 Heart Attack

Aired: November 23, 1985
Director: Jim Drake
Writer: Susan Harris, James Berg
Guest Cast: Dr. Harris (Ronald Hunter)
Summary: Sophia thinks she's having a heart attack after the Girls throw a house party.
Rating: 

"Sophia, I always thought there'd be a Catholic heaven, with nuns and priests and churches. And then a separate, Protestant heaven with people and cows and horses. And then a Jewish heaven with libraries... and furriers..."—Rose
"You're starting to annoy me.
You shouldn't annoy a sick person."—Sophia

This is my first favorite Sophia episode and it shows us all the depth she lends to the character. You almost can't believe the writers wrote this character before they had met her. Here, everyone worries that Sophia might die of a heart attack, as the paramedics take too long to get to the house during a storm. And that's what the show does best—mixed humor with genuinely touching moments about life and death.

A fun thing to note is that this episode was almost done live, since it only takes place in the house. But between Estelle Getty's obvious stage fright and the fact the other Girls had such different processes for learning lines, the idea was dismissed.

Golden Nuggets

I just find this episode's quote so funny because it's borderline offensive. And Sophia's response, played by Estelle who was actually Jewish, listening to the idea of a Jewish heaven with furriers is easy to gloss over. Rose is actually proposing a segregated heaven, but she's doing so in a sweet, naive way. And Sophia gets that. But the response of "don't annoy a sick person" is just solid advice.

Rose tells, as if for the first time, that Charlie died while having sex, but adds more jokes and a tender ending where they dress him before the paramedics get there.

Blanche really, truly and sincerely asks if there are a lot of men in heaven… probably not enough for Blanche.

Who hasn't tried to wake up an older person, thinking they might be dead, before realizing they just scared the crap out of someone and made them feel really old? Just me?

When an Italian mother says she "ate a little of this and that," it could mean something like this: scungilli, sausage and peppers, Fettuccine Alfredo, fried mozzarella, catalonni, mushrooms with gorgonzola, and milk duds.

1-11 The Return of Dorothy's Ex/Stan's Return

Aired: November 30, 1985
Director: Jim Drake
Writer: Susan Harris, Terry Grossman, Kathy Speer
Guest Cast: Stanley Zbornak (Herb Edelman), Chrissy (Simone Griffeth)
Summary: When Stan stops by in order to have some property papers signed, he and Dorothy almost get back together.
Rating: ❤❤❤

"Well, I'm shocked."—Rose
"I was too. You know Chrissy didn't teach him a thing."—Dorothy

If you're a big Dorothy and Stan fan, they're a hoot as the show's divorced, sometimes-reconciling but mostly arguing, always-rehashing-their-past couple. This time we get a good laugh as Sophia, Rose, and Blanche see Stan emerge in Dorothy's robe the morning after. Shock of their life right there. But the show has a touch of poignancy as we see Dorothy struggle with Stan's tempting offer—the comfort of his companionship, his familiarity. Stan isn't perfect, but we know from later on in the show that he loves Dorothy. She's just better and stronger without him, but we're not sure that he's better without her.

I get that older men leave their wives for younger women, but a pretty 22-year old stewardess marrying Stan never computed for me, mostly because Stan has no money and wasn't exactly the sexiest man alive. We never get to know Chrissy much, but this girl must've had significant issues. Also, the actress playing her was not in her early 20s, but about 35.

Golden Nuggets

Various innuendos about Stan and Dorothy's bad sex life are everywhere: their first convo at the door, Stan's poor recollection of the Honeymoon Hacienda, and Dorothy's final insult about "the dumb blonde who's not going to get any."

Only one weak St. Olaf throwback to when Rose wanted to be an actress as a child.

Bea Arthur was reluctant to do this episode because it reminded her of her own marriage.

We all know a friend who has been in an on-again, off-again relationship with an ex. After a while, you just want to kill them both or force them to stay married.

At this point, the kitchen table is designated as Crisis Central, as food is already prepared for Dorothy.

No matter what age, the struggle is real for older women thinking of taking back an ex. It's hard not to go back, but channel your inner Dorothy if you can.

1-12 The Custody Battle

Aired: December 7, 1985
Director: Terry Hughes
Writer: Susan Harris, Winifred Hervey
Guest Cast: Gloria Petrilla (Doris Belack)
Summary: Dorothy's sister, Gloria, comes to visit, causing a rift.
Rating: ❤❤

"I had an imaginary friend. But he would never tell me his name."—Rose

This episode falls kind of flat with Sophia playing the pestering mother, tormenting Dorothy about her life and comparing her to her sister, Gloria. She constantly mentions that Dorothy doesn't have a date, and should date more like Gloria, insulting Dorothy in an unnecessarily cruel way. Throughout the show, Sophia teases Dorothy about her height and appearance, but it usually doesn't seem forced. And Sophia makes fun of everyone.

But this seems too much to me for some reason. She just seems like the mean, nagging mother that wants you to think she loves you because she insults your appearance and your life all the time. Dorothy was married after all, and she does date. I came close to giving this one star because it does a disservice to my favorite character.

Anyway, the plot here is that the two daughters are fighting over who gets custody over their mother. I can't stress this enough, but I don't see this as a fight between my twin sister and me. The B story of Blanche sleeping with the theater director to get a local part in Macbeth gave me more laughs.

Golden Nuggets

Blanche's response to not getting the lead in *Macbeth*, with Rose getting Lady Macbeth, is quintessential Blanche. She takes Rose's nice gesture and flips it.

Blanche definitely gets laid often, and to rave reviews, though maybe not so much as her performance landed her the part of "Witch 3." Draw your own conclusions.

This is also Terry Hughes' debut episode as a director.

No St. Olaf, The South, or Sicily stories… usually not a good sign.

NBC had a bunch of sitcoms in the 80's that had side characters we never saw, like Vera on *Cheers* and Maris on *Frasie*r. We never meet Phil, Dorothy's brother.

The wallpaper here switches from a soft, gold color to white, printed leaves.

Check out Gloria's bedtime makeup! Good God, the makeup they put on these women to go to sleep should have gotten the makeup artists arrested.

There are definitely women that will sleep with a local theater director to get a part in a small production of Macbeth. Blanche Devereaux is that woman. And we must respect *all* the choices a woman makes. Too bad it's for the "witch" part.

1-13 A Little Romance

Aired: December 14, 1985
Director: Terry Hughes
Writer: Susan Harris, Barry Fanaro, Mort Nathan
Guest Cast: Dr. Jonathon Newman (Brent Collins), Edgar Lindstrom (Billy Barty), Jeane Dixon (herself)
Summary: Rose dates a little person and struggles with embarrassment and a possible marriage proposal.
Rating: ❤❤❤

"How big a man is shouldn't make or break a relationship?"—Rose
"Not a word, Blanche."—Dorothy

I love the outfits that Dorothy and Rose wear to the dinner party—the jewel tones are to die for. I miss the 80's. But the scene to watch in this episode is the arrival of Dr. Jonathan Newman, who comes as a great surprise to Blanche and Dorothy as Rose hasn't told them that he's a dwarf. Blanche thinks Rose is playing a joke on her, and her embarrassment in discovering that she was wrong is pure gold. Also, points to the writers for showing that although Rose is nervous about the relationship, she's genuinely attracted to him—as is Blanche for a brief moment.

What keeps this episode from being a favorite for me is the dream sequence. Dream sequences on TV shows, especially in the 1980s, always seemed silly to me. And this one—featuring Jeane Dixon, the psychic, and Rose marrying Jonathan—is a dud. Sophia thinking Rose is hiding Jonathan in the pillowcase however, gets me every time.

Golden Nuggets
The best part is a toss-up between Jonathan's arrival and Sophia discovering him. "I hope this doesn't sound rude…" We all have a friend that is a little too blunt when meeting people.

Blanche's dream of running naked through a train, while a sweaty body builder chases her *might* be sexual. Calling Dr. Freud…

Blanche begins a story that makes the audience think it's about interracial dating (which would've gotten Blanche and her beau Benjamin, killed in the 50's in the South). But the reveal is that Benjamin was a Yankee and that was what caused all the hullabaloo.

This episode is Betty White's favorite and it won an Emmy for Outstanding Writing in a Comedy Series.

Also in this episode, love exists between people of all heights, but apparently cannot withstand two different religions, in the case of Dr. Newman.

1-14 That Was No Lady

Aired: December 21, 1985
Director: Terry Hughes
Writer: Susan Harris, Liz Sage
Guest Cast: Glen O'Brien (Alex Rocco)
Summary: Dorothy finds out the man she is dating is married, and continues to date him, much to Sophia's dismay.
Rating: ❤❤❤❤

"You kids get to be middle-aged, you think you know everything!"—Sophia

There's lots of good stuff in this episode, with smart writing and witty lines all over the place. The fact that it's Dorothy who's been established as the levelheaded makes it even stronger. Also, to everyone's surprise, Blanche has never slept with a married man. Dorothy falls hard for Glen, finds out he's married, drops him, goes back to him, and then drops him again. And the whole time we don't judge her. Love is hard to find. And Glen, much like Stan, turns out to just be selfish, wanting things exactly how he wants them.

The B story works as some light humor, with Blanche selling her lemon of a car to Rose.

Golden Nuggets

The hotel room scene before Glen tells Dorothy that he's married is heartbreaking. She's just so genuinely happy and I didn't realize when I was younger how unusual scenes like this were. A woman in her 60's, in the throes of love and passion, making bad decisions and talking about how insecure she is about how she looks, was, and still is, a treasure. I still watch that and think, "You son of a bitch!"

The sex talk around the kitchen table revolves around sleeping with a married man, with one friend judging, and one friend encouraging (which, when you have two good friends, is usually the way it works out).

Behold Dorothy's green and purple silk suit. We'll see this probably more than any another outfit in the series.

Sophia sings Prince's "Purple Rain" on her Walkman, but you might not hear it on iTunes or Hulu because of permissions.

It looks like the Girls at this point are already numb to St. Olaf stories. This is probably the first truly great one, because it has a lot of levels, including Rose's husband selling insurance at eight years old.

Dorothy's supposed to be the smart one, but doesn't realize that Glen's married, even though whenever they have sex, it's in a hotel?

A tale as old as time itself. Dorothy's final moment with Glen probably takes women years to come to. Maybe now it takes less time, but it's a good scene for women of any age to watch and put in their psyche.

1-15 In a Bed of Rose's

Aired: January 11, 1986
Director: Terry Hughes
Writer: Susan Harris
Guest Cast: Al Beatty (Richard Roat), Lucille Beatty (Priscilla Morrill)
Summary: Rose awakens from a one-night stand to find the man dead of a heart attack—then she finds out he's married.
Rating: ❤❤❤❤

"You could light firecrackers in his nostrils,
you won't wake him."—Sophia

This episode is just chock full of laughs. It's strange that it comes after such a serious episode. The writers could have spaced these plot lines out better, but continuity wasn't a big concern back then.

Beyond that, Rose's guilt over another man dying in bed with her is a solid gift of hilarity. The ending, where Rose pretends she killed another man she slept with, is artfully acted by Betty White. I kind of believed her too.

The best thing to know about this episode is that it was written by Susan Harris and NBC didn't want to air it because it was too racy. Harris actually sat down with NBC executives and went over the script, line by line, and fought for the episode. She believed much of their problem was because it portrayed older women having sex and discussing it. The episode is considered a classic.

Golden Nuggets

When Rose goes to the wife's home to let her know what happened, I admit that I thought *that is a risky endeavor*. And it swings seamlessly through moments of awkwardness, embarrassment, and Rose's naiveté, though the actress playing Mrs. Beatty sometimes plays it a little too dramatic.

Rose rehashing the Charlie death story for the third time, causing Blanche to ask, "What exactly do you do in bed?" is hilarious.

We learn Dorothy doesn't make noise during sex, which makes Blanche speechless.

We get an unfortunate St. Olaf story this time, about a man Joe, who was backed over by a combine.

Note the activity level of these women. In the beginning they're heading to play golf, and at the end they're going square dancing.

Sophia's outfit to go square dancing wins the episode!

Fun fact: Blanche never saw her dead husband's corpse.

Another episode about men getting away with cheating, but in this one the man dies, the women become friends, and the woman starts sleeping with someone else. So… happy ending!

1-16 The Truth Will Out

Aired: January 18, 1986
Director: Terry Hughes
Writer: Susan Harris
Guest Cast: Kirsten (Christine Belford), Charley (Bridgette Anderson)
Summary: Rose hides from her daughter the fact that her husband didn't leave them a lot of money in his will.
Rating: ❤❤

"Dorothy, you're sleeping with a liar."—Rose
"Don't worry about it, Rose. Most of the people I've slept with were liars."—Dorothy

I'm not a big fan of episodes with visiting children or grandchildren. I think their casting leaves a lot to be desired and the actors never had any comedic chops. The episode focuses on family secrets and trying to spare your children from unpleasantness. Rose has led her daughter to believe that their father left them a lot of money, but he didn't. She acts as if she spent it all at first, but then fesses up in the end. Although it's a solid lesson on the nuances of wanting your children to believe the best about their parents, it's just not super-interesting or funny. It is of course well-acted by Betty White.

The B story, with the local tabloid murder, provides some repetitive laughs, but mostly the same joke about a dickey. And there are one-too many jokes about Sophia not understanding a basic conversation.

Golden Nuggets

The lesson between Rose and Charley, where Rose realizes that her lie has trickled down to her granddaughter, shows that the lies and secrets you keep from your kids affect later generations.

Blanche at first calls the murder case the Duncan/Osgood Case, then later on calls it the Patton/Osgood Case.

Blanche divulges an inappropriate sex story in front of Rose's grandchild involving a butcher block. You can't stop Blanche when she's being nostalgic.

Heavy makeup alert. The makeup artist really clobbers the lipstick on these ladies when they're wearing bathrobes.

Poor Charlie. We learn that Rose was in fact responsible with her money, and her husband wasn't much of a businessman, which I think was a good lesson for me when I was younger. The idea that a man is automatically more responsible with finances is not encouraged on this show. And I appreciate that.

1-17 Nice and Easy

Aired: February 1, 1986
Director: Terry Hughes
Writer: Susan Harris, Stuart Silverman
Guest Cast: Lucy (Hallie Todd), Ken Stovitz
Summary: Blanche worries about the dating habits of her visiting niece.
Rating: ❤❤

> *"If it weren't for a mouse, just like that little one in the kitchen, I wouldn't be sitting here today telling you this story."—Rose*

This episode runs into a weird problem by the name of Lucy. The actress playing her is perfectly fine and cute, but the plot is that everywhere Lucy goes, men drop their plans and ask her out. At the time, she was playing a 20-year-old who came into her looks and is suddenly getting male attention, but she still looks kind of awkward—especially for Miami in the 80s. I guess you're supposed to think she's not necessarily being super-sexual, just super-desperate.

Also, we don't really know if Lucy's sleeping with these men at all. Blanche's pep talk to her is the typical sitcom "wrap it up in 60-seconds" advice, when clearly there is a huge self-esteem problem. And we never hear about Lucy again! Which happens a lot on this show.

There's a B story with Dorothy coming to terms with her fear of mice, which is okay.

Golden Nuggets

I think the best scene is when Lucy's date Ed, who's obsessed with *Miami Vice,* ends up wanting to hang out with Rose because she's obsessed with the show too. Betty White's allure clearly had no limits.

There's an amazing Sicilian "slut-shaming story" from Sophia.

There's an OJ Simpson reference!

Was there an excessive attempt by NBC to give shout outs to *Miami Vice*?

1-18 The Operation

Aired: February 8, 1986
Director: Terry Hughes
Writer: Winifred Hervey
Guest Cast: Doctor Revell (Robert Picardo), Bonnie (Anne Haney)
Summary: Dorothy suffers a foot injury while dancing and is afraid to get an operation.
Rating: ❤❤❤

"Morton's Neuroma, I think I had that once. But how'd you ever catch that in your foot?" —Blanche

This episode is truly worth it, just to watch Blanche and Rose tap dance. Not to mention their legs look fantastic. But it also reveals a lot about Dorothy through her fear of hospitals and surgery. We also get a lot of good back-and-forth between Dorothy and Sophia, and their endless bantering about Dorothy's childhood which can be viewed as sometimes traumatic, but always amusing.

There are a few nuggets about the characters that will emerge throughout the series: Blanche has a lot of insecurities lying underneath her confident exterior; Dorothy can be a neurotic mess; Rose is not always the kind, sympathetic, nurturing type; and Sophia knows when Dorothy is bullshitting her. These characters build beyond the basic, comedic archetypes.

Golden Nuggets

The scene with Bonnie, the level-headed non-complainer who is sharing Dorothy's hospital room, is compelling. She gives Dorothy a pep talk that actually doesn't seem corny, illustrating that people are in the hospital facing much worse. And in the end, what choice do we have but to suck it up? The actress playing Bonnie nails it.

In a later episode, it's Dorothy that is revealed to have the fear of flying, and Blanche never mentions hers.

We get our second glimpse into Rose's insane competitiveness when she shows no sympathy for Blanche's stage fright, telling her that if she pees her pants, she better break into "Singing in the Rain." Rose has a dark side and we all know it.

Removing your appendix without anesthesia and biting a pillow—Sicily, love it or leave it!

Kudos to Bea Arthur for allowing Rose's "I just saw a big ugly man with a limp walk past my bedroom door" joke.

Well, it sucked to be in the hospital in the 80's and it sucks now!

1-19 Second Motherhood

Aired: February 15, 1986
Director: Gary Shimokawa
Writer: Christopher Lloyd
Guest Cast: Lou (Alan Blumenfeld), Richard (Kevin McCarthy)
Summary: Blanche ponders whether to marry a rich man with young children.
Rating: ❤❤❤

"Great, my unmarried daughter wants to spend her weekend with a toilet, now I can die in peace."—Sophia

This episode has some amazing, feminist messages in a classic, Susan Harris subversive way. The A story involving Blanche dating a rich man, breaks down because it ultimately doesn't match Blanche's needs. Even though Blanche paints herself as the ultimate gold-digging tramp, we know that she's not that woman. She likes sex and she likes money, but when she sees that her man wants her to be a mother and won't have time for her or them, she backs out. A lot of women wouldn't do that—they would either be a terrible mother or force themselves to be a person they weren't. Not Blanche.

The B story involves Dorothy and Rose redoing their bathroom once Dorothy realizes Rose knows a lot about plumbing from her childhood. But watching Bea Arthur deal with sexist plumbers who mock women is a treasure.

Golden Nuggets

Favorite scene: When Blanche tells Richard why she can't marry him.

Blanche just said on the previous episode that she had a fear of flying, but sure, on a private plane she seems okay!

This is only Blanche's third confirmed sexual relationship during the first season. In later seasons, she will seemingly become more and more sexually active. As she is in her 50s, and declares herself at her sexual peak, I say this is a win for women of all ages. It's not to say for sure she's had only three—we just don't know of the others.

Let's face it, Richard is going to find a new wife in Miami in about two weeks.

The rebellion against white male privilege might have started on this show. A perfectly good rich man gets dumped, and Lou the plumber gets told off more than once. Poor Lou doesn't get any respect, but that's what's great! His pandering, placating, and mansplaining is not for our Girls.

1-20 Adult Education

Aired: February 22, 1986
Director: Jack Shea
Writer: James Berg, Stan Zimmerman
Guest Cast: Professor Cooper (Jerry Hardin), Dean Tucker (James Staley)
Summary: A teacher offers Blanche a passing grade in her adult education class if she sleeps with him.
Rating: ❤❤❤

"Forgive me, Rose, I haven't had sex in 15 years and it's starting to get on my nerves."

I honestly don't know how many shows at this point did episodes about sexual harassment, but this was definitely one of the first I ever saw. And I think it's important to show it happening to the sexy character. She's being bribed, rather than helped, and just dealing with a sleazebag abusing his authority. But I think hearing Dorothy immediately label it as "sexual harassment" was crucial. Women of that generation would often dismiss it and say, "Well, boys will be boys," or some idiocy like that. But not Dorothy.

The B story this time involves Dorothy desperately trying to get Sinatra tickets. They get them, but try to scalp extras and get arrested, which bothers me. I hate plotlines like this!

Golden Nuggets

Blanche recapping and summarizing Rose's ticket story for brevity is amazing. We all have friends who don't know how to tell a story, and man, Blanche nails it.

The scene in the dean's office will make you wonder what sex act 7B is. The Dean has never heard of it, but Blanche tells him she's known about it for some time, and that he can do it to himself. There's a riddle.

Soda jerk! Rose was harassed by Neals Fielander, the soda jerk (and the town jerk), who arranged the ice cream in an obscene way, but she could never prove it because the ice cream would melt… when you think about it, that's a perfect crime!

These women have #MeToo stories, and then some! Dorothy once got a guy fired that was harassing her and others. It seems obvious today, but us ladies always have that ridiculous idea that it's only us. Dorothy, however, was the only woman harassed by a man wearing a corset and high heels.

1-21 Flu Attack

Aired: March 1, 1986
Director: Terry Hughes
Writer: James Berg, Stan Zimmerman
Guest Cast: Dr. Richmond (Sharon Spelman), Dave (Bill Cort), Harold (Ray Reinhardt), Raoul (Marcelo Tubert), Tommy (Tony Carreiro), the emcee (Silvana Gallardo)
Summary: Dorothy, Blanche, and Rose get the flu before a big event where they suspect one of them will be getting an award.
Rating: ❤❤❤❤

"I guess if you're an idiot with a hearing problem you do things like that."—Dorothy

If you're going to watch one *Golden Girls* episode, watch this one. It's got everything: snarky comments, the Girls going through dating prospects like they're in their 20s, each Girl demonstrating their lovable quirks, and it ends on a triple twist. The Girls make-up, only to argue about who will win, only to then have Sophia get the award which immediately brings them all together.

It's a writing triumph to have a show so steadfast in its strengths in the first season, with characters so well-drawn and so well-liked. Also, the older you get as a woman, the more this show just plays out as a fantasy—living with your best friends, having jobs, an active dating life, and going to banquets. Sign me up!

Golden Nuggets
Sophia's speech at the end steals it, with a touching note that's not too schmaltzy.

A vibrator reference was not common in the 80s and I most definitely didn't get that joke when it first aired.

Another plug for *Miami Vice*—jeez, the show did well NBC, calm down.

Sophia's "Linguine with Ear-Salve Sauce" for the win as far as gross Sicily stories go.

Their dresses for the banquet are all fun, but Estelle Getty's little sparkly number is just the cutest thing in the world.

Again, we get an obvious joke about Dorothy being unattractive from Blanche. I still wonder if they ran these by Bea Arthur first. I don't care for them.

If a friend of mine faked a date as elaborately as Blanche faked hers, I'm not sure I would ever let her live it down.

I didn't realize as a kid that a female doctor was such a big deal, and I couldn't believe that Blanche thought it was strange to be examined by one. These casting choices made a difference.

1-22 Job Hunting

Aired: March 8, 1986
Director: Paul Bogart
Writer: Terry Grossman, Kathy Speer
Guest Cast: Milton (Richard Venture)
Summary: Rose loses her job and struggles with ageism as she searches for employment.
Rating: ♥♥♥

> *"Oh it was nice. Being near Charlie was nice. But it was five years before I knew what made your eyes go back in your head."—Rose*

Having gone through many rounds of unemployment, this episode speaks to me. It's never easy being a woman looking for work. When you're in your 20s, you get a lot of offers for no money and no benefits, and then as you age, you get fewer and fewer opportunities all together. Rose's struggles regarding her age, being a woman, and being discarded in the workforce are still relevant. Here, she's in her early 60s, but Betty White was kicking ass right through to her 90s.

Not sure if the B story here is that Dorothy meets an old crush that turns out to be gay, or that a chubby chaser named Milton likes Blanche. Either way, it seems like it's an episode saying that the dating scene has some slim pickings for the Girls.

Golden Nuggets

Official kitchen table scene that includes a quintessential sex talk about how the three women lost their virginity, plus orgasm talk. It will be repeated in many flashback episodes because it's just so good.

There's so much fantastic-ness in that scene, I'm tempted to transcribe the whole thing. It's definitely a pre-cursor to the raunchier stuff we'd see in later years on *Sex and The City*.

Maybe it's me, but cheese making and Viking history on a resume would make me want to know more. I have seen some horrible resume writing in my time, so the criticisms of Rose's resume resonate with me. Honesty is not always the best policy.

When you actually go into the workforce, especially the corporate realm, you find that mature women and working mothers are often the most efficient and hardest working people out there—they seem to get every task done by 11:00 a.m.

1-23 Blind Ambitions

Aired: March 29, 1986
Director: Terry Hughes
Writer: Bob Colleary
Guest Cast: Lily (Polly Holiday)
Summary: Rose's blind sister comes to visit and struggles with the fact that she needs assistance.
Rating: ❤❤

"Get out of here. You come back more times than Shirley MacLaine."—Dorothy

This episode is fine I guess, and it takes on a serious topic that you don't usually see on TV. But it's just *too* serious for me, so I don't love it. This show had a lot of good episodes about various handicaps and illnesses, and in this one we see the realities of being blind. The actress playing Lily (best known as Flo from *Alice*) has a great scene where she confides her fears.

The episode also seems to be sending out a warning signal to people who want to change their lives to become caretakers for family members, posturing that it's a bad move and will probably ruin your life.

For the B story, the women hold a garage sale, which does provide a few solid laughs. I've had some garage sales, and it does hold true that you better want to sell items for less than you paid for them.

Golden Nuggets

It's pretty funny when Lily brags about getting across the living room without help, while the three women are running in circles keeping obstacles out of her way.

Woodstock apparently motivated Blanche and George to make love in the mud, proving to Dorothy that the 60's were a confusing time for everyone.

Rose eats 10 packs of peanuts on the plane! Ah, the days before peanut allergies.

1-24 Big Daddy

Aired: May 3, 1986
Director: Terry Hughes
Writer: Barry Fanaro, Mort Nathan
Guest Cast: Big Daddy Hollingsworth (Murray Hamilton), Leonard (Gordon Jump), Gladys (Peggy Pope)
Summary: Blanche's father comes to visit with news that he wants to become a country singer.
Rating: ❤❤

"Excuse me Rose, have I given you any indication at all that I care?"—Sophia

There are other, better Big Daddy episodes coming up. This one truly seems odd to me. Not so much that someone wants to try their hand at singing in their retirement, but that Big Daddy sells his house to do so. The writers seem to pair issues and conflicts together, and we just saw an episode about taking care of a sick loved one, and then we have a loved one making disconcerting life decisions.

Just as the show makes fun of Rose's small-town naiveté, Dorothy's tough Brooklyn sensibilities, and Sophia's corrupt Sicilian ways, we get a lot of laughs at the expense of the Old South.

The B story involving their rude neighbor not wanting to clean up the tree that fell showcases Sophia in her first demonstration of full curse-casting. Her capabilities will remain dubious, but it does appear that the universe slightly bends to Sophia's will. I wouldn't mess with her.

Golden Nuggets

The revelation that the neighbor's wife sabotaged him, and not by Sophia's curse, is a nice surprise (As is the boil on his butt).

Not an episode with a sex talk or revelation, so not a surprise that it's not a favorite.

Since McClanahan got to keep her wardrobe, I do hope that included her nightgowns.

I love how Big Daddy approaches Sophia first, kisses her hand, and then compliments her—good manners never go out of style.

Blanche goes into epic, southern craziness whenever Big Daddy visits, including saying "Fiddle-e-dee!"

Dorothy telling off the cowboy at the bar is hysterical—gotta give it to the guy for trying.

I would love to meet the writer who came up with the St. Olaf story of the first man to can tuna in its natural juices.

Women fight for everything on this show: taking care of their relatives, arguing with their husbands when they're being ridiculous, and plenty of legal battles (we will see these women in court a few times).

1-25 The Way We Met

Aired: May 10, 1986
Director: Terry Hughes
Writers: Barry Fanaro, Terry Grossman, Winifred Hervey, Mort Nathan, Kathy Speer
Guest Cast: Zelda (Shirley Prestia), the boy (Edan Gross), the produce clerk
Summary: The Girls remember how the four of them met.
Rating: ❤❤❤

"It was at that moment I realized my bosoms had the power to make music."—Blanche
"Didn't Bette Midler win a special Grammy for that?"—Dorothy

This is a fun episode, showing us that the Girls didn't always get along, when they reminisce about how they met because they can't sleep after watching *Psycho*.

At first the differences seem trivial. Rose is a country bumpkin, Dorothy is a cynical city girl, and Blanche is a sexy, Southern vixen. But grocery shopping proves to be the true test. They come to blows back at the house, until Rose tells a ridiculous St. Olaf story, that makes them laugh so hard that it bonds them. It's a simple reconciliation, but it works because being able to laugh with people is one of the truest measures of compatibility. All the other issues seem rather small, and then the clincher is their love of cheesecake.

One criticism is that Sophia is mostly absent, missing from the walk down memory lane. She scares them at the end with a knife—reenacting Psycho—which I liked, because I come from a family where people would pull a prank like this. You either come from this kind of tribe or you don't.

Golden Nuggets

Rose's St. Olaf Story: The Great Herring War (Oh, that Great Herring War!)

Rose has a cat here, but in a later episode, Rose is allergic to cats.

The sexiness is definitely all on Blanche in this episode. Blanche tells a psychic apartment hunter about her role-playing escapade where she wore a nurse's outfit with the gentleman she was dating. She tells Dorothy what food items to buy when a man is sluggish in bed, and Dorothy slyly pulls the item into her cart. She also lets us know she keeps whipped cream in the bedroom.

Rue McClanahan was nominated for an Emmy for this episode.

The "Herring Way" story is a classic as its ridiculous and its audacity is what brings the Girls together, inspiring them to try and get along as roommates.

A quick shout-out to Blanche's previous roomies, "two eccentric old ladies who used to bathe together and floss each other's teeth." We'll assume these women were lesbians. Not sure why Blanche threw them out, though I'd guess the flossing each other's teeth was the reason.

The Golden Girls

SEASON TWO

2-1 "End of the Curse"

Written by: Susan Harris
Aired: September 27, 1986
Director: Terry Hughes
Guest Cast: Dr. Barensfeld (Phillip Sterling), Dr. Parks (Vince Cannon), Patient in Psychiatrist's office (George J. Woods)
Summary: Blanche freaks out when she finds out that she's going through the beginning of menopause.
Rating: ❤❤❤

"Nobody in my family's ever seen a psychiatrist.
Except of course when they were institutionalized."—Blanche

This is a quintessential Blanche episode as she struggles with menopause. At first, she thinks she's pregnant, but unsure which of five men could be the father. Although there's a little bit of slut-shaming, one thing is evident—you cannot slut-shame a woman who's secure in her sexuality. And the girls do seem a little bit impressed. What is less impressive though, is that Blanche goes into a full breakdown when she learns it's menopause. It's weird that she had not expected this, considering that Rue is playing Blanche as about the same age, which is certainly when one would expect this.

But Blanche takes to her bed, and then to a psychiatrist to mourn her fertile years. It takes a vet coming by and flirting with her for her to return to her old self.

We get a lot of clues that the women are environmentally conscious. They're worried about the Everglades disappearing, and are animal lovers, but not enough to keep them away from a side hustle that kills animals for fur. So, they're woke, but not that woke. But man, I give them points for being engaged in life.

Golden Nuggets

I love Blanche's scene in the psychiatrist's office, and when she hits on the vet. That whole interaction is really Blanche at her best.

Stan did buy Dorothy a mink when they were married! We learned that in the episode "The Break-In."

Around the kitchen table: Excellent talk about menopause, and I think this is where I learned about any of that. I like that there's a spectrum of experiences from all four women, from trauma, to growing a beard, to relief.

Blanche's multi-colored robe is back!

Not a surprise that, because the actresses were all animal lovers, they all hated doing this episode, even though they save the minks at the end.

Boy, do I want to get my hands on *The Sicilian Book of World Records!*

The Girls back out at the end when the minks turn out to be homosexual and not able to breed. Oh, and the minks are too old! Someone really scammed them. But they keep the old gay minks. Again, I say, this show was pretty woke.

2-2 "Ladies of the Evening"

Written by: Barry Fanaro, Mort Nathan
Aired: October 4, 1986
Director: Terry Hughes
Guest Cast: Burt Reynolds, Meg (Rhonda Aldrich), Policeman (Peter Jason), The Exterminator (Phil Rubenstein)
Summary: The girls win tickets to an after-party with Burt Reynolds.
Rating: ❤❤❤❤

"I'm tired of being the Tonto of the group."—Sophia

This is a fantastically fun episode, and I was really torn about whether to give it three or four stars. The hookers in the jail scene are just so ridiculous. Also, raiding a hotel in Miami for hookers in the 80's? I'm thinking they should have been worried about the cocaine problem, but that's just me.

I enjoy so much of the rest of the episode though. I love that Sophia gets her revenge in such a splendid way, I love the idea that these three women get arrested for prostitution, and I love that Sophia takes all of the tickets instead of just one when she runs off to go see Burt Reynolds.

The scene with the men at the hotel bar mistaking the Girls for prostitutes is priceless. And again, good for the women! There's a certain age where being mistaken for a hooker is just simply a compliment.

And of course, the end with Burt at the door. It's the show's first, big guest spot. And it was an extremely big deal in 1986 to get a big movie star on a television show.

Golden Nuggets

The scene at the end when they all raise their hand as Burt asks, "Which one's the slut?" is one of the show's most famous moments, and a real insight into the fun of the show.

Rose says she's never been in jail, but in the first season she mentions that she spent a night in jail.

Blanche picks the hotel bar based on the men in the lobby, not realizing it's where men are picking up prostitutes. Is this a sitcom problem, or just a problem one could make before the internet?

Rose's "Butter Queen Story" is quite torturous.

Could you believe it when people on TV just open the front door without checking who's behind it? Still bothers me...

The actress playing the hooker that says, "It's okay to be career-oriented" is played by Rue McClanahan's niece.

It was Betty White who arranged to get Burt Reynolds as the guest host, as they were friends. Everyone just loved Betty.

For all the women at the time who worried about not having a man to deal with repairmen coming to the house, just take notes from Dorothy.

2-3 "Take Him, He's Mine"

Written by: Terry Grossman, Kathy Speer
Aired: October 11, 1986
Director: Terry Hughes
Guest Cast: Stan (Herb Edelman), Stan's date (Lana Schwab), Vinnie (Tom La Grua)
Summary: Dorothy sends Blanche on a date with her ex-husband, Stan, but gets jealous when they hit it off.
Rating: ❤❤❤

"You're wearing your toupee to bed. That means one of two things. Either there's a woman in your bed or Suzanne Somers is on The Tonight Show. *"—Dorothy*

This is a sweet episode on many levels. It's shows that Dorothy and Stan just have a connection that will always stay with them, but it also shows the complicated feelings between friends when you're jealous *and* being stupid, yet you still need that friend to just be a friend. When Blanche names that feeling between anger, jealousy, and sadness as "magenta," it really is kind of profound.

The B Story with Rose and Sophia doing a sandwich side-hustle is good for a few laughs.

Golden Nuggets

Dorothy and Blanche's reconciliation at the end is welcome.

Not to side with Stan, but there are just so many jokes from Dorothy about how he's quick in bed. Not sure their marriage had a chance because I don't think excessive emasculating was the way to go.

Behold Dorothy's green and purple silk suit!

Rose had a Belgian Waffle Stand as a child in St. Olaf. That is one weird, yet glorious, small town.

First episode that suggests Sophia's mob connections might be the real deal, as we have her Uncle Vito deal with Johnny No-Thumbs Sicily-style.

Though Blanche and Stan might have been an intriguing couple, this show is about girl power, and Blanche—as much as she touts being a tramp—chooses her friends first. She might be a one-kind-of-slut, but not the other kind.

2-4 "It's a Miserable Life"

Aired: November 1, 1986
Director: Terry Hughes
Writers: Barry Fanaro, Mort Nathan
Guest Cast: Frieda Claxton (Nan Martin), Mr. Pfeiffer (Thom Sharp), Lady at Funeral (Amzie Strickland)
Summary: Rose tries to save a neighborhood tree from being chopped down, while a grouchy-old neighbor tries to sabotage her efforts.
Rating: ❤❤❤❤

"Oh Rose, you have to put this terrible thing behind you. You killed Frieda Claxton two days ago."—Blanche

This episode is just another one that's a lot of fun. Season Two has a lot of episodes like this. The characters have been so clearly drawn that the Girls' adventures at this point complement their quirks. This is Rose at her most endearing, trying to see the good side of Mrs. Claxton. But I guess when you test Rose's kindness, she will freaking kill you with a heart attack and have your ashes buried by the tree you wanted to knock down. That is some cold-gangster stuff right there. The Celia Rubenstein mourner at the end is a good zinger too.

Golden Nuggets

So many gems, so it's tough, but the scene at the funeral home and the whole interaction with Mr. Pfeiffer (the P is not silent!) is perfection. Blanche's youth might be a little spotty, but not sure how long she was in a religious school, as we have so many later recollections from her that take place at her home.

Blanche really earns her rep this season. She's exchanging sexual favors to sign a petition and has slept with two men on the Board. And her neighbor thinks some of her sex acts are illegal.

This episode has a Southern flashback, a St. Olaf story, and Sophia talking about similarities between Brooklyn and Sicily—this is golden.

References to the The Cosby Show just seem so innocent now... Oh, to be back in the 80's, when Cliff Huxtable being an OB-GYN practicing out of his house didn't seem creepy at all.

Just a small note that the women are environmentalists, trying to save a tree.

2-5 "Isn't It Romantic"

Aired: November 8, 1986
Director: Terry Hughes
Writers: Jeffrey Duteil
Guest Cast: Jean (Lois Nettleton)
Summary: Dorothy's friend, Jean, a lesbian mourning her lover, gets a crush on Rose while she's visiting.
Rating: ❤❤❤

"I know what they're doing but I never saw anybody do it at that speed."—Blanche
"That's reverse Dorothy."—Sophia
"I did that once. It was his birthday!"—Blanche

I didn't think this episode was a big deal when I was younger, because talk about sexuality wasn't brought up as much as it is today. I didn't have any great awareness of what being gay or straight was in 1986, certainly not with any kind of negative spin, or tying it into one's religious beliefs.. Everything I learned about life seemed to be from MTV and soap operas. So, when shows like this showed a woman that dated women, I thought *well, I don't know any women that date women* and moved on with my Honey-Nut Cheerios.

This episode unfolds in such an innocent way, with everyone treating the whole thing with such humor, while being really well done. Even Blanche, who immediately wonders why Jean doesn't want her, is pretty on-brand.

The B story is extremely sex positive for older women. I mean, 82-year old Sophia brings "dirty movies" home from the video store. I sympathize with anyone who ever busted a grandparent indulging in X-rated films. I would've required therapy.

Golden Nuggets

The scene with Dorothy and Sophia in bed where Sophia laughs at Jean being in love with Rose is pretty iconic.

Blanche's first kiss was in the shower! This season brings us a lot more spicy tidbits about Blanche's sexual past, and I have to say they're all fantastic.

This episode won Terry Hughes a Director's Guild of America Award, and earned Lois Nettleton an Emmy nomination.

When Jean says she's falling in love with Rose, all I'm thinking is *Jeez, women fall fast. I mean, a crush is one thing, but love!*

This was Rue McClanahan's second favorite episode.

It's never a good move to reveal your crush when someone's falling asleep—whether you're gay or straight.

This episode is the first with a plot focusing entirely on a positive LGBTQ storyline and embraced by the LGBTQ community. Sophia's reaction to a hypothetical gay child is refreshing then and now.

2-6 "Big Daddy's Little Lady"

Aired: November 15, 1986
Director: Terry Hughes
Writers: Russell Marcus
Guest Cast: Big Daddy (David Wayne), Margaret Spender (Sondra Currie)
Summary: Blanche's father surprises her by telling her he's getting married — to a woman younger than Blanche.
Rating: ♥♥♥

"Miami... you're cuter than... an intrauterine..."—Rose

This episode gives us a frazzled Blanche, as she tends to get when her father is involved. What's consistent about Blanche throughout the show is that this is just how Blanche is. She jumps right into her family's business and walks it right back. It's all southern fire and fury. Speaking of the South, the detailed descriptions that color Blanche and her father's language when they speak is good for laughs. Or as Sophia says, "Get out the boots, he's back."

The scene where Blanche reconciles with her father has a nice monologue from him about why he is with her, and this actor (the second that plays Big Daddy) reflects a father that loves and favors Blanche for all her flaws. He truly seeks out her respect and opinion.

We also get to see Dorothy and Rose enter a songwriting contest with the spectacular "Miami." Their songwriting process is strangely accurate as far as collaborating and looking for rhymes.

Golden Nuggets

The Miami Song is great fun, as are all the practice versions of it.

The kitchen table revolves around older men with younger women, and mostly John Derek. The actor playing Big Daddy is actually 33 years older than the actress playing his fiancé—and in Hollywood, that was pretty average for the times.

The St. Olaf story this time is a great one about opposites attracting: Ollie, Molly and a play called *Hey, That's My Tractor.*

The previous actor who played Big Daddy died before he could reprise the role.

Rose wrote a one-line St. Olaf fight song!

Directed by comedian David Steinberg, who found Bea Arthur a little tough to work with, but of course, talented.

Blanche's father, we will learn, has an interesting history with women. But he certainly seems like a gentleman.

2-7 "Family Affair"

Aired: November 22, 1986
Director: Terry Hughes
Writers: Winifred Hervey
Guest Cast: Michael Zbornak (Scott Jacoby), Bridget Nylund (Marilyn Jones)
Summary: Rose's daughter and Dorothy's son sleep together, causing Dorothy and Rose to fight.
Rating: ❤❤

"Dorothy do you realize, it has been four days since I've enjoyed the company of a man." —Blanche
"I know, Blanche. I've been marking the days off on my Big Ships of the Navy calendar." —Dorothy

This episode has its funny spots, but it's not that strong, mostly because the visiting children aren't particularly funny characters. Rose's daughter Bridget is so blah, and Dorothy's son Michael takes himself so seriously. Together, they are a total snoozefest. Plus, Michael's speech to Dorothy about how he's a decent person falls kind of flat for me (Michael is probably my least favorite character of the show).

Dorothy and Rose's fight gets a few good laughs though. Rose is doubly traumatized because she thinks her 22-year-old lost her virginity to Michael, which would be pretty late and tells you a lot about Rose and how she thinks she'd be privy to her daughter's sexual escapades.

Blanche's ailing back provides humor, especially because it means she can't indulge in sex for a long period of time.

Golden Nuggets

Rose and Dorothy's fight is the highlight, but Rose gets so mean about Michael so fast, and Dorothy is so quick to call Bridget a slut, that it just seems a little out-of-character for both of them.

Lots of Blanche's sex life is divulged around the kitchen table. According to her, four days without a man is a long time. Wow. Blanche also talks of her sexually active college days in the 50's, which for the rest of the women was not common. They were from a time where, for most women, your husband was the first man you slept with. And if you had another lover, you certainly didn't brag about it.

A rare kitchen scene because Dorothy doesn't sit in the center seat at the table.

These women are not good at avoiding a spectacle when they catch two people in bed together. Also, when you have sex in someone else's home (especially your mother's), lock the door. This episode is awfully judgmental regarding one-night stands, but I get that it's annoying for the Girls to have their children visiting and having sex with each other. Rude!

Blanche expresses that she's at her sexual peak, and I didn't appreciate when I was younger how groundbreaking it was to hear a woman over the age of 40 (let alone 50) say that.

2-8 "Vacation"

Aired: November 29, 1986
Director: Terry Hughes
Writers: Winifred Hervey
Guest Cast: Rick (Tom Villard), Jacques de Courville (Stuart Pankin), Dwayne (Stephen Lee), Winston Hardwick III (Brett Porter), Toshiro Mitsumo (Keye Luke), Ramone (Paul Rodriquez)
Summary: Rose, Dorothy, and Blanche go on a disastrous Caribbean vacation.
Rating: ❤❤

"I'm not sharing a bathroom with three strange men. I don't care if it is my vacation."—Blanche

This episode is just cute, in a typical, 80's-sitcomy way. And if you already love the Girls, you'll enjoy it all the more. They get into one silly scenario after another—they fight, they make-up, and then all is well. The women get conned into staying at a hideous hotel in the Caribbean, have to share a bathroom with strange men, and get shipwrecked with their accidental roommates. It begs the questions, who would go out on a boat with three strange men on a strange island *at night*? Does anyone watch *48 Hours*, *SVU*, or any of the *Law & Orders*?

Golden Nuggets

Discovering yet another tough side of Rose, she is not scared of getting stuck on an island. Her survival instincts are strong and she goes into full Boss-Mode.

Rose reveals in a later episode that she finds plastic surgery unnatural, even though it's revealed she had her nose done.

Instead of the kitchen table, the sex talk occurs around the campfire. I love that both Dorothy and Blanche slept with Rose's cousin, Nolan, on a trip, and both of them confirm that he was bad in bed. This show is extremely empowering to women on all fronts.

Blanche having her tubes tied, Rose getting her nose done and reading Blanche's diary—this is a lot to unwrap!

Rose is definitely the person I wouldn't want to travel with, as she fills the day with touristy-adventure type stuff, when I'm more of a sit-by-the-pool, sunbathe, and drink cocktails kind of gal.

Sophia wanting the Girls out of the house so she could make a pass at the Japanese gardener was an intriguing B story. First, she was the character kids identified with and second, it was a casual nod to interracial dating, which is clearly no biggie to Sophia. It was just the sushi she didn't care for, which I can't understand. Third, Sophia makes the first move (and the second and third!). What a woman!

2-9 "Joust Between Patients"

Aired: December 6 1986
Director: Terry Hughes
Writers: Scott Spencer Gorden
Guest Cast: Andrew Allen (Reid Shelton)
Summary: Tensions grow between Blanche and Dorothy, when Dorothy takes a part-time job working with her at the museum.
Rating: ❤❤❤

"Don't explain, Rose. I used to live with a couple of bitches myself."—Rose

There seems to be a trend in Season Two where the writers were given an order that the Girls have to be fighting. And the fights seem rather brutal. "Eat dirt and die trash" is not for sissies. We also get something that is near and dear to Betty White—animal love. Bea, Betty, and Rue were huge animal lovers and part of many animal causes, so naturally the actresses especially enjoyed episodes with dogs. Dorothy starts working with Blanche at the museum during a teaching hiatus (and it's the only job she can find in Miami not dealing cocaine).

This episode does a decent job of showing Blanche's fragile ego, which has been slowly established with her vanity. Even with Jean the Lesbian, Blanche's go-to was to be jealous that Jean crushed on Rose over her. Her job is a place where she shines in a way that doesn't have to do with her sexuality, and it sucks to have someone replace her so easily, as she explains to Dorothy at the end. But boy, Dorothy could have been slicker about planning the banquet!

Golden Nuggets

Blanche pretended to be a virgin half a dozen times. This is the only admission that gives us some insights into how many lovers she had before George. At least six.

There's no confirmation on this, but how is it possible that Blanche never dates her boss?

Lucille Ball was a member of the studio audience.

2-10 "Love, Rose"

Aired: December 13, 1986
Director: Terry Hughes
Writers: Terry Grossman, Kathy Speer
Guest Cast: Isaac Q. Newton (Paul Dooley), Colin Drake (Wilfred Whitney Cheswick)
Summary: Dorothy and Blanche invent a man to respond to Rose's personal ad.
Rating: ❤❤

"I know what you mean, Sophia. I would never date a man unless I felt those sparks."—Blanche
"Fortunately, you carry flints in your bra."—Dorothy

This episode makes me a little sad and seems too silly. It brings to mind the pre-Tinder era of dating through Personal Ads, and how that used to be a much tougher numbers game. What irks me is that the concept is just so ridiculous! Blanche makes up a person and begins writing to Rose as that fictional man. It's a lot to take.

And then Rose wants to meet him, then finds one man named Isaac Q. Newton in the phone book who agrees to meet her. And yes, it's based on Rose's simple mindedness, but good grief it's a lot. And the Isaac character—though his stupidity matches Rose—somehow never returns. I think that he'd be a good boyfriend for her though. Strangely, the writing does progress nicely in some ways, but can be too much, especially if you're not a fan.

On the flip side, an annoying old man relentlessly pursues Sophia and it's only towards the end that she realizes why.

Golden Nuggets

When Sophia's suitor reveals that he's only interested because he thought she was a wealthy widow—man, that was sobering.

Blanche can't believe how long Rose has gone without companionship, even though Rose had at least two lovers in the last year. But we know from this season that Blanche thinks going a few days without sex is rough.

This show is known for celebrity burns, but I think one of the roughest is regarding Ted Koppel. He looks like Howdy Doody's illegitimate son?

I enjoy Dorothy's eveningwear in the beginning, and yet I loathe what she wears to the banquet. Both she and Dorothy really go overboard with the shininess!

Older women get a lot of dating offers on this show. Sophia is in the throes of dating drama, and Dorothy and Blanche are doing quite well themselves.

2-11 "Twas the Nightmare Before Christmas"

Aired: December 20, 1986
Director: Terry Hughes
Writers: Barry Fanaro, Mort Nathan
Guest Cast: Santa Claus (Terry Kiser), Thurber (Craig Richard Nelson), Albert (Teddy Wilson), Meyer (Sam Albertson)
Summary: A series of vignettes about the Girls preparing for Christmas.
Rating: ❤❤❤❤

"What do we look like, Charlie's Angels?"—Dorothy
"I have been told I bear a striking resemblance to Cheryl Ladd, although my bosoms are perkier."—Blanche
"Not even if you were hanging upside down on a trapeze."—Dorothy

I don't know how much money this show got for mentioning Neiman Marcus, but it's mentioned a *lot*. Anyway, this is the show's first Christmas episode, and it has four different vignettes, all well done: Blanche returning home to seduce Santa, the Girls opening up handmade gifts to avoid Christmas commercialism, the Girls being held up by a Santa at the counseling center, and the Girls eating Christmas dinner at a diner on Christmas night after their flights are canceled.

Golden Nuggets

I can't choose! I love Blanche's Santa fetish. I love Dorothy's response to receiving Rose's handmade gift. I love Rose interrupting the caroling to tell her St. Olaf story, causing the women to run to their bedrooms. I love the crazies at the counseling center and Sophia saving the day because she could tell a toy gun from a real gun. And I love Dorothy saying she could get herpes listening to Blanche's story!

Blanche's Santa fetish adds another layer to her multi-layered sex life.

The *Howard the Duck* joke is dated now, but man, that was funny at the time! Lots of really old references (*Charlie's Angels,* Potsy, The *Waltons*).

The calendar Blanche gives to the Girls, "The Men of Blanche's Boudoir" was used to prank the actresses, as the members of the crew put raunchy pictures of themselves in a calendar and handed it to the Girls. You can find a clip of this on YouTube.

Beware of pro-capitalism messages on television. So many sitcoms have this similar plot that ultimately shows that receiving homemade gifts from people sucks... Almost as if they're in the business of selling products and don't want you to second-guess spending a lot of money during the holiday season!

2-12 "The Sisters"

Aired: January 3, 1987
Director: Terry Hughes
Writers: Christopher Lloyd
Guest Cast: Angela (Nancy Walker)
Summary: Dorothy invites Sophia's sister, Angela, to Miami as a birthday gift, only to realize that the two have been fighting for years.
Rating: ❤❤❤❤

"You'll get your present, Ma. You win, you always win." —Dorothy " I know. Me and Mighty Mouse."—Sophia

I love this episode, even though it doesn't quite make sense that Dorothy doesn't know that Sophia and Angela have been fighting. Interesting to note is that Estelle Getty played Nancy Walker's stand-in while acting in New York, so these two playing sisters was inevitable (and amazing!) And though I've said that visiting-relative episodes have a high probability of not being the best ones, Sophia's sister (and later, her brother Angelo) is a score. Their relationship seems totally believable, and Walker seamlessly sells the Brooklyn back story and the Italian personality.

The resolution at the end, where they realize that their whole fight was a giant misunderstanding is actually semi-realistic. A lot of family-and-friend feuds come down to idiotic happenings like that, and people are too stubborn to talk it out.

Golden Nuggets

When the women confront each other with savage insults that ends with a "may your marinara never cling to your pasta." That's just great.

Sophia mentions they're the only ones left from the original family, but their brother is introduced later in the series.

Sophia jokes that she has only made love in one position, but we know from later episodes that she is quite sexually adventurous. So, let's consider it a throwaway joke.

Sophia's family stories never cease to unlock some weird, male sexual behavior and fetishes: Men who love cowboys in Times Square, the one who legally adopts a goat, and in this one, Cousin Vito parading around in the girdle. No mention yet of Phil's cross-dressing.

Angela's story of a veal shank, Pee Wee the dwarf getting killed by the mob, and how they took short walks, is as good as it gets.

Of course, we get a great tale from Brooklyn, but Blanche's tale of sister rivalry is also pretty fantastic (her sister being able to contort her body into the letter R).

A good lesson here is that there's always a blabbermouth in the family, or group of friends, and sometimes part of surprise party planning is dealing with them. They know who they are.

2-13 "The Stan That Came to Dinner"

Aired: January 10, 1987
Director: Terry Hughes
Writers: Terry Grossman, Kathy Speer
Guest Cast: Stan Zbornak (Herb Edelman), Rob (Rod Sabbe), Bob (Odil Sabbe), Dr. Stephen Deutsch (Steve Kramer)
Summary: Stan recovers from heart surgery at the Girls' home and drives them crazy while taking advantage of them.
Rating: ❤❤❤

"I said pull yourself together. Not talk like Sammy Davis Jr."—Dorothy

I like most of the Stan episodes and read that Bea Arthur just adored working with Herb Edelman. Also, the writers have said that when they couldn't think of anything, they would just bring Stan in. He was just so lovable while having unlovable characteristics. It's a difficult role to pull off, and here it's effortless.

He recovers from bypass surgery and completely uses the Girls for their food and hospitality. Yet we enjoy him. Maybe it's because before surgery, he confesses to Dorothy about multiple extramarital affairs, knowing that he will need her to take care of him while he's recovering.

Maybe I have an older sensibility about Stan, but he's the kind of guy that I can't help but think, *if any woman was willing to sleep with him, I can see how it was difficult for him to turn down that opportunity.* Especially since his relationship with Dorothy was mostly emasculation and heckling.

The B story with Blanche dating twins is pretty humorous, especially when Stan screws it up for her.

Golden Nuggets

Stan sees the dark side of Rose, who tells him what the Viking villagers did with men that were useless and bad in bed. *Tough village indeed.* Blanche fantasizing about dating twins at the same time is another piece to Blanche's complicated sexual mosaic.

For kitchen table talk, we have the first time Rose accidentally slips into verse while telling the hysterical sheep story. We also have the gross family heirloom where a man presents himself on his wedding night.

Dorothy is particularly gullible this episode, believing Stan's relapse. But when she comes back with her, "Happy Birthday Peter Pan," it's good-old Dorothy back on track.

This is the first of two episodes that doesn't end with one of the Girls.

With everything Stan has done, it's typical that he's ultimately alone and Dorothy is the family that has to take care of him. I think a lot of women relate to this.

2-14 "The Actor"

Aired: January 17, 1987
Director: Terry Hughes
Writers: Barry Fanaro, Mort Nathan
Guest Cast: Patrick Vaughn (Lloyd Bochner) Phyllis Hammerow (Janet Carroll); Stage Manager (Frank Birney)
Summary: A famous actor comes into town to perform in a local town, and secretly dates Rose, Blanche, and Dorothy.
Rating: ❤❤❤❤

"I don't know what you just did.
But you'd make one hell of a yodeler."—Rose

A classic episode that just shows the women going all in on an activity and getting into hijinks. I mean, what are the odds that a famous actor comes into town and all three start secretly sleeping with him? No matter. The man is just typical Hollywood—in an innocent sitcom way—and really quite complimentary and charming. I also love the number of activities the women participate in: charities, golf, acting, and more!

No B story here. It's all about the play and that's fine with me.

Golden Nuggets

How great is the part of the play where they all confront Patrick, and the audience thinks it's part of the performance?

I can't speak enough about this man's stamina. He's with at least 8-12 women from the play, in about one week. There's no indication of drug use, but I keep thinking he's like the Warren Beatty of this town, except I don't think Warren Beatty ever came into contact with women over 60 until he hit 80. I hear they used to remove them from the freeways in Los Angeles just so he didn't glance over and see one from his car. Now that's star power.

It's worth noting that Rose is not a prude anymore. And apparently, she's not killing men in bed either. Or maybe she has met her match with Patrick Vaughn.

We have our first Scandinavian word here: Kaflügenachen, Scandinavian pejorative term for someone who docks his boat in the handicap slip without a handicap permit.

Lovable, sexually deviant behavior? At the time, this might have been representing sleazy Hollywood behavior, but now doesn't this guy seem charming? A middle-aged man sleeping with women over 60? What a prince! They should move him into retirement communities.

2-15 "Before and After"

Aired: January 24, 1987
Director: Terry Hughes
Writers: Bob Rosenfarb
Guest Cast: Liz (Deborah May), Nat Bernstein
Summary: Rose develops an adventurous spirit after she almost dies at the hospital.
Rating: ❤❤

"We can do what we normally do. Talk dirty and pig out."—Rose

This episode has one funny spot, but it just veers too far out-of-character for Rose and the Girls. Rose has a health scare, and becomes a live-for-the-day maniac and when the Girls complain, she blows up at them and moves out. It's all a bit contrived, and maybe would've been funnier if they stuck with her transformation. But seeing her move out with the packing, repacking, and finding a place, then moving back in all within a 30-minute show is just a rush job. Then we have the roommates that Rose moves in with—they are sad, depressing "women of the 80s" types that are cold and unattached to anything.

But still, the hospital scene is great, and so is Rose's quick return and one-liner at the end. Man, Betty White can deliver.

Golden Nuggets

Rose's retelling of her visit to heaven is funny on more than one level, with Dorothy's interjecting with shirts that say, "Today is the first day of the end of your life" and Rose's dead relative with the lisp, guiding her through heaven.

Blanche hooked up with Tony Bennett! I'm pretty sure this is her biggest celebrity score. When did this even happen? She wasn't a widow for that long, but I guess some time in the early 80s, their paths crossed. Amazing!

And we get a St. Olaf story no one hears. One of the women Rose moves in with literally walks out during her story. That is really cold, and something her Girls never really do.

Sophia shortening her story to an anecdote and then moving to simple advice makes it clear that Sophia always adjusts to the circumstance.

Nat Bernstein, who plays Dr. Wallerstein, appears in the next episode as a different character.

This episode has jokes about Jewish doctors, but keep in mind, it's written by a Jewish writer. And I have to say, the jokes work. People do enjoy hearing that their doctors are Jewish. It's a stereotype, but one that Jewish doctors probably don't mind.

2-16 "And Then There Was One"

Aired: January 31, 1987
Director: Terry Hughes
Writers: Russell Marcus
Guest Cast: Norman (Christopher Burton), Nat Bernstein (Emily's father), Bob Henderson (Ray Combs)
Summary: The girls have to take care of children and an infant during a marathon.
Rating: ❤❤❤

"Siamese twins sleep alone more than you do."—Dorothy

When I watch this episode, it occurs to me that this town is awfully trusting of these women watching their children! Then again, it was the 80's. Norman is a bit much though. He is so mean, so one-dimensional, and he calls Dorothy the Bride of Frankenstein. The whole episode kind of works as long as you don't think too hard about the circumstances. The idea that they assume the baby was deserted and that they will have to care for it, all because Sophia forgot to relay the message is you know, eh.

The emotional strength of the episode is Blanche's touching connection to Emily. We'll see through the series that she struggles with her parenting and how she wasn't the most present parent. And in this episode, she talks about how her children ran to the Nanny, even as adults.

The B story with Sophia running the marathon is a good time. First of all, who doesn't love the fact that an 82-year-old woman is running (or walking) a marathon? But her retelling of it and thinking she's become a celebrity is pretty entertaining.

Golden Nuggets

The Girls in the kitchen talking about the challenges of parenting in the past, and possibly again in the future, is a tender moment.

Baby Emily is about six months old—there's no way her parents are expecting triplets.

Blanche's boyfriend in the fifth grade had a fake ID—that is something to think about. Her sexual history sometimes leaves more questions than answers.

Sophia's double insult to Dorothy as a baby is remarkable. She's been going after Dorothy's looks since she was a baby (both her chin and her forehead!).

St. Olaf gems: The Henry Ford Foundation and the Deep Blue Vegetable Carnival in one episode.

This show is about women continuing their lives without men, and in this episode, we see them considering raising a baby, walking a marathon, and reconnecting with their children.

2-17 "Bedtime Story"

Aired: February 7, 1987
Director: Terry Hughes
Writers: Barry Fanaro, Terry Grossman, Mort Nathan, Kathy Speer
Guest Cast: Stationmaster (Randy Bennett), Clown (Charles Bouvier)
Summary: The girls recall different times they had to sleep in precarious situations, as they ponder where to house visiting relatives.
Rating: ❤❤

"This is like the Twilight Zone. Somehow we got on a train that ended up inside Rose's mind." —Blanche

In *Golden Girls* vernacular, this type of episode is called a wraparound, because it's not a clip show with scenes the audience has seen before. They're new vignettes with a tied-in theme about how they've all had to sleep in weird situations. The vignettes are okay, but none of them really make me laugh or pack a punch. This really seems like a filler episode, randomly put together at the last minute.

The four of them sharing a bed when the heat goes out is definitely a memorable visual, but it just gets so silly: Rose thinking she hears God answering her prayers or being afraid of escaped convicts, is a snoozer; Dorothy hiding Rose's chipped beef to spare her feelings, when we all know that these women rarely spare each other feelings is a bit much; And a sweet one where Sophia takes care of Dorothy as she recovers from bronchitis and falls asleep is fine, but uneventful. The best vignette is the final one with the Girls at the small-town train station returning from a funeral.

Golden Nuggets

The stationmaster in *Appalapachobi* who totally gets Rose on a subatomic level, and is for some reason hostile to Dorothy, steals both the scene and the episode.

In the first flashback, Blanche says it's Saturday night, but Dorothy says she has work the next day, which doesn't make sense as Dorothy's a teacher.

Blanche's recap of a night with a sailor is all we get as far as sexual antics.

Bea Arthur sings "Sunrise, Sunset," from *Fiddler on the Roof.* She played Yenta, in the original 1969 production.

Blanche gives a real dig to Billy Joel, referring to him only as Christie Brinkley's big-eyed husband. Not cool Blanche!

Blanche also claims to have the exact same bone structure as Christie and doesn't want Billy coming after her, which takes, *oh my God*, a whole lot of chutzpah. Christie Brinkley at that time was arguably the most beautiful supermodel of the decade, and Blanche, though a beautiful woman, is twice her age.

2-18 "Forgive Me, Father"

Aired: February 14, 1987
Director: Terry Hughes
Writers: Terry Grossman, Kathy Speer
Guest Cast: Father Frank Leahy (John McMartin), Father Callahan (Barney McGeary), Priest (Charles Summers)
Summary: Dorothy doesn't realize that the man she has a crush on is a priest.
Rating: ❤❤❤

"And what are you serving for dessert, Blanche? Penicillin?"—Dorothy

First of all, I love that this was a Valentine's Day episode, because man, the fact that it's about a 60-year-old woman crushing on a priest just makes this show. This episode is a bit like the one where Rose surprises the Girls by dating a dwarf. This time, all the Girls find out that the guy Dorothy likes is a priest. He hadn't been referred to as "Father" at the school and hadn't been wearing his uniform either. So, this is Dorothy's second case of bad luck at school-dating (her affair with Glen being the other).

What sells this episode is some silly talk about sex, a few insults ("incidentally, you look fat" being the best), and maybe even Dorothy's sequined top.

Golden Nuggets

Frank's interactions with the Girls when he first enters are stellar. "He's a priest, isn't he?"

Blanche showing Dorothy how to hit on Frank is my favorite, but I also love Rose getting turned on by the phrase "the tushy of love." It gives us more insights into Rose's kinky side, which should be chronicled online somewhere.

I love the reference to Dorothy's outfit making her look like a *Solid Gold* dancer.

Sophia is very-much a sometime-Catholic, in that she can be extremely devoted to The Pope and certain traditions, and yet discard others.

2-19 "Long Day's Journey into Marinara"

Aired: February 21, 1987
Director: Terry Hughes
Writers: Barry Fanaro, Mort Nathan
Guest Cast: Angela (Nancy Walker), Tony (Joe Alfasa), Tony's roommate (Esther Larner)
Summary: Sophia fights with her sister, Angela, when she moves in while looking for a place to live in Miami.
Rating: ❤❤❤

"Who stabbed Sophia in the back?"—Rose
"The chef at Benihana."—Dorothy

If this were a *Friends* episode, it would be called *The One with the Showbiz Chicken*. But it's also the return of Sophia's sister Angela, who I love. The two of them just worked really well together. Their conflict works, and when they reunite to beat up Sophia's boyfriend with a bag, it's even better. Even the way they insult the Girls, in the same direct, yet indirect way—that works too!

But we must mention Count Bessie, the showbiz chicken. The chicken playing the piano is a crowd pleaser and I'm not one to go for animal tricks. I love how Blanche and Dorothy are patient with Rose, but only to a point. Also, the ending has two twists: the surprise twist that Angela didn't actually cook Count Bessie was a nice one, and Sophia finding out that her boyfriend is cheating, but not with Angela, was a twisty reveal.

Golden Nuggets

When the Girls find out that the chicken they are eating might be Count Bessie... I remember first seeing this episode and falling for it too.

Blanche seduced her sister's boyfriend right before prom. I tell ya, sometimes Blanche is difficult to sympathize with, but she sells it with, "I hardly put a mark on that boy."

Rose fights back when they try to walk away from one of her St. Olaf stories, threatening to tell it the next morning.

Bea Arthur didn't love filming this episode, because she was scared of the chicken, but was concerned with whether it was being treated well.

I enjoyed watching two women over 80 fighting over a boyfriend—it's what makes this show *golden.* Also, it's worth noting that their boyfriend has another girl on the side, while Angela is living with him, really speaking to the thriving old-geezer bachelor life in Miami.

2-20 "Whose Face Is This, Anyway?"

Aired: February 21, 1987
Director: Terry Hughes
Writers: Winifred Hervey
Guest Cast: Dr. Taylor (Joseph Whipp)
Summary: Blanche considers plastic surgery after a sorority reunion makes her feel insecure about her looks.
Rating: ❤❤

"I am upset because I was not the center of attention, and nobody said I was the prettiest!" —Blanche

This episode is a retread of a lot that has already been explored with Blanche, and it's just not done in a particularly original way. And for some reason, they give Sophia a lot of old references like Fess Parker and Gavin Macleod (which were old even then). I think the fact that all the Girls discuss plastic surgery as if it offends them, when all the actresses were coming off facelifts, makes me laugh.

Dorothy admits to having her eyes done, only to get insulted by her mother who says she only goes on two dates a year. By the way, these women all date a lot for women their age! It also has the recurring joke that Rose swears her hair is her natural color, which is a weird lie to cling to for a woman who's known to be so honest.

The episode also has the tired sitcom joke of friends mistaking a patient wrapped in bandages as *their* friend. I don't think that's ever happened in the history of time.

Golden Nuggets

Rose's torturous, nonsensical, St. Olaf story that Sophia has the sense to avoid with headphones is definitely my favorite part.

Nothing sexy going on here, except Blanche landing a date with a doctor at the end!

The Fess Parker jokes are way too many here, and I just feel like it was an outdated reference and insulting to Bea Arthur.

Blanche actually wanting to get about four different surgeries at once shows that she doesn't know much about plastic surgery. A facelift alone is quite harrowing. Even Joan Rivers didn't get four procedures done in one day.

2-21 "Dorothy's Prized Pupil"

Aired: March 14, 1987
Director: Terry Hughes
Writers: Christopher Lloyd
Guest Cast: Mario (Mario Lopez), Sam Burns (John Braden)
Summary: When one of Dorothy's students writes an essay about what America means to him, he becomes in danger of being deported.
Rating: 

"If we'd had them in the old days, we wouldn't have had to fight that disruptive Civil War!" —Blanche

This episode means more now than it did then and has strong political implications. These days it would be labeled as having a liberal agenda, but back then it was just the Girls being concerned citizens. A child in the country illegally, but doing the right thing, is often a victim of the system. Dorothy ultimately has him turn himself in, but it highlights an issue that a lot of people could relate to.

It also co-starred a very-young Mario Lopez as the child. His acting is a little sub-par, but I guess having him as the face of the illegal immigration does a lot of good. He's all dimples and sweetness, and after hearing so many horror stories about Dorothy's students, it seems so unfair that the nice one is the one that has to leave the country! Boo to the Department of Immigration and Naturalization Services!

I actually love the Viedenfrugen (personal servant) B plotline. Apparently, Rose's uncle lost the prosthetic leg of a man named Lars. To make up for it, he decided to become his Viedenfrugen. It turns out he used the leg to beat off wolves when he was setting up the bleachers.

We can't gloss over the fact that Dorothy submitting Mario's essay is ultimately what gets him busted. That would give me guilt for the rest of my life, but it's never spoken of again.

Golden Nuggets

When Dorothy asks what happened to Lars' leg, I like how she plays it. Blanche faked orgasms three times a week in the first few years of her marriage. I love that she admits it so matter-of-factly.

Besides the Lars story, we also get one where Rose and her family and friends kill an old lady with a surprise party. There is a dark side to St. Olaf if you're really paying attention. Slave labor, fatal surprise parties, and villagers that leave bad husbands to be eaten by birds?

Mario Lopez and Bea Arthur had previously worked together on a Norman Lear production called *aka Pablo.*

When I watched this as a young girl, it seemed so basic and humane that the kid should be able to stay in the country—well, these days, that makes me a liberal hippie.

2-22 "Diamond in the Rough"

Aired: March 21, 1987
Director: Terry Hughes
Writers: Jan Fischer
Guest Cast: Jake Smollens (Donnelly Rhodes), Hunter McCoy (Howard Witt), Waiter (Mike Muscat), Mr. Hinkley (Vince Trankina), musician (Glenn Shadix)
Summary: Blanche dates a caterer and is bothered by his lack of polish, but then regrets breaking up with him.
Rating: ❤❤❤❤

"Honey if you think you're confused, take a look at our horn section!"—Band Member

Oh man, I love this episode, but it might be the one that breaks my heart the most. Blanche should not have broken up with Jake. Their chemistry is electric and I think her issue with their background is just stupid, especially considering some of the clowns she dates. Rue McClanahan does a stellar job playing it sexy and vulnerable, and although she's slightly snobbish, it's with a genuine concern for her future with Jake.

By the way, how many banquets do the Girls go to over the years? This is one banquet-loving town. In this episode, it's a hospital charity banquet. I've watched this episode at least 20 times and this is the first time I even knew what the banquet was for.

Golden Nuggets

I love when Jake first meets the Girls and they all hit on him, but Blanche aggressively out flirts them. Damn, she's good!

Sophia's stories of her Sicilian courtship to Sal often changes. But this one, where they were arranged by height and she stood on a rock to avoid marrying Luigi the Pig Boy, is my favorite.

Sophia's husband Sal used to fall asleep during foreplay… I tell ya, we really get to know these ex-husbands, in every intimate way.

I think they should have had that actor do another episode in a later season and reconnect with Blanche. I looked him up and he did a guest stint as another character on *Empty Nest*.

The band at the benefit is full of trans members, and the Girls don't care because they sound great! This is another reason why the show is so beloved by the LGBTQ community. I also like that Rose didn't catch the hint that the band's name was The Great Pretenders.

2-23 "Son-in-Law Dearest"

Aired: April 11, 1987
Director: Terry Hughes
Writers: Patt Shea, Harriet Weiss
Guest Cast: Stan Zbornak (Herb Edelman), Kate (Deena Freeman), Dennis (Jonathan Perpich)
Summary: Dorothy's daughter, Kate, visits to deal with her husband, Dennis' cheating.
Rating: ♥♥♥

"Well, why didn't Desi play Desi?"—Rose
"He wasn't tall enough."—Blance

As it sometimes happens, the B story this episode is much stronger than the A story. The jokes about the *I Love Lucy* marathon, and the fact that Rose had so much sex with her husband that she never watched it, is just a turn-of-events that no one could have predicted. We're not even sure if Charlie was ultimately cheap, or a sex addict, or both, but he and Rose seemed to have more sex than Blanche and George. And *that* is saying something.

The A story tells of marital un-bliss, where Dorothy's daughter Kate flees to escape her husband's infidelity. At first, Dorothy thinks Kate's going to arrive and tell her she's pregnant, but alas, Kate's husband Dennis is a cheater. We get a great scene where Dorothy warns Dennis not to do it again, and it's reminiscent of the early episode when Dorothy tells Stan off for the first time since their divorce. All in all, this is a strong episode, both funny and sentimental.

Golden Nuggets

I love all the dialogue where Blanche explains *I Love Lucy* to Rose. Both actresses play that so well.

It's rare that all the sex talk in the episode is about Rose, but she divulges how robust her sex life was with Charlie. That's why they never had headaches and had really shiny hair.

I love that Rose didn't even know *I Love Lucy* was originally in black & white.

Sophia's Cesar-Romero fantasy comes to life in Season Seven, when he plays her boyfriend.

It's kind of awkward when Stan asks Kate if things were okay between her and her husband in between the sheets? I mean… eww.

This episode is a little man-hating. Stan is shown as lecherous, complaining how he was unhappy in bed. There are references to Betty Friedan, with Blanche saying that a man cheats for the same reason a dog licks himself—because he can.

2-24 "To Catch a Neighbor"

Aired: May 2, 1987
Director: Terry Hughes
Writers: Russell Marcus
Guest Cast: Al Mullins (Joe Campanella), Bobby Hopkins (George Clooney), Martha McDowell (Barbara Tarbuck)
Summary: Two police officers use the Girls' home to stake out, while they try and bust neighbors that are suspected jewel thieves.
Rating: ❤❤

"Nice touch, but I work alone."—Sophia

This episode is strange on many levels. New neighbors suddenly move in, who happen to be jewel thieves, and cops ask the Girls to work undercover. And with the ruse of a dinner party? And oh, George Clooney! Back in the 80's, he was by all definitions a TV actor that hit almost every single show. The best part is the budding flirtation between Al and Dorothy, which doesn't seem obvious until she turns around and says, "I'm crazy nuts about this guy" which is so cute!

The ending where Bobby gets shot, and Dorothy breaks up with Al because she's afraid of him being a cop (when he's probably close to retirement age) is just so obligatory.

Golden Nuggets

The four women on the phone waiting to hear what's happening next door is just a great visual, with them all in their robes and nightgowns.

Blanche gets herself into such a frenzy talking about love, lust, and ecstasy that she sprays herself with a water bottle. She also almost tells about the most fun she ever had standing up (on a 747, which again proves the earlier goof that she is not afraid to fly).

This is the first episode where the Girls hit Rose.

It drives me nuts how many sitcoms don't have homes with peepholes on their doors so that people can see who they're opening the door for. And no one opens the door without knowing who is on the other side—major pet peeve!

We had Blanche break up with a caterer she loved, and now Dorothy breaks up with another great prospect! I like that these women act like they have options, but no woman has this many.

2-25 "A Piece of Cake"

Aired: May 9, 1987
Director: Terry Hughes
Writers: Barry Fanaro, Mort Nathan, Terry Grossman, Kathy Speer
Guest Cast: Young Dorothy (Lynnie Greene), Mr. Ha Ha (Alan Blumenfeld), Bobby Spina (Jeffrey Webber), Sal Petrillo (Sid Melton)
Summary: The Girls remember various birthday celebrations, as they bake a birthday cake for a friend.
Rating: ❤❤❤

"Rose, where you live most people live in windmills and make love to polka music."—Dorothy

I always like the wraparound episodes. This one is about birthday parties celebrated reluctantly. The first one shows Rose and Blanche taking Dorothy to a birthday party at an annoying kids' venue with Mr. Ha Ha. The second one is just sad, having Rose celebrate her birthday alone and telling her dead husband that she's leaving Minnesota to start anew in Florida. The third one is my favorite because it shows a young Dorothy and Sophia back in Brooklyn.

We also meet Sal, who is played by the exact actor who you would pick for Sophia. And the actress playing Dorothy is the best casting this show ever did. She's totally a young Bea Arthur! It involves Sophia's 49th birthday where she finds out she's actually 50 via a birth certificate. The fourth vignette shows them throwing a surprise party for Blanche (who gets depressed on her birthday), where they accidentally invite men from her black book. This seems to reignite her passion for life.

Golden Nuggets

The end scene where Blanche gets surprised is of course great, but the fact that they surprise her again with men from her black book… well, that's extra special for everyone.

Sophia apparently has sex with her husband for at least two hours on her 50th birthday. Blanche gets all the sex cred, but Sophia was quite the dynamo. Even though, till her husband died, she only slept with her husband.

The St. Olaf story gets interrupted, but it had to do with a smoked herring hoagie house.

Betty White claims she definitely channeled feelings for her deceased husband, Allen Ludden, for her birthday scene.

You might not catch it on first viewing, but this episode has strong, underlying messages about women aging more-than gracefully. Dorothy is depressed at her celebration, but gets a good laugh when a kid comes to her defense. And with Rose, we see her bravery and optimism in leaving everything she knows with the hope that she'll meet people. And she's about 60—that's difficult at any age and I appreciate that courage. Sophia's next having birthday regrets. But with compliments from Dorothy and a make-out session from her husband, she's clearly cheered up. And then Blanche—who hates every birthday—gets her spirits raised by a party attended by all her friends with benefits.

2-26 "Empty Nests"

Aired: May 16, 1987
Director: Terry Hughes
Writers: Susan Harris
Guest Cast: Renee Corliss (Rita Moreno), George Corliss (Paul Dooley), Oliver (David Leisure); Jenny Corliss (Jane Harnick)
Summary: An attempted pilot for the original "Empty Nests" starring Rita Moreno as a neighbor who wants her busy doctor husband to work less and spend more time with her.
Rating: ♥

"They were like noisy little calendars. The minute they were in high school, I told everyone they were my husband's children from another marriage."—Blanche
"And you wonder why they're in therapy."—Dorothy

I only give this episode one star, but here it is. The one that I dare say, you can skip, and it's a complete nightmare. I love and adore Rita Moreno more than life, but it's so obviously a weak pilot. It's almost a spoof of a pilot, showing everything wrong with television writing and lacking the way real people talk and interact. How Susan Harris wrote this and *The Golden Girls* is one of the greatest mysteries of television history. And the entire plot revolves around Rita Moreno's character wanting her husband to work less. Then there's a scene with her daughter Jenny coming home from college with boy trouble, as if no one has ever met a teenager and has no idea how they talk or what their problems are.

Golden Nuggets

There really isn't much here. Blanche's advice to Jenny is probably the strongest part of the episode, but again, it's not that strong.

There was no *Nightmare on Elm Street 4* film at this time (only *Nightmare on Elm Street 3: Dream Warriors*). Also, Dorothy mentions throwing Oliver in a pool at Blanche's house—there is no pool! These are easily fact-checked, my God!

Blanche doesn't understand why Dorothy didn't kiss a boy with her mouth when she was eight. Wow.

Everyone, and that includes myself, think this is the worst episode of the series. Rita Moreno concurs, saying that Susan Harris was ill and couldn't do rewrites. It's also ranked at the very bottom of the IMDb ranked episodes, by a long shot.

Second *Golden Girls* episode that doesn't end with a shot of the Girls.

There's a creepy womanizer neighbor, Oliver, who's so poorly written and the jokes are terrible. He's almost like Larry from *Three's Company*. The actor ends up on the next spin-off version of *Empty Nest*, playing a less annoying neighbor, which is indeed a success. Did anyone ever really have neighbors that came and went like sitcoms would lead us to believe?

The episode actually ends with Rita Moreno asking her husband to promise her he'll never die! How depressing is that? And the audience applauds? Insanity.

This episode never re-airs on TV for obvious reasons—it's just a failed pilot.

The Golden Girls

SEASON THREE

3-1 "Old Friends"

Written by: Terry Grossman, Kathy Speer
Aired: September 19, 1987
Director: Terry Hughes
Guest Cast: Alvin (Jon Seneca), Sandra (Janet MacLachlan), Daisy (Jenny Lewis)
Summary: Sophia makes a friend on the boardwalk and finds out he's in the early stages of Alzheimer's disease.
Rating: ❤❤❤❤

"What were you doing in Ladies Petite?"—Rose

This is a heartbreaking episode, and possibly Estelle Getty's best. She's brilliant here on all levels. By this season, she really has the character of Sophia down, mixing the mean, nagging, and sarcastic parts of the character with the sweet and wise. And this episode shows her with a feistiness and sensitivity that is uniquely Getty's own creation.

The B story involving the loss of Rose's childhood stuffed bear, Fernando, is equally strong. It's one of the strongest B stories of the series, with Rose being slightly maniacal as she shoves a little girl out the door at the end. Betty White actually was worried this was going too far, but the audience loved it.

As I've mentioned before, Rose has a dark side, and I love it. Sometimes we see it as competitiveness, and other times we see it as pure possessiveness. Not only is she unforgiving when it comes to Blanche's mistake, but she shoves that girl with glee. When I first watched it, I really fell for Rose's "unfair" speech.

Golden Nuggets

There are two truly great moments in this episode. Rose throwing Daisy out the door was an audience pleaser for sure, and Sophia talking about getting old, as she knits a scarf for Alvin that she'll probably never give him, is a tearjerker.

Why hadn't Alvin's daughter told Dorothy he was leaving, so poor Sophia wouldn't be waiting for him on the bench?

Sophia trying to explain to Rose that she hadn't considered sleeping with Alvin because of the "myth about black men" and how Rose thinks it's a myth about men named Alvin is an odd conversation.

This kid Jenny is a little too old to be obsessed with a teddy bear. That's a red flag.

The third season unveiled a new stage at Ren-Mar Studios. You'll notice that Blanche's vase is missing by the front door.

This episode was submitted for Emmy consideration for Best Comedy, but didn't win.

It also reminds me of the Bette Davis quote, "Old age is no place for sissies."

3-2 "One for the Money"

Written by: Kathy Speer, Terry Grossman, Barry Fanaro, Mort Nathan, Winifred Hervey
Aired: September 26, 1987
Director: Terry Hughes
Guest Cast: Sal Petrillo (Sid Melton), Young Dorothy (Lynnie Greene), Marty (Roy Stuart), Russell (Ed Balin), Dave (Ed Kerrigan), Priscilla (Starr Andreeff), Announcer (Conrad Janis)
Summary: The Girls recall different get-rich schemes they've attempted over the years.
Rating: 

"Blanche, we're not dancing on our backs."—Dorothy

In a series of vignettes, we see the ladies do odd things for money. The first vignette is a little weak, with the Girls trying a catering business only for it to be sabotaged when the bride almost cancels the wedding. This concept just doesn't work, mostly because how rude would the bride be to not pay the women for the food and labor? The second is a Brooklyn flashback, with young Dorothy, Sophia and Sal. I always liked these because the actors were cast well. It's a *Gift of the Magi type* of story which always seems to work on shows.

There is a dance contest where the women quickly become competitive and brutal in order to win $1,000. This has Rose's memorable dance routine where she suddenly exhibits strong gymnastics ability, while Blanche promises sexual favors on the dance floor. It's definitely the most outlandish as the Girls try and heckle each other off the floor.

Golden Nuggets

In the world of #MeToo, Blanche is again clearly on the side of, if you want to trade sex for rewards, go for it. She has done this for theater parts before, and I don't know what sex acts she whispers to these men, but the woman knows how to work fast and get her point across. It's all about consent and that the first move comes from the woman.

Starting a catering business is a common sitcom trope, but does anyone know people who actually tried? It was probably so much more difficult before the Internet!

I love hearing Sal discover the joys of the TV Dinner. I loved those!

The body double during Rose's dance is quite obvious.

I'll say this again. These women rock as far as hobbies and jobs go, and in this one we see them at their most enterprising.

3-3 "Bringing Up Baby"

Written by: Barry Fanaro, Mort Nathan
Aired: October 3, 1987
Director: Terry Hughes
Guest Cast: Chester T. Rainey (Parley Baer), Veterinarian (Tom McGreevey)
Summary: Rose inherits a prize-winning pig from her uncle and the Girls debate whether they should take care of it.
Rating: ❤❤❤

"Blanche, the people you date are from foreign countries. They play by different rules."—Sophia

Some of this episode is pure sitcom stupidity. The idea that Rose inherits a pig is one of those sitcom problems that would never happen in real life. But some of it is explained away with the idea that the people of St. Olaf aren't the brightest or most normal group of people. So, there you have it. Also, to nitpick, Rose at first thinks she is inheriting a baby… and the Girls act like raising a baby is like raising a cat. But it works because the dialogue is funny, and the women sell it.

Raising a pig in a ranch house in Miami does sound like a code violation of some sort though. But the fact that taking care of this pig is worth $100,000 to the women, they are painted as greedy. It just seems judgmental. And I never like when sitcoms find some way to avoid giving the characters money!

Golden Nuggets

When Rose tells Baby to eat before she spanks him, Sophia thinks she's talking to her, because that's the way they used to call them for dinner at the Home. I love how dark this show was. Shady Pines was often portrayed as a hideous place to be, which was mildly informative for young kids with grandparents in retirement homes.

Just a little bit of sexy Blanche picking out pearls to ensure that she looks like a quick, easy good time. No boy-talk here, just pig talk.

Sophia gets in a dig about Dorothy being an unattractive baby. Poor Dorothy!

According to Betty White, the pig was "a real good actor."

Am I being sexist, ageist, or both to wonder how the four of them so easily consider raising a baby without a man, a bigger home, or the help of a younger person? They all work except Sophia. Blanche is certainly not one for taking care of a baby. She has admitted that many times. And Sophia's over 80 years old!

3-4 "The Housekeeper"

Written by: Winifred Hervey
Aired: October 17, 1987
Director: Terry Hughes
Guest Cast: Marguerite (Paula Kelly), Midge (Deborah Rose), Crow Man (Carl Ciarfalio)
Summary: The Girls think that a fired housekeeper put a curse on them.
Rating: ❤❤❤❤

"I feel like crawling under the covers and eating Velveeta right out of the box."—Rose

This episode is a favorite of mine because it's funny all-the-way through, has kind of a strange plot, and a bit of a twist ending. The Girls accuse their fired housekeeper of cursing them. Turns out, she's actually just not getting the housework done because she's studying for law school.

The reasons that the Girls think Marguerite is putting curses on them seem pretty valid. The painted rock, Dorothy not sleeping, the plumbing in the kitchen, and Blanche's boyfriend breaking up with her are all suspicious. And Crow Man! Listen, I don't like coincidences and I don't take chances. But you can't assume someone put a curse on you. Although, my twin and I swear that our lives were cursed one year after seeing the comedian Judy Gold perform (but we never felt it was an intentional curse).

Golden Nuggets

When Sophia walks in on them trying to woo Marguerite back, and Marguerite is wearing a tiara, is one of my favorite moments of the show.

Why isn't Dorothy going to her niece's wedding?

Parochial school outfit + silk sheet = one of Blanche's tricks for keeping a man's interest. But Dorothy apparently relies on vodka and black underwear. Both are solid choices.

Rose's grandparents got together based on a love potion, but it sounds more like a case of a nurse sexually harassing a patient. But it ended in an engagement.

The painted rock is the first wage Sophia earned in Sicily.

Betty really nails Rose's "Boy do I feel stupid!"

The fact that three sensible women are absolutely positive that their Black housekeeper (I think she's supposed to be from the Caribbean based on the accent) has put a curse on them is a little much. Then again, they live with Sophia who speaks often about curses that she cast. And in the end, they kind of look like idiots, so I guess all is well. You can't fight ignorance without showing that humans can be a bit ignorant at times.

The Golden Girls was a show that yes, was about four white, heterosexual women, and the storylines didn't feature all that many people of color. But when they did, like earlier in this season with Alvin and in this episode, the writers did interesting things: Alvin's race was not a part of the plot; he was merely a friend suffering from a disease. And in this one, the Girls do carry a bias about who Marguerite could be, but Marguerite handles it well. She understands that they are coming from a place that is a bit ignorant, though not hateful, and as Rose says, "Boy, do I feel stupid." Marguerite turns out be smarter than all of them, in that she used their stereotype against them in order to get more time to study to become a lawyer.

3-5 "Nothing to Fear but Fear Itself"

Written by: Christopher Lloyd
Aired: October 24, 1987
Director: Terry Hughes
Guest Cast: Stewardess (Meg Wyllie)
Summary: The Girls have to confront their fears while Rose has to fly to her Aunt's funeral.
Rating: ❤❤❤❤

"I would also say—you're fat."—Dorothy

This episode has St. Olaf stuff, a great Brooklyn flashback, and more than a few hilarious scenes. It starts out all about Rose being frazzled about giving a eulogy, but becomes about Dorothy's fear of flying as well. They all get stuck on a plane, trapped with men, but not the right men because it turns out that bald men on a plane scare Blanche. Which is a little specific. They all face up to their phobias, which seem pretty reasonable (okay maybe not Blanche's).

Golden Nuggets

You know it's a great episode when you can't pick a favorite scene. The Girls on the plane have some great moments, but my fave is probably them talking about their phobias in the kitchen. Also, Blanche pestering Dorothy about what she'd say at her funeral.

Of course, as is common, the years the Girls were married varies. Sophia says she was married for 52 years, when in another episode it's 45.

Blanche's dream involving Mel Gibson and oysters was funny, but has not aged well.

In St. Olaf, they pick the Valedictorian by picking straws. I love that town.

Rose's aha moment on the plane about how her aunt used to scare her and that being scared is a useful skill, is actually quite wise. Eventually, you have to be an adult that can get things done. Even if it's giving a eulogy on a plane.

3-6 "Letter to Gorbachev"

Written by: Barry Fanaro, Mort Nathan
Aired: October 31, 1987
Director: Terry Hughes
Guest Cast: Alexi (Alan Rich), Linda (Jaclyn Bernstein), Nancy (Cynthia Marie King)
Summary: Rose's worries about nuclear war lead her to write a letter to Soviet Premier Gorbachev, which gets surprising results.
Rating: ❤❤

"Your father's a doctor, your mother's a lawyer.
What are you, one of the Cosby kids?"
—Dorothy

There's a lot about this episode that makes me rank it low. The concept is silly, the logistics don't quite make sense, and it has a dream sequence which was a common trope in the 80's and 90's. And this sequence is a waste of time. For one thing, Blanche sings Happy Birthday to Gorbachev.

One forgets that the Cold War was ending when this aired, and the Soviet Union was falling. Many felt that it was an end to tyranny and an end to war all over the world, and that democracy and freedom would be everywhere. Seems naive now.

The B story is relatively weak with Sophia planning a talent show act, but it does pay off at the end with a Reagan impersonation we don't get to hear.

Golden Nuggets

Sophia's song "Thanks for the Medicare" is by far the highlight. I think it's hysterical and deserves another verse.

Don't even get me started on how ridiculous it is that there is hardly any American government involvement while Rose is supposedly giving a press conference to Russians about nuclear arms. And it all happens within weeks! And without any vetting of Rose!

Blanche's guess that a picture drawn by Rose's cadet girl is men fighting to sleep with her is the world's best Rorschach test.

This show loved to burn Hollywood actresses that got kicked off TV. Valerie Harper and Shelley Long are dissed episodes apart.

Rose's childhood experiences include yearning to be Small Curd Cottage Cheese Queen, which was apparently her town's second biggest honor, next to Large Curd Cottage Cheese Queen. If we know anything about St. Olaf, it's that they value cheese more than Wisconsin.

I always enjoy the busyness of these women. Sophia's involved in yet another talent show and Rose is leading cadet troops.

3-7 "Strange Bedfellows"

Written by: Christopher Lloyd
Aired: November 7, 1987
Director: Terry Hughes
Guest Cast: Gil Kessler (John Schuck), Secretary (Sarah Partridge), Reporter #1 (Darwyn Carson), Reporter #2 (David Westgor)
Summary: Blanche is accused of sleeping with a local politician, and when she denies it, the Girls don't believe her.
Rating: ❤❤❤

"No. It sounded like Jim and Tammy Faye on Nightline."—Dorothy

This episode revisits a common theme of the Girls accusing Blanche of slutty behavior, and not believing her. It's kind of frustrating because Blanche has established herself as being quite honest about her sexual behaviors, and what she will and won't do. She's honest with her friends and their insistence that she is hiding a one-night stand understandably hurts her. What's more, is it makes the audience feel really defensive of Blanche. We just instinctively believe her and turn out to be right. Blanche is clear about who she's attracted to, and she wasn't attracted to Gil. If she had slept with him, she would have fessed up.

The end twist that Gil was once a woman was definitely surprising. Before that, Gil's crime seemed to be that he's boring. And again, the Girls treat this news without judgment about Gil, and the reveal seems to make him end on an exciting note; which was an example of how the show always did a good job supporting the LGBTQ community. Though this would still be scandalous for a politician to confess, the Girls just deal with it as it pertains to their own particular drama. Even Sophia thinks the big news in his confession is that he's Italian!

Gil might be on to something in thinking that people are suddenly voting for him because they think he's dishonest and cheats on his wife. Look who we had in the White House.

Golden Nuggets

Blanche had lunch at The Press Club and either eventually slept with every man, or just learned their names and faces.

The Sicily Wine Crisis, when the town was ravaged by a case of Athlete's Foot! One of my favorites.

Again, these women are involved in charities, volunteer in all kinds of talent events, and are now central to a local political campaign. Why don't they run for something? Okay, okay, that's too progressive.

3-8 "Brotherly Love"

Written by: Jeffrey Ferro, Fredric Weiss
Aired: November 14, 1987
Director: Terry Hughes
Guest Cast: Stan Zbornak (Herb Edelman), Ted (McLean Stevenson)
Summary: Dorothy begins to have feelings for her ex-husband's Stan's brother.
Rating: ❤❤❤

"In here?"—Blanche
"No Blanche. In Hollywood. But they pipe it through these little wires, and it comes out here." —Sophia

This episode is fun because it has Stan, and Stan is just always fun. He's the fifth Golden Girl in many ways and the writers use him perfectly. It also has Blanche and Dorothy fighting over a man, Stan and Dorothy fighting, and Rose befuddled in some truly fantastic ways. The ending where Ted wants Dorothy to be his babysitter is a bummer. Those Zbornak boys are the worst sometimes!

The B story here is also a favorite of mine. Rose not being able to sleep seems simple enough, but her scenes get a lot of laughs—from how she counts the Jacksons before she goes to bed, right up until they realize she's drinking Atomic Zinger tea. And I do enjoy Sophia trying to knock her out with Sicilian Sominex.

Golden Nuggets

Oh how the Golden Girls can throw down—Dorothy and Blanche's fight at the kitchen table is epic! Epic slut-shaming, as only Dorothy can do, while Blanche slams her looks. But if you don't dig that kind of humor, you wouldn't be watching this show. "Join the navy, sea the world, sleep with Blanche Devereaux!"

Sophia says she didn't know Dorothy was pregnant until four days after her wedding to Stan. We know this isn't true from a number of episodes.

Blanche hitting on Ted is a bit much, even for her. She's usually a bit smoother.

Remember when I said to look for the dark side of St. Olaf stories? Some chick won a rocking chair contest for 17 hours, due to a husband with a cattle prod.

Man, the wardrobe department must've loved Blanche's nightgown!

First appearance of Stan without his mustache.

These Girls do insult each other in a brutal way, but I think it shows you how to fight and make up with your friends. The show also demonstrates how to give final payback to a guy that treats you shabbily, as in how Dorothy gets her revenge on Ted.

3-9 "A Visit from Little Sven"

Written by: David Nichols
Aired: November 21, 1987
Director: Terry Hughes
Guest Cast: Sven Lindstrom (Casey Sander), Olga Nordstrum (Yvette Heyden), Floyd McCallum (Chuck Walling)
Summary: Rose's cousin Sven falls in love with Blanche, even though he's engaged to be married.
Rating: ❤❤❤

"Were you two the cousins who played the banjo in Deliverance?"—Sophia

This is a light episode that makes fun of Blanche's dating insecurities, as well as Rose's hometown nuttiness. And for a B story, Sophia tries to get her driver's license renewed. Of course, I love that Sophia is about 83 and hopped up at the thought of impressing her friends with a driver's license. It's the kind of thing that makes the show appealing to all ages.

On the flip side, Sven is a bit much with the Nordic accent. I think Rue's acting pulls their scenes off though, as Blanche tries to make Floyd jealous, accidentally getting Sven to fall for her instead. And when the four women discover his feelings, it's all genuinely humorous. And then there's the nice surprise that Sven is a lot more intuitive than anyone's given him credit for. But of course, he's not an idiot and when he realizes he's being set up with a young, hot Swedish wife, he ends it with Blanche. But Blanche recovers well with a trip on a boat with Floyd. Miami is a tough dating scene!

Golden Nuggets

Oh, how I adore the look Sven gives Blanche after he says, "I'm in love with Blanche…" Blanche's look to the camera, and the whole dialogue between the Girls is hysterical.

Sven is way off geographically if he thinks he needs to sail near the Cape of Good Hope to get back to the Scandinavian countries.

Blanche claims to have only one gift—turning men on!

In St. Olaf, when a woman breaks up with a man, the man is allowed to shave the woman's head and make her wear an itchy hat. Okay St. Olaf.

I love when Rose gets angry and doesn't pull any punches.

Blanche's storylines can be amazing, because she flutters about competing over men that are younger than her, older than her, and always recovers quickly. It's a good lesson for women of all ages.

3-10 "The Audit"

Written by: Winifred Hervey
Aired: November 28, 1987
Director: Terry Hughes
Guest Cast: Stan Zbornak (Herb Edelman), Mr. Escobar (Tony Perez), Mr. Murray (Richard Penn)
Summary: Dorothy and Stan get audited and find out they owe the IRS $5,000.
Rating: ❤❤❤

"When was the last time someone gave you a spanking?"—Blanche
"Vegas."—Stan

Stan and Dorothy episodes always give us more insights into their marriage. Stan was clearly a fuck-up, as a man and as a husband. But seeing him try to explain to Dorothy, and to schmooze the IRS guy, really show how inept he is at basic human functioning. We all know women that married men like this in their youth. They took an early gamble and realized way too late that they got a total lemon. Not a bad guy, but just so useless in important situations.

The B story has Blanche and Rose taking a Spanish class, which doesn't pay off much except for Rose mixing up words and almost robbing a pawn shop.

Golden Nuggets

The end where Stan sells the Corvette to get Dorothy her ring back is why we love him. He knows that Dorothy is his love, even though they'll never end up together.

Blanche is increasingly sex-crazed this season. She's taking a Spanish class just to meet more men.

This season also amps up Sophia's gas jokes, joking that the smell of Ecuador is in fact, her gas. Gross.

Sophia pans a few films over the series. This time it's *Ishtar*, the Warren Beatty flop. Sophia (or the writers) do not seem to care for Warren Beatty.

The idea that Stan tried to sell tie-bibs without considering that people use napkins tells you everything you need to know about Stan!

This episode conveys the post-feminist view that not only are men not any smarter than women about money, but often it's men that screw up the finances all together. So many housewives lived responsible lives, pinching pennies, only to find that their husbands gambled or spent frivolously.

3-11 "Three on a Couch"

Written by: Jeffrey Ferro, Fredric Weiss
Aired: December 5, 1987
Director: Terry Hughes
Guest Cast: Dr. Ashley (Philip Sterling), Carl (Terry Wills), Jerry (John C. Moskoff)
Summary: The Girls head to a psychiatrist to deal with the problems they're having as roommates.
Rating: ❤❤❤

"I promise I'll do Hail Marys until Madonna has a hit movie."—Dorothy

The premise of the four women bickering so much that they need a therapist is a little far-fetched, but it does provide scenes for a wraparound episode. We have Blanche forcing Dorothy to get ready for a date, even though Dorothy is clearly sick, Rose messing up a simple errand of putting a job ad in the paper, Rose and Blanche jumping into bed with Dorothy after getting scared by the movie *Aliens*, and Sophia telling the others a tale of pepperoni swimming upstream to help them each with different problems.

Based on these stories, the psychiatrist tells them that they shouldn't live together and that they bring out the worst in each other. He might be the laziest shrink ever. He must tell couples to get divorced after ten minutes! He doesn't even ask them about the good times or what they like about each other, just focusing on the problems. And though the episode is entertaining, there are better snippets of them fighting over the first three seasons.

Golden Nuggets

The scene where Rose naively puts an ad in the Personals Column selling Dorothy's services for eight dollars an hour made me think of the original Tinder!

The Girls say they've lived together for the last five years, but any way you add it up, it can't be more than three.

Blanche has to go into her bedroom to get the Polaroid and the whipped cream.

Sophia gets in some digs at Blanche, first for her accent—which also insults *Designing Women*—then saying she's only giving when she's lying down.

Sophia defends, but also insults, the Asian neighbors, by saying not to call them aliens, but accusing them of eating dogs at the same time. Then she insults Sigourney Weaver in the movie *Aliens,* saying she shouldn't go without makeup.

Rose tells Sophia that her boss harassed her. A strength of this show is that it demonstrated that women of all ages and types were victims of harassment and gross men.

3-12 "Charlie's Buddy"

Written by: Terry Grossman, Kathy Speer
Aired: December 12, 1987
Director: Terry Hughes
Guest Cast: Buddy Rourke (Milo O'Shea)
Summary: Rose falls for an old war buddy of Charlie's, but the Girls soon realize he has bad intentions.
Rating:

"It is an out and out sin!"—Blanche
"Why do I feel like I just fell through the Looking Glass?"—Dorothy

In all fairness, I don't love this episode, but there's definitely a softness and a sadness to it. It's about Rose getting tricked on such a basic level—a man who preys on veteran's wives, by pretending to be their ex's army buddy, so that they fall in love with him, all to con them out of money. And it doesn't seem super-obvious at first—just kind of subtle. He lets Rose do all the talking, making her the perfect victim. Of course, a not-perfect victim would be a woman who didn't love her husband and didn't want to talk about him. But that is not Rose.

The B story is about Dorothy and Blanche trying to find a dress for yet another banquet!

Golden Nuggets

It's quite hysterical when Sophia emerges wearing the same dress that Blanche just brought home!

The Girls seem to be extremely old-fashioned about Rose moving in with a guy, which is true to form for women of their generation. Though in fairness, Blanche seems most concerned about the financial implications, offering advice to steal from his pants' pockets.

You can't get to St. Gustav by plane, you have to get there by Toboggan.

Buddy has got eyebrows that should be discussed at length. At great length.

Sophia tries to pedal a tale about a love affair between her and Winston Churchill.

I can't believe Sophia says if Dorothy hadn't married Stan, she would've given birth to reasonably attractive children (that might be one of her biggest burns ever!). Yikes.

This show does a good job educating women about certain practical matters with men. Research the new guy! Back then you didn't have social media to investigate a man's life and friends, but man, mutual friends looking out for you can save the day!

3-13 "The Artist"

Written by: Christopher Lloyd
Aired: December 19, 1987
Director: Terry Hughes
Guest Cast: Laszlo (Tony Jay), Victor (Monte Landis)
Summary: Blanche, Dorothy, and Rose fight over the attention of a sculptor and whether to be the star of his next project.
Rating: ❤❤❤❤

"Who's Laszlo?"—Sophia
"A Hungarian artist we've all been posing nude for."—Rose
"In the future, a simple, none-of-your-business Sophia will suffice."—Sophia

I love this episode. I love that the artist is choosing which of the three women to sculpt naked. I mean that is some positive vibes for older women. It's the kind of message that flows throughout a lot of episodes, but it's just so there and taken for granted here. I also dig that they are fighting over him as a romantic pursuit, even though he turns out to be gay.

The B story is about Sophia playing non-stop practical jokes, mostly to aggravate Dorothy. It definitely gets a few laughs.

Golden Nuggets

I'm torn between the final reveal of the statue, and the reveal of all three women posing for Laszlo as which scene is better. Also, whenever the women are fighting over a man, it's gold. But this is the only episode that has all three fighting over the same man!

Blanche's lines to Laszlo about her breasts being perfect orbs, as well as the one about holding his chisel gets me every time. That girl has a strong flirting game.

I don't think we can underestimate what a big deal it is that they have a statue created in their image. I mean that is something to put on a resume.

Another kitchen table scene where Bea Arthur is not in the center.

The twist at the end of Laszlo combining all three women to make the perfect statue, and in essence creating the perfect woman, is one of the nutshells of the whole show. The smart and practical, the sexy and outgoing, and the kind and innocent. And then hopefully, we combine all three and become Sophia, with wisdom and sass.

3-14 "Blanche's Little Girl"

Written by: Terry Grossman, Kathy Speer
Aired: January 9, 1988
Director: Terry Hughes
Guest Cast: Rebecca (Shawn Schepps), McCracken (Scott Menville), Edna (Meg Wyllie), Jeremy (Joe Regalbuto)
Summary Blanche's estranged daughter, Rebecca, returns to Blanche's life, with a sudden weight gain and a verbally abusive boyfriend.
Rating: ❤❤❤

"It is not easy being a mother.
If it were easy, fathers would do it."—Dorothy

This episode has a lot of depth as far as mother/daughter relationships. There's also a lot of shaming women for their appearance. I've talked about Sophia's incessant insults to Dorothy about her looks, but this episode is about Blanche reconnecting with her model/daughter Rebecca, who has become obese and is now in a verbally abusive relationship.

There are a lot of funny fat jokes if you find fat jokes funny. Like when Rebecca arrives and they're all stunned that she's the model Blanche had described. There's Blanche's awkward, initial interaction with her daughter. Sophia of course is blunt and relentless, and though Rebecca claims that she's happy and resists Blanche's efforts to put her on a diet (a common mistake mothers often make), we know there is pain deep down.

Obesity is never an issue with someone not knowing what to eat. It's an emotional problem, like any addictive behavior. It's a symptom of a problem, not the other way around. They're soothing their emotions and we know Blanche's history of focusing on her own beauty, so we know there's pressure that's not going to go away with a diet. The girl has no self-esteem.

This is why her becoming involved with Jeremy makes total sense. And also why, as horrible as Blanche can be, Rebecca is extremely manipulative threatening to take away her love. She's saying, "don't talk about my glaring weight problem or I'll withhold my love." Or, "Don't say anything about my asshole boyfriend, or you won't see me again." This is high-level dysfunction and would never be solved in a quick reunion. A girl like Becky would probably marry Jeremy and isolate herself from friends and family, and it would be a long time before she'd come to her senses to realize that although her mother was misguided, she at least loved her.

The B Story with Sophia negotiating for more pay is actually both comical and a subtle commentary on senior citizens being underpaid and abused in the workplace. Well-done sneaking that in Susan Harris!

Golden Nugget

Dorothy's quick, two-word comeback to Jeremy is better than a more obvious response.

Sophia's "Now I understand why she's sleeping in Blanche's bed. We know it can support the weight of an average female and two Venezuelan soccer players." is savage.

The actor who played Rebecca credits the episode getting her out of an abusive relationship.

Sometimes the writers need to chill with how mean they made Sophia. She fat-shames Blanche, Blanche's daughter, and gives a good dig to Dorothy about how dates don't call her back.

I love how quickly Blanche's face turns the minute Jeremy scolds Becky, and Becky apologizes, because that's exactly how long it takes to know someone's a jerk.

Sophia inserting herself into The Yalta Conference in one of my favorite Sophia stories, as well as the way they ultimately gain the upper hand in the McCracken negotiations.

I say this over and over, but this show was about women working and negotiating, never settling for relationships or jobs. And both the A and B stories address that.

3-15 “Dorothy’s New Friend”

Written by: Robert Bruce, Martin Weiss
Aired: January 16, 1988
Director: Terry Hughes
Guest Cast: Barbara Thorndyke (Bonnie Bartlett), Murray Gutman (Monty Ash), Maître d’ (Brad Trumbull)
Summary: Dorothy befriends a famous local author, who does not get along with Rose and Blanche.
Rating: ❤❤❤❤

“Please. Black underwear and pasties couldn’t make me look easy.”—Sophia

This episode introduces us to a bit of a villain and a threat to the Girls’ friendship. At first, it looks like a harmless rift between friends that have different interests, and Barbara just seems stuck-up. But it ends on a more serious note. Barbara is more than stuck-up, she’s a member of a restricted country club that doesn’t allow Jewish people. The fact that this doesn’t bother Barbara makes Dorothy see her for what she really is—a genuinely bad person.

Before, she had been enamored by Barbara’s being an author and somewhat cultured. It’s relatable to anyone who has ever met or become close to someone famous, only to realize they were a jerk. It’s a quick comedown for sure.

Barbara’s transgressions run the gamut. She’s condescending, she humble brags, and as Blanche points out, she apparently asks to pass the salt in Latin. All of that is annoying, but the actual bigotry is too much for Dorothy.

I recently related a lot more to this episode, as I ended a friendship with someone who appeared to be nice and complimentary to me, but was sometimes cruel, critical, and condescending to my friends and acquaintances. I didn’t see how frequently she did this until she was in my life more. So, this episode reminds me that at an older age, when someone reveals themselves to be toxic and narcissistic—and especially when your closest friends say a person is mean or unkind—you better run. Do not try and be someone’s cheerleader. Nice people don’t need a cheerleader.

Golden Nuggets

Sophia claims to have had a dull sex life with Sal, but previous episodes beg to differ.

The Girls are going to a ball, this time requiring animal costumes!

This episode is almost a direct remake of a Mary Tyler Moore episode called "Some of My Best Friends are Rhoda."

Bonnie Bartlett, the actress that played Barbara Thorndyke, got booed by the live audience after they performed this episode.

Weird that the alleged Mortimer Club is the most exclusive club in Miami, and Dorothy doesn't know it's restricted.

St. Olaf had a resident that had to legally change her name to Mean Old Lady Hickenlooper. I'm telling you, St. Olaffians are mean.

Oogle and Floogle is an adult version of Hide and Seek, and I have to say, I'm into it.

This is the only episode that deals with anti-Semitism. However, Estelle and Bea were Jewish, as were many of the writers.

3-16 "Grab That Dough"

Written by: Winifred Hervey
Aired: January 23, 1988
Director: Terry Hughes
Guest Cast: Guy Corbin (James MacKrell), Nancy (Lucy Lee Flippin), Tiffany (Kathy Andrus), Willard (Charles Green), Policeman (Ken Smolka), Stage Manager (Craig Schwaefer)
Summary: The Girls venture out to Hollywood to be contestants on a game show.
Rating: ❤❤

"Oh yeah, well I'm from Sicily and you know what our company policy is. First, I break your knees."—Sophia

Full disclosure. I never liked sitcom episodes where characters come close to winning money, then do something stupid to come back with nothing. It's a trope and cuts too close to home, as I had a traumatizing experience on the show "Who Wants to Be a Millionaire." It was the worst $1,000 I ever won (through no fault of Meredith, she was lovely). So, there's a bias here.

The Girls go through various mishaps before arriving on *Grab That Dough*. One is that Sophia gives the wrong address for the tickets, then they arrive late to the hotel, then they lose their reservation and get *the* most unhelpful hotel clerk. And, once they arrive on the show, Blanche and Dorothy swap Rose and Sophia for brothers who claim to be successful game-show contestants, only to realize that they're idiots that can't play the game.

Golden Nuggets

The final answers to the questions on *Grab That Dough*, that reveal Blanche and Dorothy made the wrong choice in choosing Willard, are the show's fun spots.

Sophia gets the number of her grandchildren wrong. She says six, and later on we learn Phil alone has 10 children.

"Better late than pregnant!" Indeed. Oh, and Sophia reveals some sort of sexual activity with her husband that used feathers attached to a live chicken. Eek.

The Sicily Game Show "Torture" sounds like a riveting *SNL* skit. "They used real lightning!" Oh and we finally get the address for "Picture it, Sicily." Two miles west of Palermo, underneath the old bridge.

Blanche senses a sexual rival in Tiffany and cuts her down pretty hard about nude photos she did for a magazine. Blanche really shouldn't sexually shame anyone...

"Girl most likely to get stuck in a tuba!" Someone should do a St. Olaf version of "Our Town."

The hand gesture Guy Corbin makes during the show is a nod to Allen Ludden.

Guy Corbin seems immune to Blanche's charms. But then I thought, he's a Hollywood guy, so he probably doesn't even look at women over 50. So, you know, that's accurate.

3-17 "My Brother, My Father"

Written by: Barry Fanaro, Mort Nathan
Aired: February 6, 1988
Director: Terry Hughes
Guest Cast: Stan Zbornak (Herb Edelman), Angelo (Bill Dana)
Summary: Dorothy and Stan have to pretend they're still married when Sophia's brother, Angelo, comes to visit.
Rating: ❤❤❤❤

"We're here collecting lingerie. for needy, sexy people."—Blanche

Angelo's first appearance and it's a fan favorite—certainly a character that I love. Sophia's siblings get the most laughs. In this one, Angelo is introduced as a priest, except it turns out he's pretending because of a promise he made to his mother decades ago. Meanwhile, Blanche and Rose are playing the nuns in *The Sound of Music* and everyone gets stuck at the house during a hurricane.

Every scene works here, but the fact that we have Angelo and Stan staying at the house, while Rose and Blanche are dressed as nuns, is just comedy gold. Stan and Dorothy insult each other like only exes can, and yet he wants Dorothy back at the end of the episode—those two are just sentimental fools for each other.

Golden Nuggets

When Sophia runs out of her room after hearing the Nazis are coming… I laugh every time. Also, Stan trying to get in bed with Dorothy by singing Gershwin until Sophia intervenes to block the inevitable disaster—that's some Italian mothering right there.

We'll see that Sophia's mother lives later than 1914 so Angelo's story doesn't make sense.

Blanche talking dirty to one of her boyfriends on the phone while wearing a nun outfit is quite the scene.

We learn a lot about Angelo right off the bat. First, he also tells stories that start with "Picture it" like his sisters. And secondly, he's a butt man.

Dorothy and Stan's passive aggressive jabs at each other are top-notch in this episode. "My feet have wings, barf bag."

Blanche expresses disappointment for not getting the lead role because of the gay theater director. This happened to her in an earlier season, when she slept with the director for the part of Lady Macbeth only to get the witch role. A lesson most actresses know—you can sleep with someone for a part, but it doesn't mean you'll get it.

3-18 & 3-19 "Golden Moments, Part 1 & 2"

Written by: Mort Nathan, Barry Fanaro, Kathy Speer, Terry Grossman
Aired: February 13, 1988
Director: Terry Hughes
Summary: Sophia considers moving out and moving in with her son Phil, because he's having marital problems, causing the Girls to reminisce about their time living together.
Rating: ♥♥♥

"I heard them howling and moaning all night.
How do you ignore something like that?"—Rose
"I'm getting used to it. You know my room
is next to Blanche's."—Dorothy

Entertaining enough for a fan and a new viewer, the second clip show of the third season is a two-parter. I guess the value lies in whether you think the writers chose the best scenes. They divide these into themes and show what are arguably some of the Girls' funniest interactions.

In Part 1, they delve into Sophia's thinking of leaving. We get one scene when Sophia first arrives from Shady Pines, two scenes showing Sophia and Dorothy in bed together (the second one is definitely the funnier one as they discuss Rose's lesbian friend), and one with the Girls piling into bed with Sophia during a cold night, because she has an electric blanket. I actually didn't think the scene from the pilot was that good, but maybe it was an introduction scene so they figured it was worth adding.

Then Sophia mentions the "yutz parade that's been through this house" and they go through some of the women's dating experiences next. They could've shown way more of these! We get Blanche mulling over whether to go out with the younger man Dirk, Dorothy accidentally asking out a priest and dressing like the mother of a "Solid Gold Dancer," the Girls opening up Blanche's homemade calendar called "The Men of Blanche's Boudoir," and Rose dating a dwarf. That whole montage is just good stuff.

On to the second episode. the Girls still can't sleep at the thought of Sophia moving out. They realize they are out of cheesecake, but thank God Rose anticipated this and went to the store to get some. So, without

Sophia at the table, they start to recall some of their best conversations about sex. Like when they talked about orgasms and how they all lost their virginity (which in hindsight, was quite a revolutionary sex talk for TV), and why menopause isn't so bad.

They also recount their St. Olaf stories and had their first laugh. Sophia enters the kitchen to complain about Phil, but also to remind the Girls about their fighting. In more flashbacks, we see Blanche fighting with Dorothy during the Flu Attack episode, Sophia being snippy with Rose, Dorothy and Rose quibbling while playing the piano for the songwriting contest, and Rose and Dorothy fighting over orange juice (again during the flu episode, one of my all-time favorite episodes).

In lieu of Sophia missing the sex-talk recap, Blanche reminds her that it's never dull around there. They flash back to when Rose accidentally shot at Blanche's vase, when Rose's date died in her bed overnight, and when Blanche tried out for a play by putting balloons in her bra.

And then the final flashbacks go to Sophia's best, random stories: the fast-talking pepperoni salesman, Sophia running a marathon but not making it to the end, and the ear-infection that became pesto due to a village idiot's misunderstanding.

The episode finishes as Sophia enters to say that she has decided to stay, and all is well.

3-20 "And Ma Makes Three"

Written by: Winifred Hervey
Aired: February 20, 1988
Director: Terry Hughes
Guest Cast: Raymond (James Karen), Duncan (Frank Smith), Waiter (Steven M. Porter)
Summary: Sophia becomes an increasingly annoying third wheel to Dorothy and her boyfriend.
Rating: ♥♥

"Just don't ruin it and sleep with him."—Sophia
"Of course not, Ma. I just do that with men I plan to ruin psychologically."—Dorothy

This episode just doesn't thrill me, though it does have a few funny lines. The truth is, a two-star *Golden Girls* episode is better than most any other sitcom. But I don't love how Sophia is just so obliviously irritating to Dorothy and her boyfriend, especially since Dorothy rarely finds love. Though she does pretty well for a woman who is about 60 years old at this point. But she lets another good one get away, because Sophia and her gang of friends are separating. The B story involves Rose working as Blanche's assistant as some sort of fashion show chair.

Golden Nuggets

The Sonja Klingenhoffer comic, as told by Rose, is just perfection. Dorothy "Why was your face pressed up against the crack?" Rose "That's what the crow said!

Blanche ponders the complications of an all-women panel voting for fashion coordinator—there is not one man she could sleep with, as pointed out by Rose!

When Sophia picks her teeth after dinner, she takes them out of her mouth—yuck!

Sophia's story takes us to Paris where she allegedly sleeps with Charles de Gaulle or Charles the Mole. Honest mistake.

An unusual St. Olaf tale about the first Eskimo that tried to fit in. It's a doozy that includes the family giving whale blubber out for Halloween, and their house melting.

3-21 "Larceny and Old Lace"

Written by: Robert Bruce, Martin Weiss, Jeffrey Ferro, Fredric Weiss
Aired: February 27, 1988
Director: Terry Hughes
Guest Cast: Mickey Rooney (Rocco)
Summary: Dorothy is troubled by Sophia's new boyfriend, Rocco, who pretends to have a criminal past, and then claims to have robbed a bank.
Rating: ❤❤❤❤

"Yesterday, she came home with Nyquil on her breath and his surgical stockings in her pocket... I don't know what it means. I just don't like the possibilities."—Dorothy

The only thing more adorable than Estelle Getty is Estelle Getty paired with Mickey Rooney! And man are they cute in this episode, where he plays a man pretending to be an ex-criminal all to impress Sophia.

The B story gets some solid laughs, where Blanche and Dorothy read an old diary of Rose's and think she's talking about them. But she was really writing about two pigs that she was taking care of to get a 4H badge (only regarding Rose does this make perfect sense).

Golden Nuggets

When Sophia starts taking her top off playing strip poker with Rocco, I truly laugh out loud. Estelle Getty plays it so earnestly!

All the jokes about Sophia and Rocco making out are joyous. Even at the end, Dorothy is scolding Sophia for staying out with her boyfriend!

I do not care for the opening joke of Sophia telling Dorothy how the beauty parlor shouldn't end Dorothy's appointment early! Mean!

Mickey Rooney was apparently quite a handful to work with. He wanted to improvise a lot, and that included grabbing his crotch sometimes.

There's an innocent Donald Trump joke referencing him as a rich casino owner. I miss having Trump as a harmless punch line *just* for rich egomaniacs.

The best episodes in my opinion have a twist at the end, and this twist is that Rocco is kind of full of it. He never worked for the Mob and didn't rob the bank. He's just trying to be a tough guy.

I can't stress enough how original it was to see a TV episode about a love affair between two characters that were over 65. And the fact that they're treated like teenagers is amazing.

3-22 "Rose's Big Adventure"

Written by: Jeff Abugov
Aired: March 12, 1988
Director: Terry Hughes
Guest Cast: George Coe (Al), Vito Scotti (Vincenzo), Don Woodward (Ernie)
Summary: Rose's bored, retired boyfriend decides to sail around the world.
Rating: ❤❤

"Looks like the road company of Cocoon!"—Dorothy

This is a ho-hum episode. Perfectly fine to watch, but seems like it's taken from pieces of other episodes. The garage renovation looks familiar, as does Rose's boyfriend situation. Every scene seems like something that was done better in another episode.

The resolution also seems kind of weak, as Al throws all his money away to sail around the world only to turn out seasick. The idea of anyone clearing out all of their retirement money and just realizing that is a really weak idea coming from the writers.

Golden Nuggets

Hands down, the best part is Rose's Scandinavian midnight snack that apparently stinks up the kitchen, but tastes like cheesecake and ice cream.

This dialogue is hysterical:

"And I read in a magazine that a woman is at her sexual peak at 83."—Sophia

"Sophia, I read that same article, honey. It was 33."—Blanche

"Really? Then all those feelings I've been having lately must be colitis."—Sophia

Whenever Vincenzo speaks Italian, it's so obvious that he and Sophia aren't actually Italian, as they speak it like students on their first trip to Rome.

This show sure had more than a few Jimmy Swaggart jokes.

Sophia gets way too much mileage telling Dorothy that she could never get a guy to sail around the world with her.

I was surprised they referenced *Moonlighting*, as it was on another network. Then I realized that it was a slam on how it was another rerun! As a kid, I didn't realize that shows couldn't mention other shows in a complimentary way.

In the previous episode, Rocco clears out his retirement account to impress Sophia. These women are over 60 and extremely inspiring! However, you should never empty out your retirement money on a whim—for anyone or anything.

3-23 "Mixed Blessings"

Written by: Christopher Lloyd
Aired: March 19, 1988
Director: Terry Hughes
Guest Cast: Scott Jacoby (Michael Zbornak), Virginia Capers (Greta Wagner), Lynn Hamilton (Trudy), Montrose Hagins (Libby), Hartley Silver (Justice of the Peace), Rosalind Cash (Lorraine Wagner)
Summary: Dorothy's son, Michael, gets engaged to a Black woman twice his age.
Rating: ❤❤❤❤

"Emilio Estevez is kind of Spanish, Dorothy."—Rose

This episode is a good example of what *The Golden Girls* did best. It takes an issue that makes the Girls look non-progressive, then shows them to be kind of forward thinking after all. It seems like such a naive, innocent time gone by, because it's really more about getting along with in-laws and getting past differences for the sake of the children. Episodes like this were considered somewhat cutting-edge at the time, and I suppose there are still plenty of families where interracial marriages are not welcomed or approved of. Of course, right now, I'm not sure if families with different political ideologies would get along well either.

There's also the age difference between Dorothy's son Michael, and his girl Lorraine—she's 15 years older and pregnant! Also, a lot of laughs out of Lorraine's family for not taking any crap from Sophia. The fact that she feels free to mock Lorraine for being old, and the in-laws are equally unimpressed with Michael, offers some solid one-liners. The older generation seems on the same page acknowledging that an interracial couple is a tough road, and yet there's no hatred or hostility amongst them.

I have to note that although I think this is a four-star episode (which I stand by), this episode was pulled by Hulu and other streaming services for the scene where Betty White's mud mask is confused for Black-face. And I just think that is about the stupidest thing I've ever heard of in my life. First off, one should know that the *Raisin in the Sun* quip is a nod to the actress playing Lorraine's mother, Virginia Capers (she was in the original production).

Beyond that, there are real racial problems in this country right now, and actual complaints about how people of color are treated. I'm positive that there were no complaints about this episode, nor should there be. It would be a glorious world right now if Betty White wearing a mud mask was a high-priority problem to solve.

Golden Nuggets

I think we can all agree that Sophia walking into—what she thinks is—a revival of *A Raisin in the Sun* is a humorous scene on many levels!

Michael's age is all over the place. In this one, they say he's 23.

Lots to unwrap from Blanche as she explains the dynamics of 40-something women dating 20-something men to Lorraine's family, and whether Black men are good in bed. Sounds like she has definitely sampled a few. Also, she wants a list of ten, young rich men, pronto!

Interracial, multi-generational love and cheesecake around the table—this is good stuff! I also would have loved a story where Blanche dates one of Lorraine's relatives, but that never came to pass.

I was oddly touched when Rose suggested joining hands and singing a chorus of "Abraham, Martin & John." I confess I was digging it. Only Betty White can sell such naïveté with a mud mask on her face.

3-24 "Mr. Terrific"

Written by: Terry Grossman, Kathy Speer
Aired: April 30, 1988
Director: Terry Hughes
Guest Cast: Bob Dishy (Mister Terrific), Lonny Price (Hastings), Jody Price (Jody),
Don Woodard (Kolak), John Wheeler (Patron), Jim Hudson (Freddy), Raf Mauro (Bartender), Ron Kapra (Stage Manager)
Summary: Rose dates a kids' TV show host and convinces him to hire Dorothy, who then gets him fired.
Rating: ❤❤❤

"You know what's funny? I was supposed to be Mr. Mailman today!"—Mr. Policeman

The end of the third season is chock full of tales about the Girls' dating lives. We've had Sophia's sexual shenanigans with Rocco, and her interfering with Dorothy's boyfriend. These Girls have men from week to week! And though Blanche—our resident sexpot—hasn't had a regular boyfriend in some time, we're reminded in the B story that she's been giving her bed enough action that she can't return a bed delivered to her by mistake.

But back to the A story, where Rose's boyfriend is "Mr. Terrific." I don't know why we don't see Mr. Terrific later on in the series as he seems like a much better match for Rose than Miles, her later-on regular beau. He truly seems to have Rose's simple childlike mind. Anyway, Mr. Terrific gets Dorothy a job where her ideas get him temporarily fired, until he pulls the stunt of pretending to jump off a ledge with Rose in his arms. But he's protected by some sort of wire, so it's not a post-firing suicide. I'm not sure this would get a guy to keep his job on a kids' show, but here it does the trick.

Golden Nugget

I love Mr. Policeman walking into Blanche's bedroom with the handcuffs. Though it doesn't look like Rose sleeps with Mr. Terrific, it looks like Blanche gets some light-bondage sex with Mr. Policeman/Mailman at the end of the episode.

Sophia's favorite Sicilian Comic Book Story, "Benito the Hood" is top-notch. And... they didn't call him "Benito the Idiot."

I love when the Mr. Terrific Show staff gets all-kinds-of-twisted after Mr. Terrific is fired—the puppets tormenting her on the live show seems strangely realistic.

I like that Susan Harris sprinkles that these women are always running into some old-fashioned male hostility and harassment (but of course, being ballsy, Dorothy plows through it).

3-25 "Mother's Day"

Written by: Mort Nathan, Kathy Speer, Terry Grossman
Aired: May 7, 1988
Director: Terry Hughes
Guest Cast: Herb Edelman (Stan Zbornak), Lynnie Greene (Young Dorothy Zbornak), Sid Melton (Sal Petrillo), Helen Kleeb (Margaret) Alice Ghostley (Mrs. Zbornak), Wesley Mann (Jacob), Terrence Evans (Sheriff), Geraldine Fitzgeralld (Anna)
Summary: The Girls recall previous Mother's Days, in a series of vignettes.
Rating: ❤❤

"I thought Virginia was the slut."—Blanche's mother

At this point, we're all used to the common *Golden Girls'* writer's tactic of vignettes in wraparound episodes. In this one, the Girls sit around the kitchen waiting for their children to call on Mother's Day. The first scene shows Dorothy and her mother-in-law during a time when Stan and Dorothy have to ask her for money. Her mother-in-law is also a drinker, apparently. We also learn that although Stan's mother pretends to hate Dorothy, she actually respects her tremendously and thinks Stan is a bit of a louse. She gives them a huge loan but tells Dorothy not to say it comes from her.

The second vignette—and my favorite—shows Blanche at a nursing home with her mother, as her mother struggles with senility. She mixes up Blanche's age, and other details, but when it comes down to it corrects Blanche's story about her wild teenage attempt at eloping, reminding her that it was Christmas Day, not Mother's Day. It's a reminder that a mother might mix up siblings' names, but she knows the real deal.

The third vignette is a sentimental story about Rose meeting a woman on her way to St. Olaf, but is more about reaching out and being kind, which is an easy sell for Betty White. The woman, Anna, confesses to Rose that she's escaped from a nursing home and visiting her daughter at the cemetery. This show always mixed humor with sadness really well—it takes a certain kind of writer not to dwell or be too schmaltzy.

In the middle of these stories, Sophia complains they haven't gone to brunch because they haven't received all their calls from their children.

They make a special point that Blanche's children haven't all called, because she isn't always on good terms with them.

The final tale is Brooklyn 1957, which Sophia says is the "Mother of all Mother's Day stories." It's decent. I certainly love the actress playing young Dorothy, and I like Bea Arthur playing Sophia's mother, but there's not much to the story except that they ask Sophia's mother to move in and she says yes.

The show ends with Blanche's hard-to-get daughter Janet finally calling, and Sophia whipping herself up some food in fear that she will never get something to eat.

Golden Nuggets

I love Blanche's tale of teen rebellion and trying to elope with her classmate's father. Rue's telling of it is an acting class in all its glory.

Blanche's teen story is so unapologetically wild and crazy that it's kind of worth it. Also, Sal believing he doesn't need to get Sophia a Mother's Day gift because she "said yes three times" is such a man thing to say. Bad Sal, bad!

Sophia's mother calling Sal the Little Monkey cracks me up.

Apparently, the Brooklyn flashback scene was a nightmare to shoot—Bea Arthur hated her makeup, and everyone was forgetting their lines.

All the stories do a decent job of showing the joys and stresses of being a mother, but it's a weak finale (just not as weak as *Empty Nest).*

The Golden Girls

SEASON FOUR

4-1 "Yes, We Have No Havanas"

Written by: Mort Nathan, Barry Fanaro
Aired: October 8, 1988
Director: Terry Hughes
Guest Cast: Fidel Santiago (Henry Darrow), Jim Shu (Ralph Ahn), Woman at funeral (Magda Harout), (Priest) John Achorn
Summary: Sophia and Blanche fight over the attention of a Cuban suitor.
Rating: ❤❤❤❤

"He probably made the rest of you feel that way too.
And looking out at this kennel club,
that was no small accomplishment."—Sophia

Great opening for the fourth season, and it's in full swing. If there was a checklist, this hits every mark: Sophia references Blanche being a slut, Rose not understanding a Fidel Castro reference, and Sophia insulting Dorothy's appearance by panning her ears.

You gotta love the main plot this time around—Sophia and Blanche competing over a Cuban cigar mogul, named Fidel. He eventually dies and they find out he was dating half of Miami. These women go big, or go home!

The B story is about Rose having never graduated high school, which doesn't actually check out with the show's canon. Here, Rose has to take a history course to finally get her diploma. Sometimes, Rose is written to be too ignorant and in this particular plotline, she never heard of Hitler.

Golden Nuggets

It's a scene-stealing episode for Estelle Getty, which culminates with her hysterical and touching eulogy for Fidel.

Rose never graduated high school? In another episode she was a Valedictorian?

This one has a lot of amazing sexual tidbits regarding Sophia. The fact that she is a viable threat to Blanche at the age of 84 is definitely pure *Golden Girls*.

The joke is on Dorothy as we learn that Hitler and Eva Braun must have hidden in St. Olaf High School as undercover teachers after the war.

With both a Molly Ringwald and Bruce Willis reference, this episode reeks of 1988!

Men are just a source of amusement here. You watch two characters in the throes of dating drama, while the other two are involved in bettering themselves career-wise—Rose finishing her education, and Dorothy teaching the class as a side hustle.

4-2 "The Days and Nights of Sophia Petrillo"

Written by: Kathy Speer, Terry Grossman
Aired: October 22, 1988
Director: Terry Hughes
Guest Cast: Claire (Frances Bay), Clerk (Nick DeMauro), Store Manager (David Selburg), Abe (Allen Bloomfield), Mrs. Leonard (Ellen Albertini Dow), Woman in hospital (Darlene Kardon), Wanda (Marian Wells), Esther (Peggy Gilber), Sam (Kokko Burnaby)
Summary: During a rainy day, Blanche, Rose and Dorothy attempt to be productive, while worrying that Sophia's losing her zest for life. Meanwhile, Sophia is having quite a busy day!
Rating: ❤❤❤❤

"Let's rent an adult video, drink mimosas,
and French kiss the pillows."—Blanche

I love this episode, mostly because it's a lovefest for Sophia mixed with great Girl talk. There's also the maybe-not-so subtle message about how the young often sit around, thinking they're living a fuller life than older people. While the Girls are having a lazy, rainy day—albeit, an amazing one—Sophia is kicking ass in productivity. Her list of errands includes buying a nectarine, helping her friend get a refund at the market, playing in a charity boardwalk band, and doing volunteer work at a hospital.

Golden Nuggets

When an episode has three segments around the Kitchen Table, you get a lot of good Blanche sex stories, and inevitably some nonsensical St. Olaf stuff and one Brooklyn story. I can't even pick my favorite, but the sheriff still writes...

Dorothy's story about her grandmother being 94 when she was six doesn't make sense, because in another episode we see a grown Dorothy wheeling her grandmother in a wheelchair.

Blanche's Chattanooga escapades are a longtime favorite. But we also get an earful about her college beau Preston Bougainvillea.

We're not sure about the lesson of Rose's story, but we do learn that it takes 45 minutes, which is long even for Rose.

NOOPRL: Network of Older People, Retired but Living and OREP: Organization of Retired and Elderly People are not to be messed with!

The ultimate *Golden Girls* Shot Game must include mentions of Neiman Marcus.

I'm pretty sure that Sophia getting her friend to pay for her nectarine is a better negotiation maneuver than anything in *The Art of The Deal*.

This episode has the show's first reference to AIDs, without using the name, which is telling. The victim is a little boy named Sam, conveying that the disease was hitting everyone in society. Later on, a whole episode focused on the fact that AIDs was not a bad person's disease.

4-3 "The One That Got Away"

Written by: Susan Harris, Christopher Lloyd
Aired: October 29, 1988
Director: Terry Hughes
Guest Cast: John Harkins (Ham Lushbough), Tom Dahlgren (Major Barker), Nick Toth (Waiter)
Summary: Blanche tries to seduce the only man that ever turned her down in college; a boyfriend who's suddenly bald and plump. Meanwhile, Rose and Dorothy think they spot a UFO.
Rating: ♥♥♥♥

"Blanche, no woman ever looked better than you look right now. And no woman ever will." —Dorothy

After two episodes where Sophia really shined, this one is quintessentially Blanche, showing her in all her sexy and confident audacity. She wants to cross an old boyfriend, Ham Lushbough, off her list, get back at her sister, and throw it in her face. It's romance and revenge, southern style!

Then we get the B story, with Rose and Dorothy contemplating whether they saw a UFO. Dorothy flirting with Major Barker is hilarious, as is Rose and Dorothy's conversation regarding life on other planets, and how it might impact *ALF* storylines.

Back to Blanche trying to seduce Mr. Bald and Chubby. Sophia fat-shames him when he picks her up, and though fat-shaming is now frowned upon, I somehow find it refreshing. Maybe I don't care if his feelings are hurt because this guy looks like a combination of Roger Ailes and Rush Limbaugh.

Golden Nuggets

Sex Positive in the 50s—we get a strong picture of Blanche as a young, tempestuous seductress, running through men in college and without regret.

It took a long time for me to think about this, but how exactly does a band spell out, "Maybe some other time, Blanche."

Sophia's romance with Fabrizio Rabbino ended violently by Destiny… Destiny Rabbino.

Rose "Planes aren't that thin or that bright." Dorothy: "Neither is Oprah Winfrey, but that doesn't make a flying saucer." The joke's on them because Oprah turned out bright enough to become a billionaire.

Learn a thing or two about how to get a man's attention from Blanche Devereaux. All you have to do make a big speech at a restaurant about how badly you want to have sex!

4-4 "Yokel Hero"

Written by: Martin Weiss, Robert Bruce
Aired: November 5, 1988
Director: Terry Hughes
Guest Cast: Ben (Jim Doughan) Sven (Doug Cox) Len (John Moody) The Driver (James Lashly) Fred (Valente Rodriguez) Dr. Harry Weston (Richard Mulligan)
Summary: Dorothy and Blanche lie about Rose's accomplishments in order to get her to win St. Olaf's Woman of the Year.
Rating: ❤❤

"I just found out I'm the most boring person alive."—Rose
"Did something happen to Regis Philbin?"—Sophia

This episode is just okay for me. Maybe it's too much focusing on the stupidity of St. Olaf, so the jokes get a little tired. And Betty White, bless her heart, delivers it with such innocence and authenticity, but this ongoing theme for a whole episode just doesn't rise to the top for me.

It is a good reminder of the little things one does on resumes to enhance job descriptions. This episode takes place before social media, and it makes me think of all the additions that usually reek of bullshit. There's so little honesty, and when you *are* genuine, it's usually criticized as needing to be punched up. Sometimes, even when the job requirement is just to answer phones and take notes, you still have to add six bullet points about your filing system. It's rare that someone spots the Roses of the world and rewards them.

Golden Nuggets

I love that Sophia tells Rose that she's here because the rhythm method was popular in the 20's. I have to say, bad birth control is still probably the reason many people are here.

It's just bad manners to not let your travel buddies know that it's going to take days.

This is the first episode featuring Dr. Harry Weston (played by Richard Mulligan) and his dog Dreyfuss, who would later star in the spinoff series, *Empty Nest*.

4-5 "Bang the Drum, Stanley"

Written by: Robert Bruce, Martin Weiss
Aired: November 12, 1988
Director: Terry Hughes
Guest Cast: Stanley Zbornak (Herb Edelman), Dr. Jerry (Ben Rawnsley), Dr. Cauley
(William Denis), Woman in Wheelchair (Helen Duffy), Timmy (Matthew Brooks)
Summary: Stan encourages Sophia to fake serious injuries after a baseball incident, so that they can get a big settlement.
Rating: ❤❤

"Sometimes just lying motionless is
the best thing a person can do."—Stan
"That didn't sound right when you said it on our honeymoon,
and it doesn't right now." —Dorothy

I don't love a heavy-handed morality play, and that's how this episode comes off. It also comes after an episode where Rose chastises Dorothy and Blanche for their dishonesty for fudging her St. Olaf Woman of the Year credentials. There's a trend here of teaching lessons, possibly by these two new writers (Bruce and Weiss). I don't care for that.

Full disclosure, Sophia does have a spotty reputation with Dorothy. She cheats at cards and games, constantly steals from her purse, and brags about coming from a family connected to organized crime. The episode concludes with Dorothy constructing an elaborate trick to guilt Sophia into confessing. The boy in the doctor's office—and the rest of the patients—turn out to be actors to give Sophia a last moment of conscience.

The B story of Rose and Blanche practicing for the role of *Cats* is mildly amusing and supplies a few laughs, the best one being Dreyfuss the dog chasing her.

Golden Nuggets

I love when the fat, sweaty man parks himself next to Dorothy at the baseball game.

Rose turns right to her bedroom, when in other episodes, her bedroom would be left.

It's worth noting that whenever the Girls try to slut-shame Blanche, all it does is remind her to call a random boyfriend. Remember ladies, you can't be slut-shamed if you don't think of yourself as a slut.

I feel like if a lady over 80 gets slammed in the head by a baseball at a game, she does deserve some money.

4-6 & 4-7 "Sophia's Wedding, Part 1 & 2"

Written by: Mort Nathan, Barry Fanaro
Aired: November 19, 1988
Director: Terry Hughes
Guest Cast: Max Weinstock (Jack Gilford), Caterer (Raye Birk) Sal Petrillo (Sid Melton), Preacher (Harvey J. Goldenberg), Fritzi Burr (Ruth)
Summary When Sophia's old friend dies, she reunites with her friend's husband, whom she had been fighting with for decades.
Rating: ♥♥♥♥

"Ma, what is going on here?"—Dorothy
"Afterglow."—Sophia

I love this episode and it encapsulates Sophia's close relationship with Dorothy. But it also has a decent and non-intrusive B story with Blanche and Rose starting an Elvis fan club, which brings more than a few laughs and even ties into Sophia and Max's wedding.

Jack Gilford as Max is absolutely adorable—even more than Mickey Rooney was as Sophia's love. I can't help but mention how many boyfriends Sophia comes up with after the age of 80. And this one marries her!

Part 1

We learn that Sophia had been mad at Max for decades for gambling away a business that he shared with her husband, when the real story is that it was Sal that gambled the money away. When Sophia finds this out, they reconcile and even shack up after the funeral. Did I say shack up regarding 80-year olds? On this show, it seems appropriate.

Anyway, Dorothy gets kicked out of the Elvis Club because she cracks a joke at Elvis' expense. Meanwhile, Max and Sophia decide to get married, which for Dorothy feels like she is cheating on her father. I guess Sophia's boyfriends don't bother her, but a remarriage does. I get it. And the fact that he was a friend of the family's makes it especially hard.

Part 2
Sophia and Max return from their honeymoon with no place to live and move in with the Girls. Hilarity ensues when Max ends up in the shower with Dorothy. And then in Max and Sophia's search for a new home, they decide to open her first husband's dream of a pizza/knish stand. I think this could have gone on for more episodes and I actually would've liked Max to stick around. The scene where Sophia and Max realize they're not in love enough to stay married is quite a treasure.

Golden Nuggets
There are more than a few scenes on this show where people are busted in bed with each other, and strangely, it's never Blanche. But finding Sophia in bed with Max has levels. And bless her, she is not ashamed.

Rose claims to have never fainted before, but she fainted in the episode "End of the Curse." Besides the kudos to Sophia for nabbing sex and a husband at 84, there's also Blanche's sexy call to the fire department. "I'm on fire!" These women are *on fire*.

Quentin Tarantino is one of the Elvis impersonators at Sophia's wedding. He has claimed in interviews that money from this episode kept him afloat for many months in Los Angeles.

Watching Rose and Blanche act like total groupies is amazing. When the Girls fan out, like they did for Burt Reynolds and Sinatra, it's a real pleasure. But watching them ogle Elvis' half-eaten pork chop is even better.

Am I the only one who made a mental note of the sage-witchcraft advice of Aunt Regina?

Rose mixes up the wedding list with the Elvis impersonators, which I think makes for a better wedding. Relatives can be so annoying.

Blanche describes the right man as having the body of Mel Gibson, the personality of Johnny Carson, and the financial resources of Donald Trump. Boy does that line mean something different now. I can honestly say that no matter what your politics are, none of those men turned out to be the greatest husbands, in any capacity.

Rose confesses she was a smoker—wow!

The Girls working at the pizza/knish stand has a lot of standout moments: Rose getting the pot over her head, Blanche expressing her desire to be a scientist so she could turn it into a sex romp, and Sophia showing her sales technique for getting people out of the water. The gay wedding director is definitely a character that might not be written in the same way today, even though he does kind of stand his own against both Blanche and Dorothy.

4-8 "Brother, Can You Spare a Jacket?"

Written by: Kathy Speer, Terry Grossman
Aired: December 3, 1988
Director: Terry Hughes
Guest Cast: Kenny (Karl Wiedergott), Father Campbell (Matthew Faison), Ida Perkins (Herta Ware), Ben (Teddy Wilson), Bodyguard (Andre Rosey Brown), Auctioneer (Howard Goodwin), Dave (Art K. Koustik), Stan Wojno (Philip Starr)
Summary: The Girls donate a leather jacket with a winning lottery ticket to a homeless shelter.
Rating: ♥

"And I'll never get to buy that emerald pendent to dangle between my perky bosoms."—Blanche
"And I'll never get to buy perky bosoms."—Sophia

I hate, hate, hate this episode. Forced sentiment just makes me want to scream. First of all, four women winning a lottery of $10,000 in 1988 wasn't a life-changing amount of money. At best, it was enough for them to buy something special, or go on vacation, or maybe put aside for some extra security. So, when they decide to give up the money, I find it super-frustrating.

The idea that the episode is about middle-class women feeling guilty about winning a $10,000 lottery ticket just gets on my nerves. If it had been more money, and they had decided to give some of it away, okay. But to have them so guilty that they donate all of it—well, it just bothers me. I know I'm being cynical here, but I'll bet the lives of the three people the women talk to at the shelter don't change one iota because of the winning ticket. The Girls probably could've kept the money and tried to help themselves individually.

Golden Nuggets

The speech Ida gives about how getting old costs money is quite poignant.

We see Rose's competitive streak rear its ugly head again as she encourages Blanche to sleep with the congressman in order to get the jacket.

The characters in the shelter are well played and realistic, even if a little heavy handed—a young student whose life is deteriorating because of alcoholism, an elderly woman, and a retired man from out-of-state who worked all his life and just can't get a break.

I love that Rose thinks the Michael from the Pepsi commercials is Michael J. Fox. That joke is so 1988.

The show always did an admirable job demonstrating that the economy and the American dream were not quite what they should be.

4-9 "Scared Straight"

Written by: Christopher Lloyd
Aired: December 10, 1988
Director: Terry Hughes
Guest Cast: Clayton Hollingsworth (Monte Markham), Mildred (Gwen E. Davis), Lois (Nancy Priddy), Waiter (Steve Porter)
Summary: Blanche's brother visits and is afraid to reveal he's gay, so he claims to have slept with Rose instead.
Rating: ❤❤❤

"Oh, now I get it."—Dorothy
"Oh good. I thought I was going to have to draw you a picture. And I'm not sure I'd know how."—Rose

This episode is one of many that the show was famous for in its sensitive portrayal of homosexuality. Before this, they'd had a gay wedding director, and Dorothy's lesbian friend, but this time it's a member of the family coming out. And it's not shown to be an easy thing, especially in the late 80's. Blanche is arguably the most concerned about how she's perceived by other people. When Clayton confesses his secret to Rose, and she convinces him to tell Blanche, he instead makes up a lie that he and Rose slept together.

In the B story, Sophia thinks she's dying because of a nightmare. Turns out, her friend gave her a message outside her window that they have space for her on their bowling team.

Golden Nuggets

Blanche and Clayton discussing his homosexuality at the bar is an endearing exchange between brother and sister, made better by the fact that Blanche thinks it's a gay bar.

Not sure if this peephole in the front door has always existed, but they never seem to use it. Normally, they just open the door and risk their lives.

All of the Girls except Sophia have been accused of sleeping with someone they didn't—this time Rose is the accused.

Up until this point, we heard mostly about Blanche's sisters and their sexual escapades. Turns out *all* of the Devereaux children were obsessed with men.

Rue McClanahan found it difficult to play even-slightly homophobic.

Kudos to this show for not being a one-off episode. There's a follow-up where Clayton returns in a relationship and Blanche has to deal with it. The topic wasn't just a gimmick and these storylines were courageous. Not every television show had a gay character, or a member of the family coming out as gay, while also showing the challenges of coming out to your family and friends.

4-10 "Stan Takes a Wife"

Written by: Winifred Hervey
Aired: January 7, 1989
Director: Terry Hughes
Guest Cast: Stan Zbornak (Herb Edelman), Katherine (Elinor Donahue), Dr. Seymour (Tom Tarpey), Orderly (Wayne Chou), Young Doctor (Doug Franklin), Bartender (Freeman King)
Summary: Dorothy develops feelings for Stan before he remarries.
Rating: ♥♥♥

"I hate hospitals."—Dorothy
"I hate when the people put each other down on Love Connection."—Rose

Stan is the show's lovable yutz. He's imperfect, never evolves, but a good man. And he loves Dorothy and Sophia. And for this, we love him. In this episode, Sophia is rushed to the hospital with advanced pneumonia. Meanwhile, Stan has come to tell the Girls that he's getting remarried and wants to show them the ring. They bluntly tell him that it looks cheap and convince him to buy a better one. But when he returns and learns about Sophia's condition, he brings Italian food to comfort Dorothy, reigniting her feelings for him.

Dorothy considers breaking up Stan's wedding by telling him about how she feels. And I can't tell you how much I am against this common sitcom trope. In real life, revealing your love to a groom (or the bride) pre-wedding should be against the law. Also, while I'm at it, leaving someone at the altar, or answering "yes" to "does anyone think these two people should not be wed" should also be a crime, punishable with at least a large fine.

Golden Nuggets

Stan's new wife raves to Dorothy that Stan is the best lover. But even though Dorothy is enamored with Stan in the moment, she's not crazy enough to paint him as a fantastic lover. She knows his limitations. It's not a man-hating show, but it doesn't put men on a pedestal.

Dorothy's mental state borders on delusional, but thankfully, Bea Arthur's acting sells it.

The way Blanche and Rose keep Dorothy from making a mess of her life is also what *The Golden Girls* is about. Your squad is always doing damage control, from keeping your drunk friends from texting their ex, to telling you not to wear something hideous to a job interview. Your Girls will tell you the truth in the nicest way possible, but they will keep it real.

4-11 "The Auction"

Written by: Winifred Hervey
Aired: January 14, 1989
Director: Terry Hughes
Guest Cast: Jasper DeKimmel (Tony Steedman), Sid LaBass (Michael McManus), Auctioneer (Colin Hamilton) Woman (Renata Scott)
Summary: The Girls come up with a scheme to buy a painting to pay for a new roof.
Rating: ❤❤❤❤

"I brought my son Skippy home from the hospital in this towel."—Blanche
"You're lying."—Dorothy
"Damn, you're good."—Blanche

I love episodes with all four Girls getting together and scheming. There's almost a forced-morality play ending here, but they save it when Sophia gets to con the sketchy roof fixer into finishing repairs for the painting.

At the start of the episode, the Girls can't afford to fix the roof and can only manage a patch-up. So, when they find out that a big artist is dying, they decide to buy one of his paintings and profit after his impending death. The Girls then deliberate whether to profit from the man's death. Well, joke's on them, because Sophia inadvertently saves the guy's life by donating her blood.

Golden Nuggets

We know by now that Blanche's sex life involves some high-level role play. But this time, we learn a Zorro mask has been utilized.

Blanche trying to save her sexy sex towel because there are so many fond memories attached to it really says a lot about her. And those memories clearly being made attending college spring breaks in her 40s and 50s is truly delightful… just me?

Sophia attempts a mental voyage to Sardinia, but Sophia can't finish it as she doesn't have a tale about taking advantage of a man's death.

Sophia's insults to Dorothy's appearance as she enters the art show are a little much. When people go to an event, they try to look attractive, so to make it a point to tell someone they're not beautiful really seems to cut deep. I know they're for laughs, but for any of us that have seen people do this, it's awkward.

4-12 "The Blind Date"

Written by: Christopher Lloyd
Aired: January 28, 1989
Director: Terry Hughes
Guest Cast: John Quinn (Edward Winter), Billy (Kristopher Kent), Freddy (Paul Tennen), Ernie (Alan Koss), Elaine (Lesley Glassford)
Summary: Blanche struggles with her romance with a blind man.
Rating: ♥♥♥

"For God's sakes, Rose, Eisenhower used less chalk planning D-Day!"—Dorothy

This is a solid episode knowing what we know about Blanche and Rose. Blanche struggles with whether to date a blind man, when her appearance is what she feels attracts men, while Rose's competitive nature impacts a team of eight-year-old football players.

There's a lot of the usual jokes, such as Sophia's jabs at Pat Sajak and Dorothy's at Dan Quayle. But what I like most is that it begins with Blanche extremely shallow, but with Rue's acting chops, she ends on a charming note, walking the line of self-awareness and honesty with men and herself. It's such a shame that the actresses aren't around to talk to, because I totally want to tell them how brilliant they were.

The B story involves Rose being bonkers-competitive while coaching a little league football team, annoyed that Dorothy won't let the tiniest-but-best player play because he doesn't make the weight requirement. I always get a good laugh at Rose's dark side and wonder if it was Betty White's personality that made the writers give Rose that extra oomph.

Golden Nuggets

Blanche's final scene with John, where she insults his date. I still use "music lover" as code for "has a big behind."

Raymond Burr was actually married from 1948-1952.

Sophia telling eight-year-olds to compare their football strategy to her lovemaking would probably not fly on television today, but man, it cracked me up.

The women are awfully rough on Blanche for not knowing that John was blind. And by the way, John purposely misled her.

This show had some fantastic episodes about people with disabilities without it seeming like “a very special episode.” You don’t watch this episode and think, “oh, the poor blind man.” John is a fleshed-out character, who is funny and living a full life.

4-13 "The Impotence of Being Ernest"

Written by: Rick Copp, David A. Goodman
Aired: February 4, 1989
Director: Steve Zuckerman
Guest Cast: Ernie (Richard Herd)
Summary: Rose's new boyfriend suffers from a sexual dysfunction.
Rating: ❤❤❤

"Impotent, are you sure?"—Blanche
"Oh, Blanche, what would you have done?
Asked him to prove it."—Dorothy

The Girls date some not-so-great guys, but Ernest—Rose's impotent boyfriend—has a new problem that they haven't encountered. I prefer the B story, as Sophia deals with a secret message from Sicily, involving an old feud.

Anyway, Rose dates Ernest for a month before he discloses this personal information. She pretends to be patient, but our once-prudish Rose wants some nookie and wants it fast. And speaking of non-prudes, under the guise of fulfilling a vendetta, Sophia gets lucky herself. Once Rose and Ernie consummate their relationship, Rose declares that she hasn't been that happy since Charlie. But then Ernie dumps her for his ex-wife, proving he's also a jerk.

Golden Nuggets

The scene of Rose and Ernest getting hot for each other at the restaurant is a keeper.

The Girls talk frankly about sex pretty constantly, like when Blanche advises Rose on how to turn her boyfriend on, and Dorothy talks about her issues with Stan. You still don't see much of this. The only show that surpassed it was *Sex and The City*.

In the first season, Rose hadn't slept with anyone but her husband, but by Season Four, she sounds like a regular woman-on-the-prowl.

Some people might not love the stereotyping of Italians as connected to nefarious activities, but I always find this aspect of Sophia amusing. And I'm 100% Italian!

This is a rare episode where two of the women are getting laid, and neither are Blanche!

Having read about Susan Harris' struggles with having sexual topics on the show (especially since it was always from older women's perspective), I've come to appreciate how unabashedly interested in sex these women are. Rose is, after all, the goody-two-shoes character, and she's over 60. But she's written and portrayed as being extremely invested in sex as part of all her relationships.

4-14 "Love Me Tender"

Written by: Richard Vaczy, Tracy Gamble
Aired: February 6, 1989
Director: Terry Hughes
Guest Cast: Eddie (John Fiedler), Jackie (Stefanie Ridel), Maria (Shana Washington), Security Guard (Tom Simmons)
Summary: Dorothy starts a purely sexual relationship with a guy named Eddie, and Sophia tries to get her to stop seeing him.
Rating: ❤❤❤

"But I do think I should caution you.
They were meant for petite ears."—Blanche
"They'll just have to do until Disney unveils
their Dumbo line."—Dorothy

This episode has one of the best endings of the entire series. It begins with Dorothy waiting for an arranged date, set up by Sophia. This was a time before dating apps, so matchmaking businesses like the one she used were a real thing. Eddie seems like a dud, but the morning after, Dorothy confides to Rose that although the date was horrible, he's a fantastic lover and she plans to keep seeing him.

The B story has Blanche and Rose volunteering for a Be a Pal Program, but they end up set up by two juvenile delinquents for shoplifting. This part kind of drags the episode down. The girls are cartoonishly evil as they exist in some sort of realm where pre-teens set traps for older women at malls (which is pretty easy for security guards to catch, and Rose and Blanche would've figured that out anyway).

The Dorothy and Eddie stuff is gold, as Dorothy reluctantly breaks it off even as Rose and Blanche hit on him. Then, just as he's leaving, Sophia literally jumps him!

Golden Nuggets

Who wasn't surprised when Sophia climbs on Eddie as he tries to exit the house at the end?

There are two talks about casual sex and whether Dorothy can sustain it. Sophia claims to have no problem with it as a concept, just a problem with whether Dorothy can handle it. As much as I love Sophia, she's forever buzz-killing Dorothy's sex life.

It was during rehearsals for this episode that Bea Arthur cried, as she had been fed-up with jokes about her appearance. According to one of the writers, she broke down and said, “You’ve been calling me a man for 75 episodes now!”

Sophia uses the term “sport nookie” which is definitely a new one. But this is the first time that Blanche isn’t the only one interested in purely recreational sex.

Rose’s opposites-attract story, topped off by the herring juggling act is great. But Sophia’s response of, “I hate you” is the clincher.

The whole shoplifting plot seems like a crime that absolutely no teens were committing anywhere ever.

4-15 "Valentine's Day"

Written by: Kathy Speer, Terry Grossman, Barry Fanaro, Mort Nathan
Aired: February 13, 1989
Director: Terry Hughes
Guest Cast: Sal Petrillo (Sid Melton), Clerk (Pat McCormick), Young Man (Tom Isbell), Maître d' (Wayne C. Dvorak), Porter (Michael Blue), Desk Clerk (Peter Elbling), Edgar (Michael J. London), Raymond (Joe Faust), Steve (John Rice), Mechanic (John Harnagel), Waiter (Julian Deyer), Papa Angelo (Bill Dana), Julio Iglesias (Self)
Summary: The Girls think they've all been abandoned by their boyfriends on Valentine's Day.
Rating: ❤❤❤

"Please. Until I was 80, I was combing geezers out of my blue rinse."—Sophia

This is a cute episode, with four stories about Valentine's Days.

The first shows Sophia, her husband Sal, and her father stuck in Chicago in 1929 and inadvertently witnessing the Valentine's Day Massacre.

The second vignette, which is my favorite, has the Girls accidentally stuck at a nudist hotel—I have to blame Blanche and Dorothy here, since Rose screwed up their last vacation. Anyway, the Girls break their inhibitions and get naked, shocking the dinner guests.

The third is yet another demonstration of Susan Harris championing gay rights, writing them in a real way and incorporating their lives into scripts. Blanche tells a story about going to a restaurant after George died and encouraging a man to propose to his lover, not realizing his lover was another man.

And the fourth vignette is another homage to women's empowerment, as the Girls buy condoms for a cruise, and Blanche grabs the store mic to defend them.

Golden Nuggets

Blanche's impassioned speech after Dorothy yells, "Condoms, condoms, condoms" is obviously hysterical and in my mind, a feminist rallying cry.

Young actors should probably have portrayed Sal and Sophia at the St. Valentine's Day Massacre, as it occurred to me in 1929 and they would have been in their 20s.

I just love the way Rue McClanahan plays Blanche unabashedly eyeballing the naked men at the hotel.

Bill Dana, who plays Sal's father, also portrays her brother Angelo.

In Season Three's "Rose's Big Adventure," Sofia mentions witnessing the St. Valentine's Day massacre.

We all have that friend who shouldn't be in charge of travel arrangements—I'm afraid I am that friend.

This show proves once again to be a voice for the LGBTQ community. Though Blanche doesn't tell the story as anything but a humorous anecdote, the women don't treat the story as anything unusual. Hard to believe, but scenes like that did break barriers. She also tells the man before she knows he's gay that "love is love."

4-16 "Two Rode Together"

Written by: Robert Bruce, Martin Weiss
Aired: February 18, 1989
Director: Terry Hughes
Guest Cast: Sam (Freddie Jackson)
Summary: Dorothy forces Sophia into some quality time because she's afraid Sophia's going to die.
Rating: ❤❤❤

"Jeez, Dorothy, you really know how to beat a metaphor to death."—Sophia

This episode is a Dorothy/Sophia classic. On one hand, it shows Dorothy being sentimental instead of a hard-ass, and on the flip side, it shows Sophia resisting forced sentiment. This is a woman born in the early 1900s who has survived world wars and the Depression. She's a tough little cookie. Dorothy and Sophia give us a common mother/daughter dichotomy. They mean well, but are never on the same page.

We get them at their best bondingc over old photos, sparring with each other, and then reuniting. Sophia's the child in the relationship and wants to live in the moment. She wants to ride Space Mountain, not look at videos and talk about her life. Yet it's difficult to not sympathize with Dorothy as she talks about staring at Sophia watching television, to memorize her face. That was great writing.

The B story involves one of my favorite St. Olaf stories—*Toonder the Mediocre Tiger* becomes *Toonder the Magnificent*. Blanche gets inspired by Rose's story and they begin working on a children's book.

Golden Nuggets

I laugh every time I watch Sophia ramble into George Bush's "Thousand Points of Light" speech.

As with so many episodes, ages don't make much sense. Dorothy's baby photo of 1932 wouldn't match her high school years in other episodes.

It's worth mentioning that Blanche using the word synergism to describe what goes in a motel room caused me to look it up.

Who wouldn't love to see Rose author a book of St. Olaf stories!

Notice the insult to *Mr. Belvedere.* This show was famous for trashing celebrities and television shows (not NBC ones of course).

Sophia constantly swapping friends because they're dying is a relevant joke. Her whole attitude is that life is for the living, a sentiment that probably emerges from seeing a lot of death.

The fact that St. Olaf had a classic fairy tale called Hansel and Hansel is a slick wink to the LGBTQ community.

4-17 "You Gotta Have Hope"

Written by: Barry Fanaro, Mort Nathan
Aired: February 25, 1989
Director: Terry Hughes
Guest Cast: Bob Hope (Bob Hope), Seymour (Douglas Seale), The Donatello Triplets (Eadie Del Rubio, Milly Del Rubio, Elena Del Rubio), Bodybuilder (Andre Rosey Brown), Phyllis (June Claman), Frieda (Linda Rand), Misha (Daniel Rosen), Man in Locker Room (Patrick Stack)
Summary: Blanche and Dorothy discover that Rose believes that Bob Hope is her biological father.
Rating: ❤❤❤❤

"I have to remember to stop using your towels."—Dorothy

This episode has a great twist ending, with Bob Hope becoming a surprise guest star. When I first watched it, I really didn't see that coming, much like the Burt Reynold's finale.

The show opens with the Girls watching auditions for their charity benefit. Man, these women keep busy. I'm pretty sure they're running Miami. We learn that the talent is terrible and relies too much on the hiring of the MC. The only decent talent are the Donatello triplets, who Sophia's using as leverage to get her boyfriend on the show. Yes, Sophia has yet another boyfriend this season!

But the whopper comes when the Girls find out that since Rose was a child, she believed Bob Hope was her biological father. And scene after scene, she emphatically states that if she really needs him, he will come to their aid. Later on, she realizes she sounds crazy and makes an announcement at the benefit that Bob Hope won't be performing. Just then, he comes out of the magic closet in Sophia's boyfriend's act. Apparently, they were old war buddies. It's an absolutely ridiculous, yet wonderful, plot contrivance.

Golden Nuggets

The Bob Hope surprise (I have to admit) really got me!

Rose says that her adoptive parents' name was Nylund, but we know that is her married name from many episodes.

Blanche's amazingly specific, sexual fantasy: "Sweaty Argentinian cowboys whipping things while they ride naked on the backs of Brahma bulls."

Rose's Clovis the two-headed mule that skis backwards on cottage cheese as an offhand anecdote! Holy moly.

Bob Hope apparently asked to be paid in jokes. Hope told the writers he wanted 10 Reagan jokes for a golf event, in exchange for his guest appearance.

Lots of celebrity disses (Joan Collins, Gene Shalit), but the best is a Ryan O'Neal hit: "I realize I have no talent. So, I decided to become an agent. Why Ryan O'Neal hasn't come to the same conclusion I'll never understand."

4-18 "Fiddler on the Ropes"

Written by: Kathy Speer, Terry Grossman
Aired: March 4, 1989
Director: Terry Hughes
Guest Cast: Pepe (Chick Vennera), Charley (Alfred Dennis), Woman at audition (Pamela Kosh)
Summary: Sophia invests the Girls' money in a Cuban prizefighter.
Rating: ❤❤

"...Oh pussycat, get some sleep. The big fight's tomorrow."—Sophia
"Words that have echoed between mother and daughter since time began."—Dorothy

This episode is cute, albeit silly, playing on the fact that the Girls are ignorant thinking that they can "buy" a Cuban boxer. This unfolds as Sophia returns from what was supposed to be a trip to the bank, but instead became a transaction for the boxer on the bus. This would be an unforgivable offense, though when Sophia does it, it's almost endearing.

The Girls are angry, but upon further investigation find out that the deal was legit. When they don't see Kid Pepe the night before the fight, they rifle through his things and find him at a building rehearsing for a violin audition. Furthermore, Pepe's teacher doesn't want him to ruin his hands boxing, but the women are willing to risk it to get their money back. All goes well at the end, and they get an excellent return on their investment. There's a double twist though with him throwing the fight because he can't remember his violin piece and has to improvise with an acting monologue to pass the audition.

There's a soft lesson here about stereotyping people. It's not a huge lesson, but it's your average soft-sitcom stuff.

Golden Nuggets

Extremely quotable for superfans is when Pepe switches his performance because of Dorothy's "Because you're Cuban..."

As disclosed during kitchen table talk, Blanche's engagement story has got many layers—a bad ring, a closeted football player, and Blanche being extremely shallow and naive.

Love the rules for dining in a clam bar in Italy and how they're similar to boxing tips.

The women having a smart conversation about money is a clever way to demonstrate that yes, investing is something women can do well.

I saw this episode mentioned as an example of how the Girls seem prejudiced, to which I say, please. If you're looking at the world right now, and you've come up with this as an example of bigotry, you're living in a world of privilege that I cannot imagine. At worst, it's about stereotypes leading to the wrong conclusions.

4-19 "Till Death Do We Volley"

Written by: Tracey Gamble, Richard Vaczy
Aired: March 18, 1989
Director: Terry Hughes
Guest Cast: Trudy (Anne Francis), Jack (Robert King)
Summary: When Dorothy's best friend, Trudy, pays a visit, their pranks on each other get out of control.
Rating: ❤❤❤❤

"We can't all come from places as socially acceptable as Brooklyn."—Blanche

This is a classic, with jokes all over the place. It's one of those episodes where I have trouble picking my favorite lines for sure! And I wish the character Trudy had returned for more prank episodes.

We learn that Dorothy and her best friend used to play merciless practical jokes and were endlessly competitive with each other. When Trudy comes to visit for their high school reunion, the rivalry continues, but turns out to be one of affectionate playfulness.

The teasing seems to turn fatal when Dorothy's tennis challenge causes Trudy to drop dead, and she has to tell the graduating class. But Trudy shocks the group by showing up and saying it was a joke, only for Dorothy to reverse it by saying she knew and pranked Trudy by pretending to hop into bed with Trudy's husband. Oh, the hilarity. This is one fantastic high school reunion!

Golden Nuggets

When all the pranks are revealed at the end, and Dorothy is caught in bed with Jack, the stakes really reach insanity.

Why would Dorothy's Brooklyn high school reunion be at her house in Miami, and why would it be so small?

"How does it feel to get your butt whipped?" You must be careful when you ask a question like that in front of Blanche.

A whole wall of "Kick Me" signs was part of Rose's childhood home's décor.

The Alleged Great String Cheese War… did it really happen? Not even Sophia knows for sure. But her story about screwing around in the bedroom when there are important things to do outside is a keeper.

I wonder if this show holds the record for most shows with passing gas jokes (Sophia has a good one in this episode).

By Season Four, Bea Arthur became increasingly upset about jokes regarding her looks, yet she relished in making a joke about Trudy not looking fabulous in a tennis dress. The writers wanted to change it because the actress clearly would look great, but Bea was adamant she would make it work.

4-20 “High Anxiety”

Written by: Martin Weiss, Robert Bruce
Aired: March 25, 1989
Director: Terry Hughes
Guest Cast: Sy Ferber (Jay Thomas), Heather (Nancy Black)
Summary: The Girls discover that Rose has a decades’ long addiction to painkillers.
Rating: ❤❤

“If I wanted this kind of abuse, I’d be directing The Roseanne Barr show.”—Sy

In this episode, Rose reveals that she’s addicted to pain meds. Keep in mind, this is decades before America was ravaged by opioids and benzodiazepines. We’re never given the name of her medication, but it’s from an old back injury on the farm.

Meanwhile, Sophia gets to star in a pizza commercial, but Rose’s erratic mood swing screws up the filming and they end up on a professional set where Dorothy flubs the lines. It’s always funny to watch actors pretend to be terrible actors. They switch Dorothy’s role and Sophia backs out because the pizza is horrible. I just don’t buy that—Sophia is always looking to make a quick buck.

The Girls help Rose pull an all-nighter to power through her withdrawal and realize she’ll have to check herself into rehab. The episode ends with her returning and claiming that though she’ll never be cured, she can just take it one day at a time.

Golden Nuggets

Dorothy says Rose is allergic to cats, but in “The Way We Met,” we see that Rose had a cat when first she met Blanche.

Confirmation that there is definitely camera equipment set up in Blanche’s bedroom.

Blanche’s wild story about attempted celibacy with the surprise twist that her brother-in-law tried to hit on her is well done.

Bessie, the old woman pulling the plow, and St. Olaf Monopoly are both fantastic examples of this small town’s insanity and eccentricity.

It's mentioned on IMDb that this episode is Season Four, episode 20 and that 4-20 is a common code for "getting high," though usually pertaining to marijuana. Could that be a coincidence?

It turns out the scene where Bea Arthur rewrites the lines for the commercial wasn't far off—Arthur and Getty were known to be grammar nerds.

Eighties' sitcoms used to have a huge problem like addiction addressed and solved in one episode and never dealt with again. Almost everyone knows that struggles with a pill addiction would creep up at some point in the future, yet Rose's addiction is never mentioned again.

4-21 "Little Sister"

Written by: Christopher Lloyd
Aired: April 1, 1989
Director: Terry Hughes
Guest Cast: Holly (Inga Swenson), Gary Tucker (Jerry Hardin)
Summary: Rose's troublemaking sister, Holly, comes to visit.
Rating: ♥♥

"Why is there a big, hairy beast in my living room?"—Blanche
"My guess is he bought you dinner."—Sophia

A mediocre episode. Holly, Rose's conniving younger sister, moves the plot along, but since she's just mean to Rose, it's quite forgettable. Blanche and Dorothy think Rose is crazy because Holly seems charming on the surface. But she turns out to be a tramp that sleeps with Blanche's beau. This episode repeats the theme of two of the Girls not believing the third for whatever reason.

The more amusing part is Sophia dog-sitting Dreyfuss and losing him. This begins with Sophia begging Dorothy for the chance to prove her responsible nature, only to lose memory for a few days and misplace this rather large dog. This is Sophia at her best, playing the rascally child character, against Dorothy, the parental figure. They eventually find not one, but two Dreyfusses at the animal shelter, and have to return one of them.

Not surprisingly, the Girls bust Holly hooking up with Blanche's new boyfriend and Rose tells her off, with Holly revealing a lifelong jealousy over Rose's ability to keep friendships. Just a tip: Don't sleep with people's boyfriends. Anyone else have horrible ex friends who complain about how people didn't like them growing up, and you mention that it could possibly be because they were a bully that did horrible things to people? Just a wild guess.

Golden Nuggets
It's a neat farm trick when Rose shows Sophia how to figure out which Dreyfuss is which, and Sophia stands there befuddled.

Rose swears on her mother's grave, though there had been no mention of her death.

Blanche had a sexual escapade with twin rabbinical students! I'd like to know more.

Jerry Hardin has a knack for playing a sleazeball in Blanche's life, as he played her harassing teacher in "Adult Education" and here plays her philandering boyfriend. He said that Estelle Getty was the funniest of the ladies in real life.

This is the second appearance for Dreyfuss—our favorite neighborhood dog—who was named Bear, and was a St. Bernard and Golden Retriever Mix.

Rose and her sisters were clearly named after flowers, though that's never said explicitly.

I could have easily solved the initial double-dog problem. Since Blanche is the one with the real dog, because that's the Dreyfuss that came to the house, the one with the leash Blanche used is the real Dreyfuss! (This kind of expertise comes from watching a lot of detective shows.)

4-22 "Sophia's Choice"

Written by: Tracy Gamble, Richard Vaczy
Aired: April 15, 1989
Director: Terry Hughes
Guest Cast: Lillian (Ellen Albertini Dow), Dan Cummings (Ron Orbach), Orderly (Mark Morocco), John Gale (Stanley Ullman)
Summary: Sophia busts her friend Lillian out of a retirement home because of the poor conditions, and the Girls try and take care of her.
Rating: ❤❤❤

"Not one boy was ever interested in my mind."—Rose
"Get out of here."—Blanche

This episode did really good spotlighting the plight of the elderly, often being pushed into retirement homes with substandard conditions. This show could be so funny, while being informative and sensitive. I was a kid watching this for the first time and took for granted that the women all lived together in their cute little wicker-filled house. It didn't seem like a luxury then, but for a lot of people, it's a fantasy. Meanwhile, Blanche gets a work bonus and plans to use it on breast implants.

Sophia's friend Lillian is being moved from Shady Pines, the retirement home Sophia always complains about. Most people think they all pretty much suck the same way, but Sophia knows better and breaks Lillian out, only to realize she's too much work.

And though the episode ends with Blanche using her recent bonus, the Girls acknowledge that this isn't really a happy ending. Most elderly people aren't lucky and get stuck in horrific places.

Golden Nuggets

All the jokes about the pictures of Blanche's breast photographs lying on the table are pure gold!

Poor Dorothy's honeymoon was spent picking up beer cans left by Stan's poker buddies.

Blanche goes super-Southern with her Ben story and gets called Jethro by Dorothy!

Blanche proves to be kindhearted and generous when it matters, taking money straight out of her bosom.

Rue McClanahan told guest star, Ellen Albertini, that she had been their best guest star.

The episode has a heart-rending ending when Rose asks the Girls what will happen when, even if they promise to take care of each other, there's only one left. Sophia replies that she can take care of herself, but the scene has a double meaning. Estelle Getty wasn't actually the eldest actress, Betty White was. And it was Betty White that outlived the other three actresses.

4-23 "Rites of Spring"

Written by: Eric Cohen
Aired: April 29, 1989
Director: Terry Hughes
Guest Cast: Stan Zbornak (Herb Edelman), Hairdresser (Lloyd Bochner) , Yvonne (Hilary Shepard)
Summary: The Girls recall past attempts to get in shape.
Rating: ❤❤❤

"I feel like I'm free to love everybody."—Stan
"You said the same thing after your vasectomy."—Dorothy

This is yet another wraparound, incited by an upcoming beach party. In complete juxtaposition is Sophia, who's upset that she's lost one pound—tipping the scales at 98 pounds! The other women get on the scale, prompting them to walk down the memory lane of dieting and weight-loss struggles.

In the first vignette, they go to an 80's health club where a salesgirl convinces Dorothy and Blanche to buy ridiculous, black and silver workout gear, making them look like aliens. Rose proves to be the smarty-pants by not falling for this, but also can't decipher when the instructor is suffering from a Charlie horse.

The second makes me laugh the most, as the women get their hair done from Eduardo, a handsome, debonair hair stylist that Sophia recommends. In one of the show's greatest reveals, they shut their dryers off and have Sophia's hairdo.

The final vignette shows Stan trying to convince the Girls to join a cult-like self-help group called Realizations. After they throw Stan out, they read the brochure and have Dorothy describe her best friend. Dorothy says it's all of them, making them feel good. Then she lets Sophia know it's really just her. I think Dorothy combined all of them.

The Girls discover that they have an extra day, and as women do with dieting, they figure they can still pig out and worry about bathing suits tomorrow!

Golden Nuggets

The three women sitting at the salon with Sophia hairdos is a favorite shot of mine.

Lots of jokes about Blanche's flexibility in various positions in the exercise class.

Eduardo, played by Lloyd Bochner, also played Patrick Vaughn, who was also lusted after by the women.

This is one of two episodes where Stan refers to himself as the New Stan.

Not sure how younger viewers will deal with how much the Girls are all comfortable mocking each others' weight gain. I think it's kind of healthy, but I'm not a millennial.

4-24 "Foreign Exchange"

Written by: Harriet Helberg, Sandy Helberg
Aired: April 29, 1989
Director: Terry Hughes
Guest Cast: Dominic Bosco (Vito Scotti), Philomena Bosco (Nan Martin), Gina (Flo Di Re), Dr. Watkins (Marcia Firesten), Lab Technician (Grant Moran)
Summary: Sophia's friends return from Italy and reveal that Dorothy might have been switched at birth.
Rating: ❤❤❤❤

"And the world takes a collective sigh of relief!"—Sophia

I love this episode because it has a cute twist at the end, but also a strong Rose and Blanche B story. There's also the twist of Blanche being not-so-great at sexy dancing. The *Dirty Dancing* lessons provide a lot of jokes about her awkwardness with her body, but end with an amazing final scene of Betty and Rue in the living room, nodding towards the camera, and getting busted in each others' arms.

The story is that an Italian couple (Dominic and Philomena) suddenly think Dorothy is their real daughter and not Gina, the one that they raised. The weirder part is that based on the info, I agree with them. Gina took a blood test that didn't match the parents, and when you see how Gina resembles Sophia, it seems logical. Since Sophia and Dorothy don't wait for the results at the hospital, we can only assume that Dorothy isn't her biological daughter giving us the answer to the 10-inch height disparity between them.

We also understand why Sophia doesn't wait. By all accounts, whether biological or not, Dorothy is her daughter and you can't just change things 60 years into a lifetime.

Golden Nuggets

Blanche's final dirty dance with Rose is an audience crowdpleaser, proving that she can move after all.

Rose eggs Blanche on to dance like a sex-crazed maniac by questioning her sexcapades, which is one of the signs that Rose is a secret evil genius.

The writers are the parents of Simon Helberg (Wolowitz) from *The Big Bang Theory*.

How funny that the DNA test at the hospital takes about an hour!

With all this DNA testing going on right now, I imagine Dorothy and Sophia's children and grandchildren would be taking these tests and realizing that something is in fact, amiss.

Sophia's endearing story about watching little Dorothy interact with evil little Debbie in kindergarten, then ripping up the blood test results is just classic Sophia and everything you need to know about her. Great writing. Great scene.

4-25 & 4-26 "We're Outta Here, Parts 1 & 2"

Written by: Barry Fanaro, Mort Nathan
Aired: May 13, 1989
Director: Terry Hughes
Guest Cast: Stan Zbornak (Herb Edelman), Mr. Yakamora (Ralph Ahn)
Summary: A Japanese businessman, Mr. Yahamora, makes Blanche a generous offer on the house, prompting the Girls to reminisce, as Blanche ponders selling.
Rating: ❤❤❤

"I'm wound up tighter than the girdle of a Baptist minister's wife at an all-you-can-eat pancake breakfast."—Blanche

This is a clip show and if you're a fan, of course you like watching snippets and flashbacks. What any good clip show does is explain enough of the show's characters and plot lines for a newcomer, while a fan could watch their favorite scenes. And these two episodes do a good job of both. My one criticism is that some flashbacks are a bit too long. The writers must have been really attached to those particular episodes, because they don't just show a part of a scene—they go for practically the whole thing.

Part 1

In this first part, we get the time the Girls first meet and move in together, the dance marathon where the Girls compete for $1,000 and the one where Uncle Angelo first visits and Dorothy and Stan pretend that they're still married. There's also the time when Sophia's sister Angela, and Rose's cousin Sven visit.

The episode ends with Mr. Yakamora doubling his offer, and Blanche deciding to sell.

Part 2

The second episode we see Rose debating going on the cruise with Arnie, and then the kitchen table convo where Sophia, Blanche and Dorothy discuss sex; Blanche and Rose's tap dance when Dorothy has her foot surgery is here as well, along with Sophia's rendition of "Thanks for the Medicare." There's the one with Count Bessie the Chicken's alleged slaughter, Dorothy and Rose singing the "Miami" song, the Girls getting mistakenly arrested for prostitution, and the Burt Reynolds' surprise ending. Lastly, we get the one where Daisy holds Rose's teddy bear Fernando for ransom.

The episode concludes when Mr.Yakamora rescinds his offer on the house because he spends too much money, which I actually like more than if it had been because of some sentimental reason. When someone offers you twice the value of your home, you should take it. Especially at their age!

If I had to pick, I'd say the second episode definitely has the stronger scenes, but I think the first episode has a little bit more set up. In all honestly, I never got the clip show that I really wanted. I'd love one where you see some of the emotional roller-coaster scenes like when Dorothy first tells off Stan, or when Rose expresses how scared she is that she's unemployed, or when Blanche reveals to the shrink that she's afraid of getting older. I would mix those scenes in with the funny ones, so that a new viewer would really grasp the mix of humor and solid acting that the show delivered.

Golden Nuggets

The singing and dancing scenes are much better than a Suzanne Somers special.

When Stan comes by with his pizzeria scheme, and claims his true desire is to work at the office and tease high school girls, it is so specifically creepy.

Sophia grabs Blanche's nightgown and discovers that Blanche apparently wears elaborate undergarments to hold herself in. Keep in mind, this is before SPANX.

When Rose counted cows jumping over her bed, she is speaking literally.

Sophia's father did not, in fact, own The Vatican.

I couldn't find an online list of Sophia's Hollywood disses, but she nabs Suzanne Somers in this one as she compares the bad acting, bad singing, and bad dancing in the house to a Suzanne Somers Special.

The Girls mention that they're going to order pizza and Chinese food at 4:00 a.m. Was this really a thing in Miami?

In the 80s, there was a constant theme in movies and TV that the Japanese were taking over the world. You'd see it in a lot of action films, but it seeped into sitcoms. It was usually the Russians and the Japanese. Now it's mostly the Russians and the Chinese.

The Golden Girls

SEASON FIVE

5-1 "Sick and Tired" (Part 1)

Written by: Susan Harris
Aired: September 23, 1989
Director: Terry Hughes
Guest Cast: Dr. Stevens (Jeffrey Tambor), Dr. Budd (Michael McGuire)
Summary: Dorothy deals with a chronic illness but becomes depressed when she's unable to get a diagnosis.
Rating: ♥♥♥♥

"Ribs? Why don't you just kick the dentures out of my mouth?"—Sophia

This episode is Bea Arthur at her strongest and most vulnerable, and the start of an emotional two-parter that criticizes the healthcare system—especially how older women are treated by doctors. Written by Susan Harris, this was based on her battle with Chronic Fatigue Syndrome, which she was going through at the creation of the show.

Dorothy—who we know as a sane and vital woman—becomes scared of ongoing flu symptoms that won't go away. She's dismissed by condescending male doctors, with Jeffrey Tambor being especially good at acting arrogant.

The humorous spot is the B story with Blanche's attempt at becoming a novelist, which is more hilarious to me as I'm writing about the episode.

Golden Nuggets

The end scene where Sophia reveals that she's afraid of Dorothy dying is so heartfelt.

Blanche reveals that she was getting a pedicure when she found out her husband died. In a later episode, Blanche says that she received a phone call from a police officer telling her that he was in an accident.

Rose pondering the meaning of Blanche's loins being on fire, and Sophia equating Blanche's loins with a loin of pork is like, wow, how did they get through that without laughing?

When I was 30, a male doctor asked me if I was single. He wasn't trying to be rude, but I swear I wanted to drop-kick him. This episode reminded me of that.

Lady Chatterley's Lover by D.H. Lawrence is the book that inspires Blanche to write.

When I watched this years ago, I was naive about these realities. The way that Dorothy has to constantly prove that her symptoms and her suffering are real caused the show to get a whole lot of mail from women experiencing the same ordeals.

5-2 "Sick and Tired" (Part 2)

Written by: Susan Harris
Aired: September 30, 1989
Director: Terry Hughes
Guest Cast: Dr. Budd (Michael McGuire), Dr. Chang (Keone Young), Helen Budd (Bibi Besch), Oliver (Glenn Walker Harris Jr.), The Waiter (Eric Poppick), Dr. Harry Weston (Richard Mulligan), Laverne Todd (Park Overall)
Summary: Dorothy finally gets a diagnosis of Chronic Fatigue Syndrome.
Rating: ♥♥♥♥

"He cut off his ear."—Dorothy
"I have too many earrings."—Blanche

Part 1 of "Sick and Tired" was good, but Part 2 is even better, packing in what might be the best Dorothy speech, along with the B story's seemingly infinite Blanche laughs, as she goes bonkers trying to write a sexy romance novel.

Meanwhile, Blanche comes into the kitchen fresh off an all-nighter and steals the scene with her delirium, comparing herself to Van Gogh. This is Rue exhibiting a delightful state of vapidness, and this whole episode represents the show at its peak—and not floundering in its fifth season as some shows might. These women know their characters, what makes them lovable, funny and strong, and it's on full display. As Sophia says as she exits, "I hate to leave a show like this."

But back to Dorothy. She speaks for so many women, especially women of a certain age dismissed by doctors.

Golden Nuggets

Dorothy's impassioned speech at the end, written by Susan Harris and inspired by her experience, as she went through her Chronic Fatigue diagnosis is incredibly memorable.

The speed at which Blanche gets turned down does not compute. Is it days, or a week?

We learn a little bit about Laverne Todd—Harry Westin's nurse—from the spinoff *Empty Nest*, who believes strongly in having sex outdoors.

I still want to try Sophia's champagne trick at a fancy restaurant and see if they fall for it. Maybe I should say it's for research.

This is a prime Dorothy episode, plus some stellar Blanche scenes. I'd say that although the second season "Flu Attack" is probably the best way to introduce someone to the show, this one is a close second in demonstrating the Girls at their best.

5-3 "The Accurate Conception"

Written by: Gail Parent
Aired: October 14, 1989
Director: Terry Hughes
Guest Cast: Rebecca (Debra Engle), Dr. Manning (James Staley), Receptionist (Kelly Ann Conn)
Summary: Blanche is embarrassed when her daughter Rebecca reveals that she wants to conceive a baby through artificial insemination.
Rating: ❤❤❤

"Buy? Well, sperm used to be free. It was all over the place!"—Blanche
"Oh boy, we're going to a sperm bank."—Sophia

It's not controversial now, but back then, artificial insemination and single motherhood were topics that were deemed non-traditional. It creates some great fodder for the Girls to discuss that the times were changing, and for women, the desire to have a baby on their own was on the rise. It's also worth noting that in real life, none of the actresses had issues with insemination.

But this episode was also controversial in a way that was not thought of as controversial at the time. When the Girls describe that they all conceived in different ways, Dorothy explains that she was "totally unconscious." Sophia then jokes that she never bought that story and then Dorothy replies, "I swear. [Stan] must've slipped me something" to which Sophia gets a huge laugh with "apparently." In today's woke culture, this looks like jokes about a date rape, and that our beloved Stan character was a date raper.

My opinion is this. First of all, this story is inconsistent with how it's told in other episodes and just seems like a few laugh lines that go too far. In other instances, Dorothy says Stan begged her to sleep with him because he was leaving for the war and she agreed. Most often, it's explained that she got very drunk, but was clearly conscious. Other times, she explains that it happened so fast that she wasn't sure anything happened. So, with everything we know about Stan, can we assume from this dialogue that he spiked a drink and knocked her out and raped her? I don't think so.

Are the writers making a joke about two drunken teenagers in the 1950's who had sex, and perhaps Dorothy passed out at some point? Possibly. By all accounts, this is the first time Dorothy had gotten drunk in her youth and when you miscalculate your liquor intake when you're young (and old for that matter), there's often a memory lapse. From the description, she doesn't sound like she was dosed—more like drunk. When you're dosed, you lose a lot of time. Nothing about Dorothy retelling this, or in the ways she has told it before, portrays Stan as a sexual predator. It definitely doesn't seem like the most romantic story in the world, but a common one.

Golden Nuggets

The scene of them discussing Becky's decision around the kitchen table is a quintessential *Golden Girls* scene, with the four of them going over their children's rogue life choices, their own sex lives, and unusual ways of conceiving.

Not to be a stickler, but Rose shouldn't really be able to pinpoint when her children were conceived, since we know from an earlier episode that she and Charlie had sex more than once a day for most of their marriage.

As mentioned above, this scene has it all, even talk of cows looking for sex, and Sophia and Sal getting frisky at a festival behind the sausage and peppers stand.

Rose's story of the mighty swimming sperm that came over by mail is extra special.

This is another example of the show being progressive, but not in-your-face about it. Generations have different ideas about raising families, and they struggle, but *The Golden Girls* always conveys that the love for parents and children overrides everything.

5-4 "Rose Fights Back"

Written by: Marc Sotkin
Aired: October 21, 1989
Director: Terry Hughes
Guest Cast: Enrique Mas (Chick Vennera), Terry Franco (Beth Grant)
Summary: Rose tries to get a second job when she can no longer collect her husband's pension fund.
Rating: ❤❤❤

"Why don't we just set each other on fire?"—Dorothy

This episode is about a lot of things that the show touched on and did very well. Unemployment and age discrimination among elderly women isn't the sexiest television topic, but *The Golden Girls* always kept it lively—these are real moments when Rose worries about her pension being cut off. She needs to get a second job and though she is clearly hard-working and full of energy, she can't find work. She's not living an extravagant life either. So, Rose goes about proving herself to consumer rights advocate Enrique Mas by becoming a production assistant. Truth be told, that is an exhausting job, but Rose seems up to it.

The B story with Sophia buying in bulk just reminds me of my mom spending my inheritance at Costco. As my father often said, he's never spent so much money saving money.

Golden Nuggets

Rose's monologue about the homeless woman is so well acted by Betty White. I like how she takes her time with it. Bravo.

Is Dorothy's father dead for 27 years or 15 years? Seems like a huge difference.

Blanche didn't become loose till she was 12—not when she first started shaving her legs at 11 (old wives' tale be damned!). I love when Blanche gives us flashes into her childhood and we find that little Blanche was such a vixen.

This episode introduces us to Rose's new employer, Enrique Mas.

Best nickname ever might be "Rose with the hairy legs!"

It always amazes me that companies don't specifically go after middle-aged+ women. In my years of corporate experience, women over 40 always seemed to be the ones who get the most done in the shortest amount of time. They don't screw around!

5-5 "Love Under the Big Top"

Written by: Tracy Gamble, Richard Vaczy
Aired: October 28, 1989
Director: Terry Hughes
Guest Cast: Ken (Dick Van Dyke), Judge (Mel Stewart), Fisherman (John DiSanti)
Summary: Dorothy dates a successful lawyer who wants to give up law to become a full-time circus clown.
Rating: ❤❤❤

"I just didn't fit in with the other clowns' wives."—Dorothy

This is a quirky episode that allows Bea Arthur to be in an actual functional relationship with a stand-up guy, even though it doesn't work out. Her beau Ken starts out as a prominent Miami lawyer, but decides that he wants to turn his volunteer act into a full-time circus gig. Oh my, that is strange. But I have to say, Dorothy does seem a bit too particular here. Let him retire and follow his passion! I assume he has money saved. But I guess she really doesn't love him enough. I feel like I did when Blanche broke up with her chef-guy Jake—maybe hold on to these guys a little bit longer ladies, as the post-50 dating pool is extremely unforgiving.

The B story with the Girls protesting the tuna fishing gets a lot of laughs, but also gets the women to show us their off-screen passion for animal rights.

Golden Nuggets

Ken's final summation has some great gags, but it's really Dick Van Dyke that just sells the whole thing. He's a perfect guest star and boyfriend for Dorothy—immediately likable but doesn't stand in the way of the Girls being outlandish and charming.

Rose gets most of the sexy talk here, and again we get the feeling that she's got some twisted turn-ons. She gets hot talking about a hypothetical circus boyfriend, and then gets too detailed talking about bears mating with mice. But let's not forget that Blanche does plan a drool-inducing pirate party in her mind to save the mammals.

Blanche has a point about Dorothy's outfit.

We learn Blanche calls herself "Waterlily."

Sophia has a point blaming Dorothy repeatedly for Ken's life decision, yelling, "What did you do to him" works every time!

I love the jokes about the circus couples that Dorothy and Ken go out with ("call them Little People").

The issue of dolphins getting tangled in plastic was more of a Pacific Ocean occurrence than an Atlantic, but the writers hoped the audience wouldn't notice.

5-6 "Dancing in the Dark"

Written by: Phillip Jayson Lasker
Aired: November 4, 1989
Director: Terry Hughes
Guest Cast: Miles Webber (Harold Gould), Gayle (G.F. Smith), Lillian (Mimi Cozzens) Harry (John Ingle), Elise (Channing Chase), Mr. Morelli (Edgar Justice), Paul (Al Berry)
Summary Rose begins a romance with a college professor named Miles.
Rating: ❤❤❤

"Cabbage she says? In 10 minutes, I could be sky riding."—Sophia

Behold Miles! It took five seasons, but in this episode one of the Girls finally reels a man in for some long-term commitment. And that Girl is Rose, with Miles Webber, a college professor played brilliantly by Harold Gould. Miles is Rose's ballroom dancing partner, and she has reservations because he's so smart which makes her feel they have nothing in common, and nothing to talk about. She ends up sending Blanche on a date with him, and since she's going through a dating drought, she goes. But Miles and Rose are a match, and they end up getting together for the rest of the show.

Golden Nuggets

The scene with Rose forcing Blanche into going out with Miles, and then calling her a slut behind her back, is just the kind of scene where Betty White kills. She just kills it.

Blanche goes through a sexual drought that leads her to try and pick up guys at a hardware store. I wish I cared about anything as much as Blanche cares about picking up men.

I'm sorry but anyone who doesn't like Rose's tale of "You can't go home again…" isn't anyone I would want to hang out with. Miles clearly gets the genius behind her stories.

Rose's lines at the dinner party are actually kind of interesting. I would want to know what to serve to any two people in history. And I like that she has Jesus coming over for dessert.

There are a few episodes that brush up on this topic and it's humorous here, but Blanche really shouldn't have gone out on that date. Rose is clearly crushing on Miles hard, and if anything had happened, that would have just gone against the true best-friend code!

5-7 "Not Another Monday"

Written by: Gail Parent
Aired: November 11, 1989
Director: Terry Hughes
Guest Cast: Martha (Geraldine Fitzgerald), Maître d'(Jayson Kane), Young Man (Doug Cox), Young Woman (Bonnie Urseth), Bartender (Robert Neches), Dr. Harry Weston (Richard Mulligan)
Summary: One of Sophia's friends is depressed at the prospect of old age and illness, and requests Sophia's assistance in her suicide.
Rating: ❤❤❤❤

"If this were Sicily, you wouldn't have any lips left."—Sophia

This episode is a strong one in every way. It packs an emotional punch about aging, yet has so many laughs. The Martha character is played with such realism by Geraldine Page, whom I love from one of my favorite films, *Arthur*. She was also in Season Three's *Mother's Day*.

The melancholy is offset by Sophia nailing the comedy and drama. It's reminiscent of her fourth season work in "Old Friends." I love the scene with the waiter. As Sophia's friend contemplates suicide, the Girls babysit a newborn and we get a lot of fantastic zingers about Blanche's aging eyes, and the Girls breaking into Mr. Sandman to put the baby to sleep. All gold (pardon the pun).

Golden Nuggets

Tough to pick here between "Mr. Sandman" and Sophia at the restaurant, and then the tearjerker where Sophia talks Martha off the edge. So, I'm doing a three-way tie for my favorite part!

As a kid, Dr. Weston being so turned off by Blanche always bothered me. But now I see how intimidating a man of his era could find such a forward woman.

Sophia's dream, Blanche's fear of losing her looks, and Dorothy encouraging Rose to tell a story with an order to make the end come as close to the beginning, make a perfect scene!

Two words. Meanest ventriloquist. St. Olaf has everything.

It's been a while since I've mentioned them but Blanche's negligees are my life goals for sleepwear. But Dorothy's right—the earrings are too much.

Being 4'9, I totally empathize with Sophia needing help getting on that bar stool.

Though Rose is the one who boils it down to ethics, Dorothy sees it as being hard for Sophia on an emotional level. Sophia's hesitations come from her belief in fighting for life and leaving it to God. But there's no judgment towards Martha, which is why it works as well.

5-8 "That Old Feeling"

Written by: Tom Whedon
Aired: November 11, 1989
Director: Terry Hughes
Guest Cast: Jamie (George Grizzard)
Summary: Blanche develops feelings for her late husband's brother, when he comes to visit.
Rating: 

"Why don't we go real high fiber and spread ketchup on cardboard? Pizza damnit, get pizza!"—Dorothy

This is an emotional episode that demonstrates how Blanche is still looking for romance and is nostalgic for her old life with her husband. She finds it in her brother-in-law when he comes to visit, misinterpreting their friendship and making a pass at him only to feel rather foolish by his rebuff. And I have to say, this show always got me to really feel bad for the ladies when men turned them down. For the audience member, we thought they were just perfect. But yeah, Jamie was correct. She was just romanticizing her past life.

Meanwhile, Sophia starts driving behind Dorothy's back creating some laughs. The best part is that she has to sit on phone books in order to drive their cars.

Golden Nuggets

When Blanche confesses her feelings to Jamie at the restaurant and mixes up Jamie's name with George's, it hurts.

A literal sex-education recap from Jamie as he points out that Blanche used to purposely mix up tentacle/testicle in biology class and never blush.

Per Sophia needing phone books to see over the steering wheel, I have to say that as someone 4'9, I never needed a phone book. Though I think older cars might not have had the same adjustment settings.

Just for fun, drink a shot of something whenever Blanche says "many, many men!"

A few episodes ago we had Blanche going after Rose's crush, and now she's going after her brother-in-law. I think this speaks to the bigger issue of loneliness, especially for a woman that isn't just sex-obsessed, but still very much a romantic. I so wish we had seen her find someone at the end of the series.

5-9 "Comedy of Errors"

Written by: Don Reo
Aired: November 25, 1989
Director: Terry Hughes
Guest Cast: Roger (Oliver Clark), Gloria Schmidt (Linda Rand), Comedian (David Jay Willis), Jimmy (Tom La Grua)
Summary: Dorothy decides to fulfill her high school dream of performing standup comedy.
Rating: ❤❤❤

"You can still be Homecoming Queen.
It'll just be a different kind of home."—Sophia

This episode is unique in that it has three plotlines which becomes more and more frequent at this point. Besides Dorothy's standup comedy goals, we have Blanche dodging the IRS and Rose trying to get a coworker to like her. It touches nicely upon the Girls' insecurities.

As a substitute teacher that's clearly smart enough to be a teacher, Dorothy's always the character struggling to reach her potential. She's probably the easiest to relate to as she goes through her high school yearbook, seeing her bucket list of unfulfilled dreams.

Blanche on the other hand can be quite a rascal, in love and in finances, so of course she'd be the one scamming the IRS. Then we have Rose's dark side. She's sweet on the surface, but clearly borders on compulsive behavior. So much so, that she displays some serious boundary issues with a coworker, Roger, who finds her annoying. We get a quick psychological explanation, tracing it to how as an orphan she learned that you have to be nice to win people over.

Since I've dabbled in standup, I can relate to Dorothy's performance and her initial sweating and stammering. It's all pretty realistic and a good first performance when she finds her voice. When you find that magic, and that connection, it's wonderful. It can even be addicting when a performer finds that mix of being all-knowing and yet self-deprecating.

Golden Nuggets
Dorothy's standup set goes well in a realistic way, and the age jokes are timeless.

The last time Blanche got audited, she got money back from the government. She is unapologetically admitting that she swapped sexual favors with the U.S. government.

Sophia's critique of Dorothy's comedy is actually quite astute.

The Golden Girls never did a Thanksgiving episode, and honestly, that's one of the things I liked about the show.

Truth be told, I stopped keeping a Bucket List, because the minute you make them, you resign yourself to "Oh, one day, I might do that." I think it's better to have, "This Year Lists" and that resonates more than ever during the pandemic.

5-10 "All That Jazz"

Written by: Robert Bruce and Martin Weiss
Aired: December 2, 1989
Director: Terry Hughes
Guest Cast: Stan Zbornak (Herb Edelman), Michael Zbornak (Scott Jacoby), Make-up Man (Stan Roth), Enrique Mas (Chick Vennera)
Summary: When Dorothy's son, Michael, loses his job and fights with his wife, he moves in with Dorothy and drives her crazy.
Rating: ❤❤

"That's where the job-job comes in." —Dorothy

By now you know that the character of Michael is probably my least favorite. He causes problems for Dorothy every time he visits, he sleeps with Rose's daughter, surprises Dorothy when he gets engaged to his pregnant fiancé, and now he's unemployed and crashing at her place. And in this episode, he wears out his welcome, moves in with Stan, and reluctantly returns to his job. He's just so annoying and he keeps coming back to be even more of a pest. His lines are flat and not well delivered.

Rose's B story, and Stan's scenes make the episode tolerable. Rose getting super-stressed at work as a consumer research assistant for Enrique Mas, works well enough. I also like that Rose's job is portrayed as a difficult one, not one that she just automatically eases into.

Golden Nuggets

Seventeen men used Blanche's name as a mantra at a meditation retreat. Sure, it's probably an exaggeration, but man it's a good one. She's so inspiring that I might try it myself.

It looks like Blanche is reading *Lady Chatterley's Lover* again in the scene where she mixes up *Rough Love* and *Tough Love*.

Few shows joke about family members sleeping with farm animals, but apparently, Sophia's Uncle Nunzio openly slept with a goat. It's one of the more disturbing throwaway jokes on the show in my opinion.

Rose's Charlie was so well endowed, that he would have made a bull jealous.

I enjoy Enrique Mas, a positive Hispanic character, when there weren't that many on television. He's a sympathetic boss to Rose and provides a lot of humor in his brief scenes.

5-11 "Ebb Tide"

Written by: Marc Sotkin
Aired: December 9, 1989
Director: Terry Hughes
Guest Cast: Virginia Hollingsworth (Sheree North), Howard (Steven Gilborn), Peter (Paul Eiding), Maddy (Brandis Kemp)
Summary: Blanche is despondent when she finds out her father, Big Daddy, has died. While she attends the funeral, Sophia rents the house out to strangers.
Rating: ❤❤❤

"How about $100 and we show you a good time?"—Sophia

This is a melancholy Blanche episode as we watch her go through the five phases of grieving after Big Daddy dies. The denial is deep as she initially doesn't believe he's dead. She's too busy getting ready to be Queen of a Ball—a festival so important, she slept with a man twice to be named Queen, as well as to be described as 35 years old.

Blanche argues with her sister once in Atlanta, then somberly goes through family albums with Dorothy and has a tearful monologue at Big Daddy's gravestone. When she arrives home in her final stage of acceptance, she no longer cares about the prized plate she was awarded as Queen and has a seemingly renewed outlook on life.

The B story, with Sophia trying to make money by renting the house to strangers, involves Sophia being delightfully sneaky and duplicitous.

Golden Nuggets

In two small snippets of dialogue, Blanche says so much: "There's no one to be proud of me anymore," tied with "I'm nobody's little girl anymore."

We learn it's the law in St. Olaf to have a cow in a rented room.

OMG, Sophia singing with the couple from Iowa is so adorable. Then when she comes in, counts her money, and says, "Hide me" when Dorothy calls—it's just absolute perfection.

The impact of Big Daddy's death was shocking when I first watched, and that's the point. The abruptness of losing your favorite person in the world just because you're in the middle of, well, life. And how we take everything and everyone for granted. But Blanche is so-very much daddy's little girl, and it's one of a few episodes where she has to reluctantly, truly, grow up.

5-12 "Have Yourself a Very Little Christmas"

Written by: Tom Whedon
Aired: December 16, 1989
Director: Terry Hughes
Guest Cast: Stan Zbornak (Herb Edelman), Father Avery (Matt McCoy), Homeless Person (Cynthia Lea Clark)
Summary: The Girls find out that Stan is homeless when they volunteer at a church during Christmas.
Rating: ❤❤

"Dorothy said you'd like something crotchless!"—Rose

Another Christmas episode that begins with the Girls frustrated by shopping. They decide they will pick names out of a hat and only buy for one person, but the problem is none of them want a gift from Rose. They also get a quick stop-by from Stan trying to con them into giving him money. This time it's for $1,000 each, which I have to say is a ballsy move for someone desperate for cash. See if they have a few hundred first, Stan. Jeez.

So, the Girls go to Rose's church to donate extra food, and the episode gets very "message-y." There were always these holiday episodes guilting people about doing more for the less fortunate, and I just don't think they ever really motivated people. The fourth season homeless shelter episode is a little bit stronger showing how ordinary people can lose everything. This one has some guy explaining it to Rose like she's an idiot. Anyway, Stan shows up as a homeless Santa, and then rebounds by coming back to give the kids toys.

Golden Nuggets

I like when the Girls gather at the kitchen table trying to avoid getting picked by Rose in their Secret Santa.

Blanche tries to tell a wholesome Christmas story, but it veers off into a naughty Veteran's Day story.

Eels are apparently part of the traditional Sicilian meal on Christmas Day. To which I say, eww, gross. I only like eel sushi rolls.

A St. Olaf Christmas with only Two Wise Men, a lot of smoked kippers, and animals sleeping inside houses caused racy rumors around town.

This is the last episode where Stan's third wife, Katherine, is mentioned. It's assumed they get divorced some time before Dorothy and Stan's sixth season reunion.

My humble opinion is that Oprah Winfrey was the only person on TV that ever made a real difference. I miss those days when she would talk about an issue on a Friday, and it was solved by Monday.

5-13 "Mary Has a Little Lamb"

Written by: Harold Apter
Aired: January 6, 1990
Director: Terry Hughes
Guest Cast: Mary (Julie McCullough), Merrill (John Dennis Johnston), Fred (Lorry Goldman)
Summary: The Girls take care of a pregnant teenage neighbor who's trying to reconcile with her father.
Rating: ❤❤

"Break out the finger sandwiches,
Mr. Astaire looks like he's hungry."—Sophia

This episode is a little hokey, because as you know my opinion is that the show wasn't strong in writing about the teen issues of the 80's and 90's. Their strength was writing about middle-aged and senior-aged women dealing with life. The actress playing Mary is convincing and she's better known for playing Kirk Cameron's girlfriend, Julie, on *Growing Pains.* At least until Kirk (allegedly) wielded his power and threw her off the show for previously posing for *Playboy* Magazine. Allegedly. You know, cause he was a devout Christian.

Meanwhile, the B story is better than the A story in humor. Blanche misjudges her prison pen-pal, Merrill, in that she thinks he's going to stay in prison. But lo and behold, Merrill comes a-knocking and ends up tying up Sophia and robbing the joint. But it's hilarious.

In the meantime, the Girls try and appeal to Mary's father, Fred, to convince him to take her back, but he's unmoved. But he comes around due to Dorothy's last-ditch St. Olaf story. When Rose finds this out, she is downright gleeful.

Golden Nuggets

Merrill steals the episode when he ogles Sophia with the, "What about you, cutie?" and prompts Sophia to sit on top of Dorothy.

Blanche's sexuality is so complete that she even writes erotic love letters. It's kind of tragic that we never saw Blanche discover the internet and explore fan fiction.

St. Olaf's justice system was so progressive that their mantra was *Use a gun, go apologize.*

Blanche's jewelry gets stolen a few times over the course of the show, but she always seems to have more.

Another fun side gag is that Sophia is afraid of Fred's dog, because she thinks the dog ate her friend Ida—so much so, Sophia turns back at one point to yell, "What'd you do with Ida?"

There are two types of women: One who would take the call from the prisoner and tell him what she was wearing, and the other who would be Dorothy.

5-14 "Great Expectations"

Written by: Robert Bruce and Martin Weiss
Aired: January 13, 1990
Director: Terry Hughes
Guest Cast: Stephen (Robert Mandan), Mary Ellen (Michele Pawk), Woman (Kat Sawyer), Nurse (Kathy Bendett)
Summary: Blanche struggles with long-term commitment and Rose joins a positivity seminar.
Rating: ♥♥♥

"Pussycat. You got your roast beef. Don't push it."—Sophia

This season for me seems to be defined by B stories that are more entertaining than the A story. The A story, involving Blanche's reluctance to commit to her boyfriend, is just okay. It deals with the usual trope of Blanche's shallowness and vapidity. When he has a heart attack, she doesn't visit him right away in the hospital, causing him to get back together with his ex.

The funnier part is the Girls joining the positivity group. Rose encourages them to attend a seminar of smiling weirdos, and Dorothy begins to consider that her negative outlook does have an effect on her life.

Golden Nuggets

The scene with the demented positive-thinking group does remind me of all these cult groups in the news (Scientology, NXIVM). Personally, I'd rather hang with a group of cynical pessimists who insult their children and don't smile so much.

Dorothy's pregnancy age is mentioned as 19 here, but sometimes, it's said to be 17.

Stephen and Blanche, for whatever reason, pretend to play tennis while having a rendezvous. Seems like a lot of work.

The Great Denture Swap at Shady Pines is one of my favorite Shady Pines references. I just have an image of old people sitting around with each other's teeth.

One of my favorites as well is the one where Sophia says she slept with Pablo Picasso (apparently as a teenage girl). The tale has nothing to do with Blanche's predicament, but man it's a doozy.

A Shady Pines/Sicily flashback, and a St. Olaf story make for a perfect trio! Here we get a special version of Ponce de Leon's Fountain of Youth that begins with a search for intelligence and ends with a case of cholera. These writers were packing a lot into this episode.

Blanche does have a real fear of commitment, but what she really has is a fear of dating a guy that might die. The Girls and Stephen judge her harshly, but I feel like with the modern world of dating and Covid, this behavior doesn't seem so bad because ghosting for no reason is so frightfully common.

5-15 "Triple Play"

Written by: Gail Parent
Aired: January 27, 1990
Director: Terry Hughes
Guest Cast: Miles Webber (Harold Gould), Caroline (Molly Hagan), Thomas (Ronnie Schell), James (William Cort), Delivery Boy (Lance Wilson-White)
Summary: Miles' daughter, Caroline, tries to sabotage their relationship.
Rating: ❤❤❤

"Enough to have you rubbed out if you rat on me."—Sophia

First off, one of the strongest episode openers is Sophia asking who Cecilia is, and Dorothy saying it's their cousin who only has weeks to live. "Next time I'll accept the charges." So savage. This episode is so close to a four-star episode for me, because it gives all four women lines that are perfect for them.

But there's also a valid emotional conflict. In this case, it's Miles' daughter and she's a bit of a manipulative snit. She corners Rose and guilt-trips her about dating Miles too soon after her mother's death. In reality, having Rose as your father's girlfriend is about as good as it gets. You can get her to do just about anything (wait, am I a manipulative snit?).

The B story, as per usual, is where the real fun is. Blanche concocts a trick to meet more men. Yes, more men! She puts an ad up saying she's selling a Mercedes to entrap rich men. I gotta tell you… it's a good plan. The flaw is that the men are actually interested in the rented car. So, not a perfect plan.

The C story is that Sophia's getting extra Social Security checks due to some sort of accident. Her walking around the house, handing out hundreds with a bag of cash in her bedroom is some amazing gangster stuff. That's the kind of government I want. Not socialism, or capitalism. Anyway, Dorothy the Buzzkill guilts Sophia into giving the money back. Then Dorothy ends up on a date with one of Blanche's prospective suitors, so Blanche reports the Mercedes stolen to get them pulled over by the police.

Golden Nuggets

When Sophia claims the car is haunted. "You look fine." "I'm 28 years old." Bwahaha.

Sophia's epic slut-shaming. We can only wonder what her response is to "I can't believe anything that beautiful is so cheap."

This episode is named "Triple Play" because it has three separate stories running simultaneously, instead of two.

One of the most savage Sophia burns: "I had that recurring nightmare. You know the one where I'm in bed with Warren Beatty and he says, 'Sorry this is too sick, even for me."

Dorothy's guilt trip to Sophia about what this country means to her, as she convinces her to return the money, is a bit much. I wish Sophia kept a few thousand for fun money. She's about 85!

5-16 "Clinton Avenue Memoirs"

Written by: Richard Vaczy and Tracy Gamble
Aired: February 3, 1990
Director: Terry Hughes
Guest Cast: Sal Petrillo (Sid Melton), Young Sal (Kyle T. Heffner), Mr. Hernandez (David Correi), Young Sophia (Flo Di Re), Young Dorothy (Jandi Swanson)
Summary: Sophia's memory problems start to worry Dorothy and prompt them to return to Brooklyn
Rating: ❤❤❤

"Isn't it good to be in the old neighborhood. Watching the kids play stickball on the corner?" —Sophia
"Ma, they were beating a man."—Dorothy

This episode touches on that horrible feeling of getting old and forgetting things—your sense of self, and the people and places you hold dear. Here, Sophia gets triggered when she and Dorothy argue over an old picture. Sophia believes that in her kitchen, her husband drew a heart that said, "Sal loves Sophia." Dorothy thinks that the wall has her and her siblings' heights. This questioning proves to be too much.

Sophia plans a trip to Brooklyn to prove Dorothy wrong. Of course, this is a huge gamble that could easily have been painted over. But what do you know? Dorothy's right. But the heart is in the bedroom which perks Sophia up. Meanwhile, she talks to Sal's ghost in the bedroom, as one would do.

The B story is a bit of a snoozer. Blanche works for Rose for some side cash on a project helping elderly people that have been taken advantage of by healthcare companies. Blanche doesn't take it seriously at first, but realizes the horrors of older people getting scammed. It's heavy-handed, but just not particularly memorable.

Golden Nuggets

I like when Sophia brags about her prowess in the bedroom with, "Kitchen? Bedroom? I knew it was a room I was good in."

Eww, to the pre-*There's Something About Mary* joke about which part of the moose Mr. Ingrid of St. Olaf uses to keep your hair in place.

Estelle Getty got an Emmy nomination for this episode.

Expensive healthcare for the elderly, say what? It's funny. Watching this as a kid in 1990, I didn't think every single thing would have political spin, but it turns out, something so obvious yesterday would mean something totally different today. If you aired this today, it would be all about which party was at fault. And which solution was socialism, etc. It's just worth noting that the problem was there in 1990.

5-17 "Like the Beep Beep Beep of the Tom-Tom"

Written by: Phillip Jayson Lasker
Aired: February 10, 1990
Director: Terry Hughes
Guest Cast: Simon (Robert Culp), Dr. Stein (Peter Michael Goetz), Orderly (David Jay Willis)
Summary: Blanche has to get a pacemaker, which causes her to question whether she can continue her sexual lifestyle.
Rating: ❤❤❤

"If a 5,000-year-old Indian shows up, tell him, I want to know more about his people." —Blanche

This is an entertaining episode that hits all the same notes that we've seen before, with Blanche freaking out about aging and her love life suffering because of it.

The episode starts with Blanche's concerns over her heart trouble and getting a pacemaker. Once she has the surgery, she becomes afraid of starting up her sex life and uses her recovery period to carve random objects out of wood.

No real B story here, which made me almost give this two hearts. Rose is trying out consumer products for a few laughs, but that's it—no real sub plot. But the truth is, I laughed out loud more than once. And I will never think of the song "Over There" the same again.

Golden Nuggets

The ending, which happens often, is the highlight, when the Girls come home and hear Blanche in her bedroom singing.

Lots of info about Blanche's sexcapades, including that men are being oversensitive when they get mad about her calling out other men's names.

Sophia's "Who's for popcorn?" line is actually from a deleted part about how microwaves affect pacemakers. It's not just Sophia interjecting with nonsense. She's actually joking about sabotaging Blanche's pacemaker and perhaps killing her!

This show was big on spiritual epiphanies that occur from near-death experiences. Blanche's is the only one that leads to celibacy.

Sal and Sophia went through a sexless period when her mother-in-law lived with them as newlyweds. Apparently, this sicko slept between them.

Sophia does some epic trash-talking this episode. I counted at least five. It's part of the show's humor: friends mocking each other for a rampant sex life, a lack of a rampant sex life, being stupid or being old. If you can't take it, this is the wrong show for you.

5-18 "An Illegitimate Concern"

Written by: Marc Cherry and Jamie Wooten
Aired: February 12, 1990
Director: Terry Hughes
Guest Cast: David (Mark Moses)
Summary: Blanche finds out that her husband had a child out of wedlock.
Rating: ❤❤❤

"Oh I couldn't sleep. It must be from living with old people."—Blanche

A man arrives at Blanche's doorstep pretending to be a salesman, then comes back to tell her that he did investigating and found out George Devereaux was his father. Blanche delves into this further and realizes he's probably telling the truth. The Girls discuss their husbands' infidelities and Blanche mourns her own marriage.

We learn some fun facts about the women, such as Rose's Charlie did cheat. We learn that Andy Rooney once propositioned Blanche, and that she, even at her most romantic and starry-eyed, is never too starry-eyed to skip appraising a diamond gift.

The best part, which makes it a three-heart episode, is the few minutes of Dorothy and Sophia rehearsing their impersonation of Sonny and Cher singing "I Got You Babe." The studio audience clearly went bananas. It's just brilliant!

The actor playing George's son, Mark Moses, is a familiar face, having starred on everything from *Homeland* to *Desperate Housewives.*

Golden Nuggets

Rose tells Blanche that because of Charlie's rumored cheating, she and Charlie didn't have sex for a year, but in an earlier episode, she says they had sex every day, without fail.

We learn that Blanche dumped a high school boyfriend to date the coach. *Way* before the #MeToo movement.

St. Olaf's encyclopedia salesmen ran around with 26 books in each hand. And the 60's were tumultuous because of opposite-side-of-the-street parking. Also, strict divorce laws meant the wife gets to keep everything that doesn't ferment.

I love the ongoing Sophia vs. Gladys Goldfine feud. She's so passionate, and yet disappointed when Gladys turns out to be losing her marbles.

This episode marked Marc Cherry's first writing experience on *The Golden Girls*.

This makes me think about how DNA websites are uncovering family secrets. Let's face it. You either have siblings you don't know about, someone in your family's a serial killer, or your family's partially a different race or nationality than you originally thought.

5-19 "72 Hours"

Written by: Richard Vaczy and Tracy Gamble
Aired: February 17, 1990
Director: Terry Hughes
Guest Cast: Doctor (Tony Carreiro), Receptionist (Peggy Walton-Walker)
Summary: Rose finds out that she might have been infected with HIV from a blood transfusion during a gall bladder surgery years ago.
Rating: ❤❤❤

"I'm usually not like this. I've been using your toothbrush for months."—Sophia

This is an important episode—more important than I thought it was when I first watched. I grew up watching television shows introducing the idea of AIDs, and I remember first seeing it mentioned on newspaper covers in the summer of 1985. My views, even as a child, were progressive. I didn't grow up around homophobia or any "gay is evil" nonsense. So, I thought a lot of television shows demonstrating such bigotry were heavy-handed nonsense, almost insulting to small-town people. Were people really that ignorant?

Then I grew up and learned, oh yes, it's bad out there! In reading *Golden Girls Forever*, you can learn more about how much hokey episodes like this meant to them. Not just the fact that they mentioned AIDs by name, but that it's Rose who's in danger. The line where Blanche says, "AIDs is not a bad person's disease" brought tears to one writer's eyes.

It's also worth pointing out that Estelle Getty was such an early AIDs activist that she really didn't like having to play the scenes where she's afraid of drinking from Rose's cup. But these scenes were important, because they had to show everyone reacting differently—Dorothy is reasonable, Rose is petrified, Blanche is suddenly compassionate, and Sophia is paranoid.

Also, in the passages about the first few years of AIDs, I can't help but see the Covid correlations and how some people were ignoring the problem or just didn't care. People in the entertainment industry were watching their family members and friends die, and there was an attitude in many places that they deserved it. Estelle Getty's nephew had been HIV-positive at the time. All the actresses had been amazingly supportive to some of the writers who had people close to them dying. It's so reassuring to find out, in reading about actresses that I loved, that they were actually amazing women in every respect.

By the way, the B story of having Dorothy doing more charity work is a bit much. We get a serious issue episode about AIDs, but on top of that they pick a preachy B story. What nut came up with that? There should've been some silly Dreyfuss shenanigans or something going on.

Golden Nuggets

The scene between Dorothy and Rose is actually effective and it packs a whole lot in a few minutes—distracting yourself when you're sad, joining groups in high school to fit in, and just having a friend there when you need them most.

Blanche became a woman in a bayou. Or at least officially. Less officially in either a hot-air balloon or a pancake breakfast. But hats off to Sophia's sex talk to Dorothy as a child "Never let a boy touch you 'you know where.'"

Just a sidenote, but this ranch house has four bedrooms and two full bathrooms? That's pretty huge!

One of the best St. Olaf stories! Rose volunteers to be a sacrificial dumbest virgin to save her town… as only the dumbest virgin in St. Olaf would do.

Blanche admits that she had already gone for an HIV test, which is extremely responsible and progressive of her character. Go Blanche!
Saving the Wetlands is Dorothy's pet cause this week and she's doing press releases and a banquet. Holy moly! These ladies are really trying to save the world.

5-20 "Twice in a Lifetime"

Written by: Robert Bruce and Martin Weiss
Aired: February 24, 1990
Director: Terry Hughes
Guest Cast: Miles Webber (Harold Gould), Buzz (Eddie Bracken), Maria (April Ortiz), Malcolm (Douglas Seale)
Summary: Rose's ex-boyfriend Buzz causes a love triangle with her boyfriend, Miles.
Rating: ❤❤❤

"This is why when I was a kid, I had an imaginary mother."—Dorothy

The episode starts with Sophia hanging with a new crowd, asking Dorothy for money. By season five, she has established herself as the rebellious teen character, with she and Dorothy in an obviously reversed mother/daughter dynamic. Sophia's rebellious attitude ultimately lands her in a new apartment.

But the big story in this episode is the love triangle between Rose, Miles, and Rose's ex-boyfriend Buzz. Yes, Miles is back and getting pretty serious. Buzz is quite a character—an eccentric musician who left St. Olaf for show business. Miles pretends not to be jealous, and Rose pretends not to mind him *not* being jealous. But when Buzz wants Rose to leave town with him, Miles has had enough and fights for her. And Rose enjoys this.

Sophia's debacle concludes when she returns home and needs an alibi for the night before.

Golden Nuggets

The kitchen table discussion has a lot of strong moments, even without Sophia there (though her absence is noted by the ladies).

Lots of great quotes here!

"Is it possible to love two men at one time?"—Rose

"Set the scene, have we been drinking?"—Blanche

"I'm gone a few days and the slut's in here acting dumb, and the dumb one's out there acting like a slut."—Sophia

Sophia gets lucky with a retired jeweler named Shlomo. Blanche offers guidance on MFM threesomes and talks about a baseball player that had a hold over her. Wow, this is a lot.

Buzz is inherently a St. Olafian-type weirdo. His whole family is named Buzz. I also appreciate Little Yemini Raised by the Wild Moose who put him through medical school.

The Girls complain that Sophia isn't there in the middle of the night. Apparently, Blanche and Rose have been using her as a nightly therapist (who portions out hard candy).

This begins the slow reveal of Rose having over 50 boyfriends in high school.

Buzz left Rose to work in the Spike Jones band, and the writer cleverly lifted Sophia's goodbye/Adios joke from a Spike Jones record.

5-21 "Sisters and Other Strangers"

Written by: Marc Cherry and Jamie Wooten
Aired: March 3, 1990
Director: Terry Hughes
Guest Cast: Charmaine Hollingsworth (Barbara Babcock), Magda (Marian Mercer)
Summary: Blanche thinks her sister Charmaine's newly published, risqué novel is based on her life.
Rating: ❤❤❤

"You had no right to use my life for your book. I earned that A in History."—Blanche

By the fifth season, we know the women and their family drama. But like the first season episode between her and Virginia, it looks like Blanche and her sister are getting along. Charmaine is in good spirits and about to publish a novel, but the strife begins when Blanche believes the novel, *Vixen: Story of a Woman,* is about Blanche's sexual escapades. She raids Charmaine's book signing and accuses her of stealing Blanche's life stories.

On the B side, Stan's cousin Magda is staying with The Girls. Magda has left Czechoslovakia after the fall of Communism, but spends most of the time talking about how bad America is. She reminds me of a Russian girl that went to my high school. She wouldn't say the Pledge of Allegiance, bragged about eating bacon in Russia, and complained that I used to apply my makeup before class. I enjoyed that she spoke her mind all the time.

The episode ends with Charmaine telling Blanche that no, the book is not about her, but Blanche's ego got the best of her. They make up, Blanche gives her Big Daddy's watch that she had been promised in the will, and all is well.

Golden Nuggets

When the doorbell rings and Sophia says, "I hope it's death," I sympathized.

Sorry, Magda, Slurpees do not taste "natural and fruitlike."

Blanche and Charmaine had been busted by their father for skinny dipping, and Blanche tried to say they were practicing baptizing.

The City That Never Naps! Officially my least favorite city, but they taught Rose the street-smart savvy of coming in out of the rain.

I love Dorothy's Mrs. DooLittle story, recounting her sister Gloria, breaking her favorite doll. If any of my sisters wrecked my stuffed monkey, Hot Lips, there would be hell to pay.

The Girls have ongoing sibling feuds that don't end in middle age, which is one of the aspects of the show that I truly enjoy. Their relationships might evolve, but they carry the tumult of childhood right into old age.

5-22 "Cheaters"

Written by: Tom Whedon
Aired: March 24, 1990
Director: Terry Hughes
Guest Cast: Glen O'Brien (Jerry Orbach), Mr. Kane (Sam McMurray), Nun (Nancy Lenehan)
Summary: Dorothy begins dating Glen (the man she previously had an affair with) again.
Rating: ❤❤❤

"Self-respect is for losers like Rose." —Blanche

I like this episode because it actually follows up on one of the men they dumped a few years back. Dorothy's Glen is played by Jerry Orbach, my favorite *Law & Order* actor! It's an interesting spin to show that though the married guy sometimes does actually get divorced, you may not want him, even if he wants to marry you. Dorothy wisely sees that there's something sneaky in the way he says he's alone when his wife calls, even though they're getting divorced. Then again, maybe my horoscope lady is right—my standards are too high.

Anyway, the B story has Sophia and Blanche getting in trouble at the mall, where they get conned by a man and a woman dressed as a nun.

Golden Nuggets

Dorothy sort-of looks at the audience and says, "I guess it's a bad day for mothers," which Bea Arthur said this was her favorite line of the series.

Blanche's amazing advice to counter Sophia's "act like a lady" warning—If she's going to keep her feet on the floor, wear something you can throw over your head. By the way, Glen puts the moves on Dorothy pretty quickly.

It's suspicious that, in all the shacking up that Dorothy and Glen did in Season One, Dorothy is just finding out that he grew up in Brooklyn.

Pigeon drop (also known as Spanish Handkerchief) is a confidence trick in which a mark or "pigeon" is persuaded to give up money, in order to secure a larger sum of money or more valuable object. Two con artists pose as strangers to each other and manipulate a mark into finding a large amount of "lost" money.

The Boy Who Cried Continuously sounds like a perfect fable for that strange little town.

The Lupara (a solution to divorce, a sawed-off shot gun).

Most women wouldn't be so quick to leave as Dorothy. But when someone's instincts are to lie about where they are, and who they're with, that's the essence of who they are. And who wants to freaking deal with that?

5-23 "The Mangiacavallo Curse Makes a Lousy Wedding Present"

Written by: Phillip Jayson Lasker
Aired: March 31, 1990
Director: Terry Hughes
Guest Cast: Mangiacavallo (Howard Duff), Doug (Stuart Nisbet), Jenny (Tanya Louise), Man (Paul Collins), Waiter (Jonathan Schmock), Groom (Myles Berkowitz)
Summary: The Girls go to a wedding of the daughter of a man (Mangiacavallo) Sophia cursed years ago for jilting her at the altar.
Rating: ❤❤❤❤

"Is it just me or did anybody else notice the buns on that priest?"—Rose

Finally, a four-heart review! I love the whole spirit of this episode. And come on, a nonsensical curse that says, "May you be sterile, and may all your offspring be sterile." Good stuff. "May your socks always slip down your shoes." Even better! Coming from a jilted, 14-year-old Sicilian girl? That's the kind of rage you want to instill in a child early on.

The B story is that Dorothy reluctantly borrows one of Blanche's "many, many men." She rightfully thinks Blanche holds out on the good ones, and won't really give when it means something, which is on-brand for Blanche. And when Blanche finally delivers Doug, she flirts with him the whole night. Dorothy then fights with Blanche and ignores Rose, who they're supposed to be supervising because of her penchant for getting slutty at weddings (which we're just learning about now, but it's quite entertaining to watch Betty White play this). She ultimately goes to the airport to meet up with her boyfriend Miles.

Sophia ends the curse when Mangiacavallo announces to the wedding that Sophia was the one who left him and that she turned down his marriage proposal again, and he's now gay. That's how you enact revenge Italian-style—a 70-year waiting period and a public shaming. Also, the married couple makes up, Blanche and Dorothy reconcile, Doug delivers Rose to the airport, and Sophia and Mangiacavallo dance the night away.

Golden Nuggets

I love Sophia's face when Mangiacavallo's socks start to fall down and she realizes the curse is working.

Rose's problem has evolved into a serious fetish. She runs around wanting to take her clothes off and do the Hokey Pokey.

Apparently, Sophia had the "longest legs in the village."

This episode is light and sweet, but there's a message that one should probably hold on to love, passion, grudges, and friendships. Sophia does this well.

5-24 "All Bets Are Off"

Written by: Eugene B. Stein
Aired: April 28, 1990
Director: Terry Hughes
Guest Cast: Donald (Michael Ensign)
Summary: Dorothy struggles with a gambling problem she thought she recovered from years ago.
Rating: ♥♥

"Fine. I'll eat a bowl of chili and we'll talk later in your bedroom?"—Sophia

This episode is okay, but I have trouble with the premise. It gives us a sudden background tidbit about Dorothy that we never heard before—we learn that she had a pretty severe gambling habit. It's treated fairly realistically, and with humor, but it's out of left field and it bothers me. Kind of like when we learn Rose has a pill addiction. It also keeps her from getting a promotion. Maybe if this had been developed over the season, it would make more sense, but this show didn't do much as far as having a storyline evolve over episodes.

Anyway, Dorothy starts helping Rose out with her sudden painting obsession (also out of the blue), and gets addicted again, then later acknowledges her problem after trying to con Rose out of money to pay off a bookie. She finally agrees to go to Gambler's Anonymous.

The B story is funnier as Blanche gets frustrated by her coworker playing hard-to-get and keeps trying to seduce him. When he finally tells her that he has a rule about dating coworkers, he quits his job, and she decides that is when she will play hard-to-get. You gotta love that logic!

Golden Nuggets

Dorothy's brother Phil was not oiling his baseball glove in the bathroom as a child. According to Sophia, he was working on his simplicity patterns. And you know what, we believe her!

Blanche subscribes to something called *Slung* magazine, and I have to say, I'd love to hear some of the article titles.

Insights into Blanche's fantasy life are revealed when she thinks Rose too has the Invisible Man fantasy.

I'm coveting Blanche's nightgown game again in this episode.

The most famous religious painting in St. Olaf is (drum roll) *The Last Pancake Breakfast*.

This was the last episode that Terry Hughes directed.

Not to rain on Blanche's parade, but man, she comes on real heavy to her coworker, and then *she* feels humiliated when he turns her down. Then again, he's dating his coworker...

5-25 "The President's Coming! The President's Coming!" (Part 1)

Written by: Marc Sotkin, Gail Parent, Martin Weiss, Robert Bruce, Phillip Jayson Lasker, Tom Whedon, Marc Cherry, and Jamie Wooten
Aired: May 5, 1990
Director: Lex Passaris
Guest Cast: Agent Bell (Timothy Stack), Mr. Ha Ha (Alan Blumenfeld)
Summary: The Girls undergo interviews about their personal lives for an upcoming visit from President George H.W Bush.
Rating: ❤❤❤

"Oh, if you need to know anything else about me,
uh, I have pictures."—Blanche
"So do we."—Agent Bell

Prompted by President Bush coming to Miami to open a senior center, this is a two-part flashback show. I give all the flashback episodes three hearts, because if you like the show, you like the flashbacks. Of course, since this one is done at the end of the fifth season, we really get a full spectrum of character scenes and all the nuttiness that goes on in that house.

It begins when Blanche answers Special Agent Bell's simple "Tell me about yourself" question and we get a series of classic Blanche scenes—her romantic dry spell, her pondering breast implants, beating out the other Girls for a date with the hot caterer, and when she tried dirty dancing lessons. Agent Bell ends the meeting with a warning not to hit on the President.

Rose is next and she gets asked about St. Olaf for a change, giving us a montage of some of the silliest, like the stinky Sparehuven Krispies.

In the midst of this, Dorothy gets busted writing down issues she wants to discuss, which seems so quaint now. Like oh, Dorothy the Teacher wants to chat about public school funding? These days, it would probably be mentioned on Fox News as liberals using the media to shame Republicans. Insert nutty Ann Coulter-talking point.

This leads to two flashbacks of Dorothy's best retorts, and also some hot-button stuff like age discrimination in the workforce and sexual harassment.

Agent Bell reenters and says that the President wants to visit a more typical family. The Girls protest with some heartwarming stories, which actually works.

Sophia counters with some of their more contentious memories, like when they all fought over Fernando in Season Four. Agent Bell returns to tell them that yes, the President will be coming.

I like this episode since I can watch flashbacks all day, but I never felt like they did the perfect flashback show. As a fan, I would have wanted to see at least five of the best Sicily stories, five of the toughest Dorothy comebacks, five of the best St. Olaf tales, and the slinkiest Blanche scenes.

Golden Nuggets

Blanche and Rose dirty dancing is still way up there as far as one of the funniest scenes.

5-26 "The President's Coming! The President's Coming!" (Part 2)

Written by: Marc Sotkin, Gail Parent, Martin Weiss, Robert Bruce, Phillip Jayson Lasker, Tom Whedon, Marc Cherry, and Jamie Wooten
Aired: May 5, 1990
Director: Lex Passaris
Guest Cast: Stan Zbornak (Herb Edelman), Agent Bell (Timothy Stack), George Bush (Harry Shearer), Caterer (Raye Birk), Lou (Alan Blumenfeld), Fidel Santiago (Henry Darrow), Max Weinstock (Jack Gilford), Preacher (Harvey J. Goldenberg), Richard (Kevin McCarthy), Clerk (Pat McCormick), Bobby Spina (Jeffrey Webber), Secret Service Agent (Tom Lancaster)
Summary: Agent Bell returns to the Girls' home to discuss security for the President's visit.
Rating: ❤❤❤

"Maybe you ought to join an organization that's a little less fanatical in its devotion?"—Blanche
"Like what, Blanche, the P.L.O.?"—Dorothy

The flashbacks begin again as the Girls prepare for President Bush's arrival. It goes straight into the hilarious condom scene, with Dorothy yelling, "Condoms, Condoms, Condoms," which has become a pretty infamous meme! Then it goes into the scene where Dorothy and Rose insist on installing their first toilet, which goes on way too long.

The doorbell rings and Stan comes a knocking with a gimmick to sell at the event, and I have to side with Stan—why not give him a chance?

Agent Bell comes back at this time and says Sophia didn't pass clearance due to her little clandestine marriage to Max Weinstock, and we get three flashbacks explaining that relationship. Which of course, are some of my favorites of the series.

There's another check as to what organizations the women belong to: Dorothy is a member of the Sierra Club, Blanche is a member of the Daughters of the Confederacy, and Rose is a member of the Otto Club of St. Olaf. But more importantly, they feel the need to mention their membership to the Unauthorized Elvis Hunk-a Hunk-a-Burning Love Fan Club.

The President arrives and they have some weirdo actor doing an impersonation, surrounded by secret service agents that all recognize Blanche. Rose says something stupid about vacuuming the White House, while Sophia makes a good point about how he should have brought them a gift. And Dorothy completely freezes up like an idiot.

Golden Nuggets

The Sophia and Max Weinstock relationship unfolding is a gem.

All the Elvis impersonator guest stars! Roland August, Richard Bernard, Scott Gale, Blake Gibbons, Tally Lauriti, Rich Le Fever, Samuel Lloyd, Jay Pennick, Eddie Powers, and Quentin Tarantino.

The Golden Girls

SEASON SIX

6-1 "Blanche Delivers"

Written by: Gail Parent
Aired: September 22, 1990
Director: Matthew Diamond, James Vallely
Guest Cast: Rebecca (Debra Engle), Doctor (Ken Lerner), Tamara (Leila Kenzle), Mr. Ninervini (John O'Leary), Nurse (Marti Muller), Nurse (Diane Racine)
Summary: Blanche's daughter, Becky, arrives in Miami to deliver her baby.
Rating: ❤❤

"How come I always get the short stick?"—Sophia
"Because you are the short stick."—Dorothy

In this episode, we get a payoff from an earlier one where Becky considers artificial insemination. We find out that, yes, she did it, and yes, she is nine months pregnant. Blanche is still embarrassed. Keep in mind, this is 1990 and this was all new.

It's a weak opener that feels gimmicky, especially with the misunderstanding at the end where they call Rose's ice-skating coach by mistake. I also think that bringing in the idea that Rose wanted to be an Olympic skater at this point is left field. They get a bunch of jokes out of it, but they could have just had her take ice skating lessons.

Becky ultimately gives birth in Miami (with the obligatory television birth scene, with the mother screaming and everyone yelling "push") much to Blanche's chagrin, and Rose finally gives up her alleged ice-skating dream. Sophia continues to chastise Dorothy for her life choices, while Blanche and Becky find momentary peace with some dialogue where Blanche calls her brave. Also, Sophia professes her love to Dorothy after insulting her throughout the episode.

Golden Nuggets

Becky would not have been allowed to fly so late in her pregnancy.

She wants to conceive in a clinic and give birth in a bedroom (she has everything backwards). Blanche does make a good point.

There's a yawner of a joke regarding Blanche mistaking the baby's umbilical cord for a penis. Blanche, who has many children, shouldn't be so vapid.

Gross St. Olaf story alert: Lucky Gunther, delivering babies and handing out corn. Eww.

The theme of this episode is that parents are never satisfied with their children. Sophia heckles Dorothy, Rose is still trying to make her dead parents' dreams come true, and Blanche can't hide her dissatisfaction with Becky. But in the end, your kids have to do what they want.

6-2 "Once, in St. Olaf"

Written by: Harold Apter
Aired: September 29, 1990
Director: Matthew Diamond
Guest Cast: Brother Martin (Don Ameche), Dr. Warren (Scott Bryce), Attendant (Michael Goldfinger), Dr. Bob (Tom Henschel), Dr. Tess (Alicia Brandt), Man (William Bumiller)
Summary: Rose meets her biological father, a monk, while she's working in a hospital.
Rating: ❤❤❤❤

"I can't believe the last words I said to her were, 'Shut up, Zulu.'"—Dorothy

Most of the best episodes have a strong A and B story that somehow intersect, and that's the deal here. Rose accidentally meets her biological father, Brother Martin (played by Don Ameche), a monk who got her mother pregnant. Meanwhile at the same hospital, Sophia's having hernia surgery. In the midst of all of this, the Girls give Dorothy the guilt treatment for causing Sophia's hernia, because Dorothy had asked Sophia to help move furniture. That's a lot of shenanigans to keep track of, and it's all done seamlessly.

Rose flips out upon discovering the story of her pregnant mother being abandoned. Apparently, the monk chose the Order and then her mother died in labor. Rose treats Brother Martin at the hospital, and they reconcile.

Beyond Rose's paternity drama, Sophia's afraid that Dorothy is scamming her into returning to Shady Pines. She then gets misplaced in the elevator, providing some rich, comedic hijinks. She assumes she's in purgatory. When Dorothy and Blanche finally discover her, Sophia confesses that Dorothy shouldn't feel guilty because her hernia was caused by pulling a prank on a friend, not moving furniture.

Golden Nuggets

All references to Zulu, Queen of the Dwarf People crack me up.

We never find out why Ingrid's family never found out about the baby born in St. Olaf. The young girl got pregnant, gave up the baby and died, and no one ever reached out to the parents?

Blanche, once again, lands on the other side of the #MeToo movement, not knowing that you *don't* give sponge baths without consent. Oh, and Blanche's fantasy neighbors are Masters and Johnson.

This whole episode is a *back in St. Olaf,* but I love the tale of the baby in the basket, left with the crackers that didn't go with anything.

There's a nice acknowledgment that Blanche's father was a bigot, and it makes the future mammy episode more intriguing.

6-3 "If at Last You Do Succeed"

Written by: Robert Spina
Aired: October 6, 1990
Director: Matthew Diamond
Guest Cast: Stan Zbornak (Herb Edelman)
Summary: Stan finally becomes a success.
Rating: ❤❤❤

"Hey Stan, could I be a pothead?"—Sophia

Although the show didn't follow through with a lot of guest-star subplots, they did create an authentic arc for Stan. In this episode, he finally finds legitimate success. All his years hustling within the novelty business pays off with the Zbornie—his gadget for peeling baked potatoes without burning your hands. Stan becomes a millionaire overnight and wants to share his success with the ladies, but Dorothy isn't falling for it.

We know by now that Stan's not that bad, and that he's trying to make good on his failures. He's the ultimate underdog. And part of *The Golden Girls'* appeal is that it's about the underdogs that are older women. And Dorothy is probably the biggest underdog of them all. Now Stan being the one who threw Dorothy away, does make him somewhat unlikable, but the show was written smarter than that.

We know that Stan values the Girls as friends, and we see that he loves Sophia no matter how much she insults him. Stan and Dorothy smooth things out in the end and venture out to a business dinner, rekindling some of their old chemistry.

For the B story, we have Rose selling her junk to Blanche for 50 bucks, who finds old war bonds worth $50,000 which would inevitably bankrupt St. Olaf. Dorothy guilts her into destroying them, only to find out that St. Olaf could have paid for the bonds with their emergency statue budget. I think Rose owes her $50,000.

Golden Nuggets

It feels kind of weird knowing what Stan named his penis.

Beware of "attack cows," St. Olaf's secret weapon, parachuting onto enemy lines, trying to pull a ripcord. "No one expects trouble from a cow."

I wish we'd get a follow-up of whether there is a Blanche statue sitting in St. Olaf.

Stan buys Sophia presents, becomes a decent businessman, and expresses fears and vulnerabilities, all while planting a big whopper of a kiss on Dorothy at the end.

6-4 “Snap Out of It”

Written by: Tracy Gamble, Richard Vaczy
Aired: October 13, 1990
Director: Matthew Diamond
Guest Cast: Jimmy (Martin Mull), Emcee (Danny Breen), Mrs. Taylor (Lenore Woodward)
Summary: Dorothy tries to convince a hippie shut-in to leave his apartment.
Rating: ♥♥♥

“My mistake. I thought that because you looked like Yoda, you were also wise.”—Blanche

When Sophia delivers her Meals on Wheels in an apartment complex, Dorothy meets a man that was traumatized by the tumultuous 60’s and has become agoraphobic. She befriends him, trying to get him to leave his apartment. But she seems to be biting off more than she could chew here. When Jimmy decides he wants Dorothy to move into the apartment with him, she sees that she’s got a nutcase on her hands. But since this is a light sitcom, Jimmy comes around and becomes relatively cured by the end, even after a scare at the supermarket of being the 1,000th customer.

Special kudos to Sophia’s zest for charity work and staying engaged with the people she delivers too. Plus, the jokes about the woman who thinks Jewish people control the planet get me laughing every time.

The B story is about Blanche’s birthday approaching, and Rose planning a party against her wishes. Not only does Blanche not want the party, she doesn’t want her age disclosed.

Golden Nuggets

I love the end with Jimmy running out as Blanche walks into her party.

Blanche boasts the ability to make Mel Bushman’s head snap back, but this is called into question when Rose calls him Old Pez Head.

The sixth season is more overt in calling Big Daddy a racist, and this time Dorothy slips and refers to him as Grand Dragon.

Oh God, I’m older now than Blanche’s make-believe age. Sobering thought.

Based on the envelope Rose uncovers, we have to assume Blanche slept with a Florida governor, or he was just a big fan. My deductive reasoning leads me to think it's Bob Graham, Democratic governor from 1979-1987, or Bob Martinez, a Republican governor from 1987-1991. Both would have been married at the time. Hmm...

6-5 "Wham, Bam, Thank You, Mammy"

Written by: Marc Cherry, Jamie Wooten
Aired: October 20, 1990
Director: Matthew Diamond
Guest Cast: Mammy Watkins (Ruby Dee), Mrs. Contini (Peggy Rea), Jack (Richard McKenzie)
Summary Blanche's former Mammy reveals the shocking reason that she deserted Blanche as a young girl.
Rating: ❤❤❤

"Now listen up, you withered up Sicilian monkey."—Dorothy

We get a bit of a payoff here for all the references to racial bigotry regarding Big Daddy, clearly a man of a certain place and time. We get the revelation that he had a long, interracial affair with Blanche's nanny. Now some might look upon this and wonder if the power disparity between them negates consent (this was Georgia in the 1930's/40's), but the picture presented is this: Mammy returns upon hearing that Blanche is selling some of Big Daddy's belongings, and she wants a music box that she gifted him. According to her Mammy (played by iconic actress Ruby Dee), they were very much in love. So much so that they exchanged passionate and sexy letters for over 50 years. Blanche knew none of this as a 10-year-old child and just thought her Mammy left. I think this relationship is reflected as complicated, and I think Rue and Ruby do a great job showing it.

Meanwhile, for the B story, Sophia uses a matchmaker to fix Dorothy up with a felon. I feel that yes, Sophia oversteps some boundaries here, but there's an authenticness to her not wanting Dorothy to be lonely. And Dorothy's a little quick to dismiss white-collar criminal Jack as a suitor—he seems fine to me.

Golden Nuggets

The revelation that some hussy gave Big Daddy a music box. Bonanza!

Blanche learned as a teenager that smoking after sex is optional.

Anyone else think Mammy's delusional when she says that she and Big Daddy would have been married?

Rose trying to tell two St. Olaf stories at once. She's becoming quite the storytelling powerhouse.

I love the Girls' recollections of walking in on their parents having sex, with the highlight being Sophia telling a young Dorothy, "Mommy needs help."

Ruby Dee was the same age as Betty White, but made to look older.

Blanche states that Big Daddy was a Republican and therefore wouldn't have had an affair with Mammy, but actually it was Democrats that legislated Jim Crow Laws from 1865-1968. So, Big Daddy would've most likely been a Democrat.

6-6 "Feelings"

Written by: Jerry Perzigian, Don Seigel
Aired: October 27, 1990
Director: Matthew Diamond
Guest Cast: Dr. Norgan (George Wyner), Coach Odlivak (Robert Costanzo), Father O'Mara (Frank Hamilton), Kevin (Christopher Daniel Barnes)
Summary: Dorothy gets local pressure to pass a football player in her English Literature class. Meanwhile, Rose deliberates how to respond to her dentist groping her.
Rating: ❤❤❤

"Ma, you had relatives that threw priests out of windows!"—Dorothy
"That was business."—Sophia

This episode deals with Dorothy and Rose being disrespected by men for entirely different reasons. Dorothy tries to take a stand, by not doling out a passing grade to a slacker-athlete. She receives tremendous pressure, first from the coach, then a priest, then a dead fish at her door, until she relents.

Rose, on the other hand, gets molested by her dentist. The show always introduces these topics well. In an earlier season, a professor harassed Blanche by making her a lewd offer to sleep with him. So, they do a good job of showing that this happens to women of all ages. And now Rose, who is in her 60s at this point, is taken advantage of while under nitrous oxide. This dentist is a friend of hers too, and she's sure of what happened, but still second guesses herself.

I also appreciated that when Rose tells the Girls, they believe her and advise that she report it. They don't second guess or say that she was imagining it. They know this woman and they can tell by her body language that she's telling the truth.

Golden Nuggets

When Dorothy reads *A Tale of Two Cities* to Kevin in the hospital, it's endearing and lets us know that she is more than just a hard-ass substitute teacher.

Apparently, Blanche's name comes up in a lot of confessions. Oh, and Sophia claims to have slept with Freud.

Honorable mention to "*The Art of the Deal,*" a little book by a man named Donald Trump. I wonder what happened to that guy.

Rose's retelling of the St. Olaf Farm Animal race is a hoot.

Sometimes what sitcoms are fantastic for is giving us the right language for some of life's little hiccups. And now we know how often these little hiccups with creepy men happen. Report them if you can. And don't be the idiot that assumes women are mistaken or lying, because it's extremely rare that a person lies about being molested. The odds are excellent that a person's telling the truth.

6-7 "Zborn Again"

Written by: Mitchell Hurwitz
Aired: November 3, 1990
Director: Matthew Diamond
Guest Cast: Stan Zbornak (Herb Edelman), Abby (Siobhan Fallon Hogan), Mr. Percy (Dion Anderson), Cop (Stan Roth)
Summary: Dorothy considers getting back together with Stan, while Rose deals with an annoying coworker.
Rating: ❤❤❤

"Sticks and stones may break your bones, but cement pays homage to tradition." —Sophia

I love most Stan episodes. He blended right in and, except for maybe one episode, all the shows with him are good ones. This one begins an important subplot of Season Six: Dorothy and Stan getting back together. They just can't help themselves and are good together. And a little bad. Yet I liked them together. So, I'm just as confused as Dorothy.

Rose's dealing with a needy coworker has its moments, especially when Sophia tells the girl off, and the girl ends up becoming her supervisor. Yikes.

Golden Nuggets

The shock of seeing Dorothy and Stan naked, making out in the car, and getting busted by the cop was a solid shocker. But the following kitchen scene is the gold standard.

I love that Blanche's self-confidence extends to believing Dorothy has the hots for her. She is the "fatal blossom" indeed.

Rose divulges that she is a psychology aficionado because she read *The American Journal of Abnormal Psychology* in St. Olaf. She seems to have a good grasp of the term "cognitive dissonance" and of course her accurate read of Blanche as a "psychosexual bitch."

New info: Blanche reads comics, *Marmaduke* and *Apartment 3G.*

Fantastic stuff all over the place, from Rose's recap of her and Charlie's last night, to Blanche trying to analyze her best sex, then Dorothy's post-op Stan call, and Sophia realizing why they're all sitting around talking about sex.

This must be the fourth time that Rose tells the story of her last night with Charlie, and the women act like they've never heard it.

There are worse things than your supervisor being emotionally attached to you. Meanwhile I was thinking, "Wow, lots of women in top positions at that company. Good for them!" I guess it's all in the outlook.

6-8 "How Do You Solve a Problem Like Sophia?"

Written by: Marc Cherry, Jamie Wooten
Aired: November 10, 1990
Director: Matthew Diamond
Guest Cast: Mother Superior (Kathleen Freeman), Arthur Nivingston (Paul Wilson), Sister Claire (Lela Ivey), Sister Anne (Lynne Marie Stewart)
Summary When Sophia's friend, Sister Agnes, a former nun dies, Sophia decides to become a nun herself.
Rating: ❤❤❤❤

"10 days celibate!" —Sophia

In this episode, Sophia is at the top-level of her mischievous self and Blanche is at her best nonchalant, self-centeredness. It's endlessly quotable for a fan with tight one-liners and also endearing as Sophia joins a convent to honor her dead friend. Not all that believable as far as the plots are concerned, but passable in a sitcom world.

The B story where Blanche crashes Rose's car picking up rich guys, getting Rose sued, is even more fun. Blanche is relentlessly unsympathetic, but ultimately helps Rose set up the man faking his injuries, giving the audience one of the strongest laugh-out loud finishes.

Golden Nuggets

I like the finale, but the snippets of Sophia causing trouble in the convent, playing poker and rebelling are my favorite.

The things we learn about these ladies' sexual pasts never ceases to enlighten, and here, Sophia revealing that she wanted to become a nun when she was younger until Sal put his hand under her blouse, is the leading revelation.

Scientology threatened to sue *The Golden Girls* because of a scene where a nun catches Sophia with a copy of *Dianetics*, and Sophia says, "I thought it was Diuretics." That really speaks to Scientologists' lack of a sense of humor and pulling their weight around. I'm not a fan of such bully tactics, but the joke was pulled to save money.

Sophia loses a lot of best friends during this show and we never really meet any of them.

The Rorschach Test given by the nuns is actually something done as a nun screening process, as discovered by the writers.

The emotional punches in the show always demonstrate that the women are still trying to reinvent themselves and look for life's meaning. Sophia, in her 80s, prays to God and is still asking that question. That scene is what made her character so beloved and relatable to all ages.

6-9 "Mrs. George Devereaux"

Written by: Tracy Gamble, Richard Vaczy
Aired: November 17, 1990
Director: Matthew Diamond
Guest Cast: George Devereaux (George Grizzard), Sonny Bono (Sonny Bono), Lyle Waggoner (Lyle Waggoner), Policeman (Todd Jeffries), Maître d' (Brad Koepenick)
Summary Blanche's late husband George returns and reveals he faked his death. Meanwhile, Dorothy finds herself in the middle of a celebrity love triangle.
Rating: ❤❤❤

"Excuse me, I've had some experience in marital discord myself."—Sonny Bono

Normally, I'm not a fan of dream sequence episodes, but this one has such a whimsical nature and heart behind it, that I really like it. And Sonny Bono! I like the final reveal that this is a recurring dream of Blanche's, and that she finally gets to hug George, her husband. It's some well-deserved sort of closure.

And the wild dream subplot, with Dorothy choosing between Sonny and Lyle Waggoner is just quirky and imaginative. Why Blanche's recurring dream has a subplot where men are fighting over Dorothy is a mystery, but hey, dreams are weird. I like that the Girls all know about the dream at the end, and Dorothy asks if she picked Sonny. It's a great, humorous touch.

Golden Nuggets

Dorothy singing "I Got You Babe" on the phone with Sonny is just great. I love when Blanche tells George that she's only been with two men since he died. The real George would've never fallen for that.

Sophia's unexplained hatred for Lyle Waggoner is never explained.

The fact that it's a dream makes me wonder about George's confession that he always wanted to be a dancer. That is a strange seed in Blanche's subconscious.

Rose's tale of St. Olaf's famous OB/M.A.G (Obstetrician/Magician) is a quick one, but I relish in the details.

Lyle's comeback to Sonny when Sonny asks him, "How many gold records do you have?" is definitely worth the price of admission. Sonny Bono must have been a great sport (unlike the Scientologists).

6-10 "Girls Just Wanna Have Fun... Before They Die"

Written by: Gail Parent, James Vallely
Aired: November 24, 1990
Director: Matthew Diamond
Guest Cast: Tony (Cesar Romero), Miles Webber (Harold Gould)
Summary: Rose and Sophia take romantic pointers from Blanche, with disastrous results.
Rating: 

"Where did a sweet, Sicilian girl learn to do those things?"—Tony
"I live with a slut."—Sophia

This episode is a wild ride. Sophia takes Blanche's advice and hooks up with her crush, Tony, played by silver-fox Cesar Romero. And Rose abstains from sex with Miles to help bring aid to a St. Olaf drought. She avoids alerting Miles to her reasoning, because Blanche insists this will make him more attentive, but it just pisses him off instead.

Sophia gets a makeover and comes out in a red dress, in a scene that only the dynamic Estelle Getty could have pulled off. Well, Blanche's words get the Girls into trouble. Sophia tells Tony she loves him, but he doesn't return the words, while Miles gets frustrated with Rose. It turns out that Blanche's tutelage only works for superficial relationships.

Golden Nuggets

Sophia coming out in the red dress is epic.

Blanche confesses to 143 "relationships" so for superfans, that's a solid tally to work with. Now, she does say "relationship" so can we assume these are sexual partners?

Rose's hometown has a Department of Water and Coffee. During droughts, they remind people not to send water in envelopes. They also encourage abstaining during droughts (except for Ulf, the Umbrella King who has suffered enough).

This could have been a *Sex and The City* episode with Miranda, Samantha and Rose. We see Sophia unabashedly expressing her desires as she confesses that she just wanted to hear someone say "I love you" one more time. Blanche even discloses that she cries once a week, because her dating life doesn't quite meet all her needs. Rose, who's in the most stable relationship, is still making adolescent mistakes by not telling Miles what's going on.

6-11 "Stand by Your Man"

Written by: Tom Whedon
Aired: December 1, 1990
Director: Matthew Diamond
Guest Cast: Ted (Hugh Farrington), Librarian (Tom Nibley), House Boy (Andy Goldberg), Dreyfuss (Bear the Dog)
Summary: Blanche arranges a date at the library without realizing that the man is in a wheelchair.
Rating: ❤❤❤

"Well, mercy me, looks like my little magnolia just turned into a big ho."—Sophia

This is one of the many episodes where Blanche's love life doesn't work out, but there's a twist. It starts out in the same vein as the episode where Blanche dates the blind man and has to overcome her shallow limitations. But then she finds out Ted—the blind guy—is married. He's a disabled jerk in a wheelchair. It's actually quite heartbreaking when Blanche wants to reach out and commit, only to realize he's married. She recovers quickly, but it still stings. Also, sidenote, I personally didn't trust how he was sitting there in the library in that that argyle sweater.

The B story is a weak but harmless one, with Rose trying to sneak one of Dreyfuss' puppies into the house. Boy, is that puppy cute!

Golden Nuggets

Sophia pretending to be Blanche's mother/grandmother with a passing Southern accent, recounting fake childhood moments is definitely fun.

You'd think that the showstopper here is Blanche sleeping with a man in a wheelchair for the first time, but on a re-watch it seems the more spectacular revelation is that Dorothy slept with a pilot in an airplane bathroom. *Who are we to judge her?*

It is strange to me that Blanche doesn't ask a man over 50 whether he's married.

Dorothy's Bird on a Stick story is particularly depressing, encapsulating Sophia's insensitive parenting style. But hey, immigrant parents in Brooklyn, NY in the 20's were tough.

All men are created equal… and infuriating! What made this episode a standout about disabled people is that it showed them truly as imperfect. Not as heroic or overly sympathetic. Ted is a cheating married man, who just happens to be in a wheelchair.

6-12 "Ebbtide's Revenge"

Written by: Marc Sotkin
Aired: December 15, 1990
Director: Matthew Diamond
Guest Cast: Angela (Brenda Vaccaro), Father Salerno (Earl Boen)
Summary: Sophia's son, Phil, dies and she takes out her grief on Phil's wife, Angela.
Rating: ❤❤

"This is too funny, I have to go get my camera from the car."—Blanche

This is a funeral episode, but most importantly, it's a representation of the show again being supportive in its representation of the LGBTQ community. Even though we've come to understand Phil was not gay, but liked to dress in women's clothing, nowadays he would be considered a cross dresser. It's quite progressive, and this plays out with all the characters being quite open about it, while seeing the humor in it, but not making fun of the deceased brother.

But still, it is a kind-of-downer-preachy episode with no B story, which makes it kind of eh. It ends with a melodramatic scene where it's discovered that Sophia's hostility towards her daughter-in-law is because she's embarrassed about the cross-dressing. It might seem dated now, 30 years later, but it doesn't demonize Sophia nor did it shy away from the comedy in Phil being buried in a teddy. But it ends on a note of simple love between a mother and son, that defies sexuality.

Golden Nuggets

Funerals can be dramatic, like when the veiled "women" come to the funeral and Blanche calls them sluts.

Dorothy's sister, Gloria, doesn't show up at the funeral. That's just sloppy writing!

Besides the obvious LGBTQ-themed plot, Blanche wants to be buried as a majorette, which has some weird death and sex undertones (or maybe overtones).

Cher was a huge fan of the show, but turned down a few guest roles including the part of Angela. Ironic that Sonny Bono appeared in a previous episode.

Rose actually reunited Sophia and Angela with a story about her Cousin Ingmar.

This episode was nominated for a Writer's Guild of America Award.

Estelle Getty was reluctant about this episode, because she didn't want to do a scene where she walked up to her son's grave. So, they rewrote it where she says she doesn't want to.

Estelle Getty also had the writers remove jokes about Sophia insulting Phil because she didn't think a mother would be that heartless. As much as the show had the women being snippy with each other, there were lines they wouldn't cross.

6-13 "The Bloom is Off the Rose"

Written by: Phillip Jayson Lasker
Aired: January 5, 1991
Director: Matthew Diamond
Guest Cast: Miles Webber (Harold Gould), Rex (Mitchell Ryan), Flight Instructor (Don Mirault)
Summary: Rose eggs Miles on to be more adventurous, while Blanche becomes involved in an abusive relationship.
Rating: ❤❤

"Now I'm confused."—Miles
"And you know, I feel like I'm getting smarter." —Rose

This episode is your typical cautionary tale about women in abusive relationships, and it gets heavy handed. Part of the problem is that the audience doesn't get to see the abuse evolve in a realistic time period. Everything wraps up nicely and you never see Rex again.

So, Blanche's beau demonstrates some monstrous verbal abuse, which Dorothy warns her about. But Blanche dismisses all of this as Rex being a challenge, against Dorothy adamantly calling it abuse. Blanche deflects by saying that he never put his hands on her.

Meanwhile, Rose pressures Miles to be more adventurous, eventually landing the two of them a skydiving lesson. It's there he learns that Rose has been comparing him to her dead husband, which inspires Miles to go through with the skydiving to impress her. Except it lands him in the hospital, while Rose backs out. Pretty funny.

Golden Nuggets

The reveal at the end that Rose didn't jump out of the plane, for me, is the best part. Not a lot of laughs for me in this episode.

We learn a little bit about Rose and Miles sex life, which can go on for about four hours—apparently Rose spends a lot of time playing hard-to-get.

The joke about Blanche not knowing how to pronounce "bleach" might be the weakest joke of the entire series.

This is another episode that I think gets dragged down by the Dorothy-insults, from Blanche and from Sophia.

Per Miles' comments that he makes a better salad dressing than Paul Newman: Harold Gould (Miles) actually starred in two films with Paul Newman: *Harper* (1966) and *The Sting* (1973).

For me, this episode did raise awareness about physically abusive relationships and how they often start with nitpicks, insults, and demeaning someone in front of their friends and family.

6-14 "Sister of the Bride"

Written by: Marc Cherry, Jamie Wooten
Aired: January 12, 1991
Director: Matthew Diamond
Guest Cast: Clayton Hollingsworth (Monte Markham), Doug (Michael Ayr), Irving (Lou Cutell), Susan Doff (Mimi Cozzens)
Summary: Blanche has trouble with her brother, Clayton's decision to marry his boyfriend.
Rating: ❤❤❤

"Sleeping arrangements? What will the neighbors think if they see two men in my bedroom?" —Blanche
"They'll think it's Tuesday."—Sophia

This episode is basically the sequel to "Scared Straight" where Clayton, Blanche's brother, confesses to Blanche that he's gay. Although it seemed that she was okay with it at the time, this shows the reality as Clayton is planning to marry his boyfriend. As open and progressive as people might say they are, they often can't handle their relatives and friends being openly gay/bisexual or transgendered. It's probably a little bit better now, but not that much.

Homosexuals still get bullied, face job discrimination, threats of physical violence, and are ostracized from their families and religious institutions. Blanche is a character that wouldn't do any of that, but she's still embarrassed and as a result, is perpetuating homophobia. At that time, many relatives of gay people would have advised them not to go public. (Sidenote: I like the sentiment of the episode, but I don't think Clayton's very funny and I kind of wish Blanche's brother was as quick-witted and sassy as she was.)

On the B plot, Dorothy and Sophia are planning a banquet, and Sophia's promising sexual favors from Dorothy for lower prices. I couldn't help but think, how nice that there are so many eligible men that want to have sex with Dorothy? I mean Sophia's getting 40% discounts, so I guess, good for her?

As a C side plot, Rose becomes obsessed with winning the banquet award and we see her twisted nature. Here, she's completely joyous that an old woman (her award competition) has died, and then freaks out when they give the woman to the award posthumously.

Golden Nuggets

Sophia's speech to Blanche about why Clayton wants to get married is touching and so well-acted by Estelle Getty. Simple and to the point.

One of the most interesting sex education topics is brought up by Sophia when she asks Blanche, "why do men have nipples?"

This episode received lots of hate mail, which one of the writers saved.

I've lost count of the banquets on this series, but this banquet, which is for charity, and filmed in the same banquet hall as all the other big events of the show, is called the Volunteer Vanguard Award.

What many *Golden Girls'* episodes do really well is portray the gray area where we might not realize we're doing harm, even though we think we're trying to protect those that we love. Blanche struggles, but she loves and accepts her brother.

6-15 "Miles to Go"

Written by: Jerry Perzigian, Don Seigel
Aired: January 19, 1991
Director: Matthew Diamond
Guest Cast: Miles Webber (Harold Gould), Gladys (Mary Gillis)
Summary: Rose and The Girls find out that Miles is really in the Witness Protection Program and has to be relocated.
Rating: ♥♥

"Thank you Sheena, Queen of the Slut People."—Sophia

While The Girls are at Miles' house for an evening of poetry, he finds out that the Mob guy he snitched on, The Cheeseman, is allegedly dead, prompting him to confess to Rose about how he had worked for the Mob years ago as an unknowing accomplice.

But it's Rose who struggles, because much like the audience, she doesn't feel like she knows Miles anymore. Yet, he seems like the same perfectly boring dude. Except, oh no, The Cheeseman turns out to be alive and Miles needs to go back into hiding. Naturally, this turns out to be too much for Rose (duh, she's only been dating Miles for like, a year). It's an okay episode, with a preposterous plotline, and it's not one of my faves.

The B story has Blanche returning expensive dresses to retail stores after she wears them, with the tags still on them.

In a C story, Sophia is fighting with her friend Gladys, because Gladys is taking another friend to a Tony Bennett concert. I love Gladys—she's the only friend of Sophia's that doesn't seem to die.

Golden Nuggets

The kitchen scene where Sophia fights with Gladys made me laugh out loud.

Sophia and Gladys get a little raunchy when they act like absolute groupies for Tony Bennett and Tony Martin, with Gladys confessing to throwing underwear from the audience.

Love the St. Olaf story about the friend who thought that the chihuahua puppy was a rat.

This is the first episode where we get to see Gladys.

The writers were split on the ridiculousness of the Witness Protection plotline, and Harold Gould didn't care for it. Meanwhile, Betty White didn't even know it even existed.

This episode develops a story arc for Miles that devoted fans can never quite resolve. Before this, we knew him to be widowed and a college professor, and Rose even met his daughter. What the heck?

6-16 "There Goes the Bride: Part 1"

Written by: Gail Parent, James Vallely, Mitchell Hurwitz
Aired: February 2, 1991
Director: Matthew Diamond
Guest Cast: Stan Zbornak (Herb Edelman), Cop (Jack Yates), Lois (Toni Sawyer)
Summary Dorothy and Stan decide to remarry against Sophia's wishes.
Rating: ❤❤❤

"I'm from Sicily. You know what the #1 export of our village is? Ransom notes!" —Sophia

In this episode, Dorothy and Stan are still sneaking around behind Sophia's back. I love this two-parter because if you've been reading this (and I truly thank you), you know I love Dorothy and Stan, and all their dysfunction. I like them fighting, apart, and I like them trying to get back together.

When Dorothy finally confesses the relationship to Sophia, she fakes chest pains (as an Italian mother might do). Then, after Dorothy agrees to Stan's "ring-in-a-potato" proposal, Sophia sticks her head in the microwave (as a desperate Italian mother might do). Standard stuff for a not-so-subtle woman, really. But I have to say, Sophia is sometimes written as uber-toxic. She is so negative towards Dorothy reconciling with him, but in other episodes recognizes that he's a decent guy.

In the B story, Rose gets harassed by a woman who thinks Rose is dating her ex. This escalates through to Part 2.

Golden Nuggets
The scene with Blanche and the cop (who she thinks is a stripper) could have just been silly, but McClanahan is just so good at being sexy.

At the end of the last episode, Miles was still in Witness Protection, but Rose says he's in Europe with students?

When Dorothy says that Stan is a solicitous lover, am I the only one who looked that word up? Solicitous: c*aring, attentive*

Sophia has some solid threats for Myra that come from her Sicilian heritage—piano wire and ransom notes. As an Italian, I'm just going to say that no, I am not offended by the stereotype. I think the jokes are funny.

The writers really hammer home how insulting Sophia is to Dorothy about her dating life, and I wonder if they wanted people to connect constantly insulting a daughter to the quality of companions she chooses. Meanwhile, Dorothy dates a lot for a 60-year-old woman and has already been married. And she seems to have friends to invite to the bridal shower. So, she's relatively likable and successful.

6-17 "There Goes the Bride: Part 2"

Written by: Gail Parent, James Vallely
Aired: February 9, 1991
Director: Matthew Diamond
Guest Cast: Stan Zbornak (Herb Edelman), The Caterer (Raye Birk), Myra (Meg Wyllie), Father Monroe (Jack Blessing), Marvin Mitchelson (Marvin Mitchelson), Erroll (Milt Oberman), Photographer (Cleto Augusto), Truby (Debbie Reynolds)
Summary: The Girls interview prospective roommates as Dorothy plans to marry Stan, as Sophia tries to sabotage the wedding.
Rating: ❤❤❤

"If I can see over the counter, I'm their new fry cook."—Sophia

I like this episode, but have to agree with the online consensus that Debbie Reynolds didn't seem like a good fit to replace Bea Arthur as the new, fourth *Golden Girl*. She just reeked of too much movie-star power. Her lines are funny enough, and God knows she delivers them well, but that character replacing Dorothy, the eternal underdog, just wouldn't have worked.

The better scenes are the rehearsal for the wedding, and Rose trying to protect herself from Myra, who is clearly a harmless old lady. Rose's ideas are so very Rose (not opening mail, doorbells that bark).

Golden Nuggets:
What a riot when Sophia comes out yelling, "The dogs are on my tail again..."

I love that Sophia wants to give Dorothy a sex talk after all these years, because she thinks she's doing it wrong. You don't hear much about mothers giving daughters this talk after middle age.

It's not that it's a surprise that Blanche didn't have underwear on at her wedding, it's that she says it was the right thing to do that gets the real laugh.

A lot of hubbub went on during the announcement of this episode, because there were rumors that Bea Arthur wasn't going to continue the show, and people thought Debbie Reynolds might replace her.

I like how on TV, so many weddings are just right in the backyard, easy-peezy. People should take this as a lesson and save about $50,000.

Blanche and Rose's bridesmaids' dresses are adorable, but Dorothy's headpiece is horrendous.

The way they end it, with Stan having his lawyer give Dorothy a prenup, feels clumsy and staged... I just don't buy it. He was a jerk, but I don't believe he would've sprung that on Dorothy that day.

6-18 "Older and Wiser"

Written by: Tracy Gamble, Richard Vaczy
Aired: February 16, 1991
Director: Matthew Diamond
Guest Cast: Mr. Porter (Don Lake), Mr. Lewis (Julius Harris), Lucille (Carol Bruce), Smokey (Bill Wiley), Sarah (Ellen Albertini Dow)
Summary: Sophia learns that her new job was set up by Dorothy to keep an eye on her.
Rating: ❤❤❤

"Maybe you know her by her Indian name—
Dances with Nobody."—Sophia

This episode was the first on a VHS tape that I brought to college, so I feel like I've seen it a lot. It's not a four-heart one for me, but it's got solid laughs and a tender heart. The idea that Sophia never lets herself fall into some of the trappings of old age is her core quality, and even though she's got the gray hair and old-lady handbag, she's active with a zest for life. When she becomes the Activities Director of the nursing home (even though it's a ruse), she really wants to bring life to the place.

The B story has quite a few twists and they're all hysterical, as Blanche gets offered to model for a Penny Saver, only to learn that they want Rose to be the hand model, and ultimately finds out that it's really a liver spots ad. Hey, a paying gig is a paying gig, you know?

Golden Nuggets

The ridiculousness of Blanche concocting an elaborate plan to retrieve all the Penny Saver copies, with Rose having to hit on a lesbian truck driver, is quite the height of *Girls Gone Wild.*

Not to go all farm-animal-anatomy on you all, but Rose mentions assisting a chicken in a breech birth... even I know chickens lay eggs... she probably meant to say cow?

More of a sex question here? What was Blanche's involvement in delaying the torch's arrival at the 1964 Tokyo Olympics? And what was she up to since she was most definitely married to George then?

St. Olaf is apparently the broken hip capital because they *actually* put their elderly on pedestals.

I enjoy "the pieces of the puzzle" anecdotes regarding Rose.

There's a good one here about Big Daddy carousing for trouble and finding "New York lawyers."

Am I the only one who thinks that this nursing home is probably nicer than most these days? It's a sad commentary, but wow, acting like this is such a bad place to end up makes me think that what was bad in 1990 is not quite the same as what is deemed bad in 2021.

6-19 "Melodrama"

Written by: Robert Spina
Aired: February 16, 1991
Director: Matthew Diamond
Guest Cast: Mel Bushman (Alan King), Andy (Tommy Hinkley), The Robber (Jonathan Schmock), Bill (Phil Forman)
Summary: Blanche tries to make her casual relationship with Mel Bushman into a permanent one.
Rating: ❤❤❤❤

"You know, I learned something tonight. A relationship is more than sex and fun and good times. Thank God this isn't a relationship."—Blanche

This is the episode where we finally meet Mel Bushman of the famous saying, "Bushman awaits" and he doesn't disappoint—because he's played by the great Alan King! This is the ultimate "Friends with Benefits" episode, and as Blanche says, "do you realize how rare it is to find out the person you're sleeping with is the person you love?"

Of course, Mel and Blanche don't end up together as she likes to date high-rollers, and Mel understands that they're truly just friends.

I love the B story here on many levels. It opens well with Rose getting the job as lead reporter, resulting in Sophia doing a spit take. But the big reveal is that she doesn't film the robbery, instead focusing on the cat show, which is on one hand moronic, but on the other a strange statement of journalistic integrity. As the Girls say, "wow."

Golden Nuggets

This is a tough choice for favorite scene, but Rose's interview of Dorothy is so good with the nursing home reveal. But the Mel Bushman/Blanche fight and make-up scene at the end is also a fantastic scene.

If you're sensitive to slut-shaming, Sophia's slams at Blanche before her date with Mel won't appeal to you. I, however, enjoyed them.

Rose does try and work within some storytelling parameters here, but ends up sending Blanche right to Mel's house.

Blanche carries keys for all her booty calls, with their names on them. That is not just trampy, but efficient. What a lifehack for sleeping around!

Blanche's character remains a pioneer in that she's unapologetically proud of how she lives her life, and that she's looking for love, but also enjoying multiple sexual partners at any given time. She not only stands up for her lifestyle, but sort of pities everyone else.

6-20 "Even Grandmas Get the Blues"

Written by: Gail Parent, James Vallely
Aired: February 16, 1991
Director: Matthew Diamond
Guest Cast: Rebecca (Debra Engle), Actress (Allison Robinson), The Director (Jonathan Schmock), Jason (Alan Rachins)
Summary: Blanche pretends her daughter is her granddaughter to appear younger to a man she's interested in.
Rating: ♥♥♥

"Wait a couple of years and Medicare will pay for it."—Dorothy

This episode is another prime example of me liking the B story more than the A. The Festival of the Dancing Virgins is a hoot, but I think Blanche pretending to be a young mother is just too silly to monopolize the plot. And six seasons in, it's just annoying that the episodes with her children are always about them being mad at her. Rebecca needs to lighten up—her mother is fun and she's a buzzkill. And as for Jason, Blanche's love interest, he always rubbed me the wrong way. He's a little too John Malkovich for my taste. At least Sophia guilts Rebecca into staying at the end.

There's a C story about Sophia lying to Dorothy about her IQ, but it feels like it's there just to take Dorothy down a notch. And by the way, an IQ as high as 173 is extremely suspicious. I mean, Dorothy wasn't even at the top of her class or really known as an honor student. It's almost like Dorothy has to be an idiot to believe Sophia here. I rarely believe anyone who says their IQ is above 150. I'll need to see that test result.

Golden Nuggets

The final festival scene where Blanche and Rebecca make up, and Sophia reveals that she lied to Dorothy, is probably the best.

I think we all know why Uncle Gino adopted the goat.

Mensa is what they called the Men's' room at St. Olaf's only Italian restaurant.

This must be some sauce. Sophia's great-grandmother added heat to the special sauce. Sophia added a mouthful of wine. Rose adds Frosted Flakes.

Tradition! I like this idea of the Festival of the Dancing Virgins and I say if you can, start it up with the women in your family, to tell the men in your life, *what kind of tramp do you take me for?* Also, develop a recipe (and one moron to do all the work for you), and throw rocks at a trollop. That's better than most holiday functions.

6-21 "Witness"

Written by: Mitchell Hurwitz
Aired: March 9, 1991
Director: Zane Buzby
Guest Cast: Miles Webber (Harold Gould), Karl (Barney Martin), Louise (Beth Grant), Woman #1 (Marla Adams), Mrs. Ward (Gloria Dorson), Woman #2 (Elise Ogden), Barbara Weston (Kristy McNichol)
Summary: Rose begins dating again, only to realize she is dating the man that's trying to find and kill Miles.
Rating: ❤❤❤❤

"Silly rabbi, tricks are for kids."—Sophia

This episode has a lot of laughs and surprises. Like many of the sixth season episodes, it has an A, B, and C story, and they culminate in an uproarious final scene. There are some twists as well. First, that Rose is dating and that the man she's dating is the Cheeseman, Miles' enemy from the Mob. Further, Miles has been hiding in the Witness Protection Program as an Amish man. Okay, it all seems a little ridiculous, but it works.

On the B side, we find out Blanche is trying to get into one of those Southern Confederacy clubs called Daughters of the Confederacy. And in investigating her lineage, she finds that her great-grandmother was Jewish *and* from Buffalo, New York. All of this while Sophia is looking for her lost glasses, running around in sunglasses as a continuous gag.

Golden Nuggets

Blanche's confession, then revelation, then begging at The Daughters of the Confederacy ceremony is a treasure.

Blanche says her mother's name was Samantha Roque. In the first season, her name was Elizabeth Ann Bennett (and Blanche's middle name is Elizabeth). Damn this show for not having a show bible.

Blanche to the rescue with the handcuffs—but they were a gift.

This episode is the first *Golden Girls* episode directed by a woman, Zane Buzby. It's also the first solo episode written by Mitchell Hurwitz, creator of the mega hit *Arrested Development.*

We get a lot of insights into Blanche's southern heritage here, but we also see that Blanche can cling to her Southern pride without crossing the line of becoming a bigot herself.

I really dig when Blanche says, "Oh you lost the war, get over it," That should be yelled at every moron that owns a Confederate flag—a flag that represents the losing side of a war from the 1860's that fought for the right to own slaves. As one of my favorite comedians, Sebastian Maniscalco would ask, "Aren't you embarrassed?"

6-22 "What a Difference a Date Makes"

Written by: Marc Cherry, Jamie Wooten
Aired: March 23, 1991
Director: Lex Passaris
Guest Cast: John (Hal Linden), Don the Fool (Sid Melton), The Minstrel (Nick Jameson), Juggler (Dana Daniels)
Summary: Dorothy finds out the real reason her prom date never showed up years ago.
Rating: ❤❤❤

"He's a guy who humiliated me."—Dorothy
"Could you narrow it down, Dorothy?"—Rose

This is another episode about how Sophia wreaked havoc on Dorothy's early life. This time, we learn that she sent away Dorothy's prom date, John Neretti, which sent her into an insecurity tailspin that probably led her to her going out with Stan and getting pregnant. Or at least, that's how Dorothy sees it.

Apparently, John wasn't dressed appropriately, and Sophia had told him to come back and change, but he never did. Dorothy scolds Sophia, but all ends well when she and John have a lovely second prom. John, by the way, played by Hal Linden, is super handsome.

The B story has Blanche trying to lose weight for her anniversary, so she can take a picture in her wedding dress as an homage to her dead husband. That is loyalty. And Blanche nearly goes nuts with one of those near-starvation diets, where you eat just one shake and one meal. She nearly kills Rose for eating her strawberry drink and "sensible meal."

Golden Nuggets

The Medieval restaurant that Dorothy and John go for their date is clever. Grog and pheasant for everyone!

Other episodes claim Dorothy went to the senior prom with Stan. The writers should've just made it a school dance or junior prom.

Dorothy gained 18 pounds once on a "weight-loss through sex" diet with Stan. This makes me want a flashback scene or episode... or maybe not.

Junior proms just for people named Junior? Uh, that's when the St. Olaf anecdotes get a little much.

Of course, Blanche celebrates her wedding day in a red dress, but I feel like Rose would've already known this, having known her for more than five years.

The waiter at the medieval-themed restaurant also played Sal, so Dorothy has her father interfering with her date from the great beyond!

I've read much criticism of the show, that the women focused on each other's bodies too much, but hello? Women talk about diets and tease each other about their bodies. Especially that generation. It's realistic and relatable.

6-23 "Love for Sale"

Written by: Jerry Perzigian, Don Seigel
Aired: April 6, 1991
Director: Peter D. Beyt
Guest Cast: Stan Zbornak (Herb Edelman), Uncle Angelo (Bill Dana), Terry (Lou Felder), Man (Tom Seidman)
Summary: Stan wins Dorothy at a charity auction, while Uncle Angelo comes to visit with a request.
Rating: ❤❤❤

"Oh God, he's proposing to her again. Will one of you raise your standards please?"—Sophia

Well, Stan is back and Uncle Angelo is visiting, so the audience should know it's going to be a good time. I can't help but love these guys. This time, Stan's Uncle Morris died and left Dorothy and Stan a building, which is a nice problem to have. At the same time, Dorothy is participating in one of those charity auctions you only see on TV, where people bid for dates. I have never heard of anyone going to one of these things, but I feel like every 80/90's sitcom had them. So, inevitably the women plan to get someone to bid on Dorothy, only to be outbid by Stan.

Meanwhile, Angelo moves into Stan and Dorothy's building and complains about everything. Worse, he tops it off by not inviting her to his party. But the theme of the episode is really that Stan's trying to keep Dorothy in his life.

Golden Nuggets

There are some silly snippets during the auction that crack me up, like the woman being sold for four dollars. I guess a personal goal of mine is that if I'm ever auctioned off, I sell for more than that.

There's a level of kink in this episode, when Dorothy expresses interest in binding and gagging. Plus, Uncle Angelo confesses to playing hide and seek with a date named Bambi. All this kink, and all Blanche wants is a better-looking gardener.

At the St. Olaf Bicentennial, livestock get treated very well, including being taken to fancy restaurants in limousines.

Angelo brings a tale of sex and woe this episode, as he arrives broken-hearted from what was clearly a relationship with a younger woman who left him for a younger man.

So... Angelo doesn't invite Dorothy to his housewarming party? I can't help but wonder if the reason why Bea Arthur wanted to end the show was because the writers made her the butt of so many jokes about her unpopularity.

6-24 "Never Yell Fire in a Crowded Retirement Home: Part 1"

Written by: Gail Parent, Tracy Gamble, Richard Vaczy, Tom Whedon, Mitchell Hurwitz
Aired: April 27, 1991
Director: Matthew Diamond
Guest Cast: Herb (Stanley Kamel), Detective Parres (Richard Riehle), Dr. Stevens (Jeffrey Tambor)
Summary: Police suspect that Sophia was responsible for the fire that burned down Shady Pines years ago—except Sophia has no recollection of how it started.
Rating: ❤❤❤

"Did you see Awakenings? Throw a ball at me."—Sophia

This episode brings us a flashback episode for one of the more ridiculous reasons—hauling Sophia off to prison, because an old lady on her deathbed confesses that Sophia set a nursing home on fire. Seems kind of flimsy to me, but it gets the women talking about the past, so we get clips.

Blanche talks to the lawyer about...

How she couldn't be a southern writer.

How Rose tried to motivate Blanche to lick envelopes for the Friends of Sea Mammals.

Sophia wakes up stressed and reminisces with The Girls about...

Mixing up Martha Ray and Madge jokes.

One of the best Warren Beatty jokes I've ever heard.

The time she discussed 10 days without a bowel movement.

The Girls in the Kitchen reminisce about all the times they told stories in times of crisis

Sophia's tale of being Picasso's lover.

Sophia and Dorothy try and de-stress Rose when Charlie's pension runs out.

Sophia tries to knock Rose out with a pan when she can't sleep.

Rose's stories about being level-headed

How she volunteered once as the town's dumbest virgin.

How she led a protest against tuna fisherman.

How she tried to get Dorothy to a meeting with a story about her "fricken" cousin.

Dorothy attempts to soothe Sophia with flashbacks of...

How Sophia had her back against that jerky doctor that tried to tell her she wasn't sick when she had Chronic Fatigue Syndrome.

How Sophia and Dorothy dressed up as Sonny and Cher.

How Sophia broke Dorothy's watch trying to do a magic trick.

Sophia and Dorothy fighting about Sophia staying out too late.

Sophia and Dorothy fighting about going to the doctor.

As the flashbacks roll in Part 1, Sophia becomes more convinced that she might have been involved in the fire, causing Sophia to contemplate jumping bail and moving back to Sicily.

Golden Nuggets

It's a small thing, but I love that Rose tells the lawyer that she's the level-headed one.

As much as I love the idea that the fire occurred on my Aunt Marilyn's birthday, the pilot mentions that it's June, so one of these episodes has that date wrong!

It's in the flashbacks, but Sophia getting lucky with a jeweler named Shlomo is still a testament to how active her sex life was for an 80+ year old. Blanche getting lucky was par for the course.

Having two pigs on her back and pushing a wheel barrel is apparently a method to relax in St. Olaf. No explanation given.

I probably would choose 80% of these scenes and knock some of them out. I can't for the life of me figure out why some of them were chosen. I figure they had done earlier clip shows, with episodes from earlier seasons, so they wanted to pick from the last two seasons.

By the end of Season Six, you'd want the best of the best, clips that show the zaniest moments, which is a challenge since YouTube has so many montages like 15-minutes of Rose's best St. Olaf stories, or Dorothy's best zingers. But Clip Shows were before YouTube, and if you're watching them, you're probably a fan of the show and this is the stuff you want to see.

6-25 "Never Yell Fire in a Crowded Retirement Home: Part 2"

Written by: James Vellely, Tracy Gamble, Richard Vaczy, Don Seigel, Jerry Perzigian
Aired: April 27, 1991
Director: Matthew Diamond
Guest Cast: Herb (Stanley Kamel), Detective Parres (Richard Riehle), Stan Zbornak (Herb Edelman), Ted (McLean Stevenson), Laszlo (Tony Jay), Ernie (Richard Herd)
Summary: Sophia becomes more and more desperate at the prospect of going to jail for the fire years ago at Shady Pines.
Rating: ❤❤❤

"And we can start by ruling out the obvious. Does Sophia have any friends who are or ever have been circus fire eaters? Would she like to meet some?" —Rose

Part 2 continues as Sophia tries to run off to Sicily, and the Girls attempt to figure out how the Shady Pines fire started. These flashbacks are a whole lot of fun, because there's a bunch of them in a row that just focus on some of the Girls best sex talks (except the first one where they just sing to a baby).

The time they sang Mr. Sandman to get a baby to sleep.

Rose persuades Blanche to date Miles.

A "birds and bees" chat the Girls have on the lanai.

The Girls have a sex talk in the kitchen that Rose doesn't realize is about sex.

The Girls talk about how they all became pregnant.

After Sophia gets busted trying to escape to Sicily, the Girls continue their trip down memory lane:

Blanche and Rose talk about how they had late-nights with Sophia whenever they sought out advice.

Blanche confesses to the Girls that her daughter wants to have a baby via artificial insemination.

Soon after, Blanche's idea for a sexy prison party gets them telling more dating stories:

Sophia tries to get more money from Dorothy, because her cash went to a male stripper.

Blanche flirts heavily with Stan's brother, who turns out to be a dud.

The Girls fawn over the Hungarian artist named Laszlo.

Rose and her impotent boyfriend get all hot and bothered at a restaurant.

Golden Nuggets

The montage of sex discussions is by far the most enlightening, and as I've stated many times, a precursor to the brunch sex talks that *Sex and The City* was famous for.

Rose learns that the Shady Pines inspector came into money days after the fire. But the real revelation comes when the song "One for My Baby" inspires Sophia to recall what happened that night. She heard the smoke alarm go off and noticed smoke coming from the heater. She realizes she's no arsonist and that she saved her friend.

A deathbed confession would be considered hearsay.

Blanche's prison party ideas confirm my notion that she would just be the best roommate.

St. Olaf has a combined prison deli? After binge watching this show, I totally want to create a live version of this make-believe town.

Sophia knows how to party—Nyquil shooters and S'Mores! I wanna say that every five years after 35, this idea becomes more and more appealing.

That's some strong investigating from Rose this early on in her journalism career!

6-26 "Henny Penny - Straight, No Chaser"

Written by: Tom Whedon
Aired: May 4, 1991
Director: Judy Pioli
Guest Cast: Frank Nann (George Hearn), Delivery Boy (David Jay Willis)
Summary: The Girls perform a school play for children when the cast catches the Measles.
Rating: ❤❤❤❤

"Off to the Rusty Anchor. Spring Break comes but once a year."—Blanche

I love this episode. I swear I saw it ranked low on a list somewhere, which is just nuts. This late in the series, I was surprised that the show came up with a gimmick to get the Girls on stage that was actually inventive *and* funny. Of course, you have to have three talents that can sing and dance, plus Estelle Getty looking absolutely adorable in an elf costume. They perform a musical version of *Henny Penny*, but Rose has issues with the traumatic ending where the animals get eaten by Foxy Loxy. I think she's right, that is scary. But it does introduce another important concept to children—don't follow strangers offering shortcuts.

The B story is amusing, even though it involves a slightly dark turn of events. A fake obituary announces Blanche's death, and she waits for flowers and grieving from the city of Miami, but even Mel Bushman doesn't seem particularly fazed. He does send flowers announcing his return to his ex-wife though.

The C story has Sophia playing a chess game via mail with her old friend in Italy.

Golden Nuggets

I like how Blanche flaunts her sexuality, even in a play geared at children. "You can learn how to be the most popular birds in the barnyard—safely."

Rose's tale of living in a burning building is absolutely ridiculous, but Betty White just makes it freaking work.

One of only two episodes directed by a woman.

Marco the Goat Boy—the Sicilian who liked fat, hairy chicks—is the reason Sophia plays chess by mail.

Fairy tales are filthy. At least, they are when you look at them through Blanche's eyes. She discusses cod pieces, *Humpty Dumpty*, and the profound influence *Snow White and The Seven Dwarves* had on her, while Rose counters with the lame St. Olaf ones. Blanche's are dirtier. And better.

The Golden Girls

SEASON SEVEN

7-1 "Hey, Look Me Over"

Written by: Mitchell Hurwitz
Aired: September 21, 1991
Director: Lex Passaris
Guest Cast: None
Summary: Rose believes Blanche had an affair with Charlie after she finds a picture of them together in an old camera.
Rating: ❤❤❤

"Look at her, the woman is hundreds of years old. She should be carbon dated."—Dorothy

Decent opening for the season, though it covers some emotions we know all too well at this point. Blanche is being slut-shamed to a degree, but if she had indeed slept with Charlie—a married man and her future best friend's husband—it's understandable that it would cause a rift. Then we have the B plot where Sophia doesn't want to get her hearing checked, but it turns out that Dorothy has the hearing problem and worries about feeling old.

Both of these plots end with sly little twists: Charlie's camera was full of double exposures, and Dorothy—who had chastised Sophia for being terrified of aging—is afraid of it too.

Golden Nuggets

Dorothy's insults to Blanche, as delivered by Rose, and Sophia's teasing of Dorothy with the microphone are great.

Blanche's initials are B.E.D in this episode, obviously to make a joke work, but in previous episodes they were B.M.D. for Blanche Marie Hollingsworth Devereaux. Also, Sophia has mentioned having a hearing aid in an earlier episode.

Blanche keeps a book record with gold stars to indicate whether she had a good time.

Rose bought Charlie a piece of land in Minnesota for his last birthday. You should have seen his face when they delivered it.

A sonata is a piano solo and would not need a full philharmonic orchestra.

By the end of the series, Sophia is the only character that has not been involved, in some way or another, in adultery.

Blanche's backstory of sexual prowess is deep in the minds of the audience at this point, and Rue plays Blanche's vacillating emotions well. She genuinely might not remember everyone she has slept with, even with her album full of dates and lovers, but I like that at this point it's an understood personality attribute—not a defect, nor something Blanche backs away from him in the slightest.

7-2 "The Case of the Libertine Bell"

Written by: Tom Whedon
Aired: September 28, 1991
Director: Lex Passaris
Guest Cast: Spade Marlowe (Todd Susman), Lieutenant Alvarez (Tony Plana), Kendall Nesbit (Richard Roat), Posey McGlynn (Claudette Sutherland), Maître d' (Nicholas Kepros), Vaczy (Zach Grenier), Waiter (Leland Orser), Gloria (Gloria Cromwell), Man (Tim Haldeman), Woman (Margery Nelson)
Summary: A pretend murder mystery becomes real when Blanche ends up the murder suspect.
Rating: ❤❤❤❤

"I take offense to that. No one in my family, ever, ever, left a body to be found."—Sophia

The concept of this episode had been done before, but it's well executed, and they had me the first time I watched it. The Girls participate on a murder mystery retreat, hosted by Blanche's employer. I guess employment was a lot more fun in the early 90's, because I have never heard of a job letting an employee and three of her guests participate in such an event. But here it is!

Blanche, once again on the flip side of the #MeToo movement, is unapologetically trying to sleep with her boss for a promotion and ends up discovering his stabbed body. After initially panicking, Dorothy gets it together and solves the murder, which turns out to be staged.

There are so many fun scenes, like Dorothy using deductive reasoning to work through the supposed murder. Dorothy and Sophia have had many interesting interactions in the series, but Dorothy taking a knife to Sophia's throat is definitely a highlight. Plus, Rose being constantly called out for being a St. Olaffian is a running gag that works every time.

Golden Nuggets

Mel Bushman is apparently still in the picture, though sight unseen.

Rose was known as the Sherlock Holmes of St. Olaf. (She figured out which one was Shinola, the hard way!)

During the fake murder, the suspects are named after Dorothy's siblings, Phil and Gloria.

Dorothy taking out a compact to check whether Sophia is breathing is a callback to the pilot, where she does the same thing.

I enjoy episodes that have Dorothy shine, and here we have her using her literary skills and streets smarts to solve both cases. The seventh season seems to want to redeem the character.

7-3 "Beauty and the Beast"

Written by: Marc Cherry and Jamie Wooten
Aired: October 5, 1991
Director: Lex Passaris
Guest Cast: Nurse DeFarge (Edie McClurg), Melissa (Alisan Porter), Woman (Barbara Alyn Woods), Clarice (Mindy Ann Martin), Stage Manager (Robert Gould)
Summary: Sophia becomes attached to a home nurse, who drives the other Girls crazy. Meanwhile, Blanche pressures her granddaughter into a beauty pageant.
Rating: ❤❤❤

"Ma, you know the rules. When we eat Mexican food, you sit at the counter."—Dorothy

This is a genuinely good Sophia episode and exhibits well how strong *The Golden Girls* remained until the last season. My ratings for the Season Seven don't really drop at all. Like other seasons, I have mostly three heart ratings with a sprinkling of two and four hearts.

This episode starts with Sophia displeased with the idea of a nurse (especially the Angel of Death from Shady Pines) after her ankle injury, but grows to love having a sort-of evil henchwoman in the house to fulfill her every need. We've seen other shows have a sick character ring a bell, but when Sophia tests the nurse by seeing how quickly she'll answer, I relished it. Nurse DeFarge quickly gets on the Girls' nerves and Dorothy tries to fire her, but Sophia pretends that her ankles aren't healed, because she likes the extra caretaking.

The B story is slightly weak, with Blanche acting as a horrific stage mom to her granddaughter. I did laugh at her mocking the other kids though, and truthfully, this isn't the harshest representation of children's pageants (it's tame by *Toddlers & Tiaras* standards).

Golden Nuggets

Dorothy's affirmation that she's Pussycat one, not Pussycat two, is so fantastic.

Whatever Blanche does at 2:00 a.m. with gentlemen callers, she could lose her balance and chip a tooth if interrupted.

Edie McClurg accidentally ran over Betty White's foot with a wheelchair on tape night, but White being such a pro, improvised so they could still use the footage.

Rose lost the Little Miss St. Olaf contest 23 times, once to an imaginary playmate. Dorothy had it worse. She lost a pageant and her mother was a judge.

Blanche never gets it right with her kids and grandkids, and Sophia and Dorothy are naturally adversarial. But don't you just enjoy Sophia getting pampered? And don't you wish Melissa would just get on stage and dance to please Blanche?

7-4 "That's for Me to Know"

Written by: Kevin Abbott
Aired: October 12, 1991
Director: Lex Passaris
Guest Cast: Don (Richard Stahl)
Summary: Dorothy finds out that Sophia was married to someone else before Dorothy's father.
Rating: ❤❤❤

"Dorothy, guess what I have under my robe?"—Blanche
"That guy from the circus?"—Dorothy

When Dorothy starts collecting information for a family history, she finds out a big secret—Sophia had a previous marriage that she fled in order to start a life in America. By the way, the guy she was going to marry was going to inherit the family business of revenge.

On the B side, Blanche is trying to build a hot tub and Rose totally snitches to the city inspector, who tells Blanche that it requires a small fee. Rose then blabs about Blanche renting to her friends, and tells her that she needs to come up with a $10,000 boarding license. The Girls vote to have someone move out and end up writing Dorothy's name, which I think is particularly mean. In the end, they come up with the idea to become owners of the house instead of renters (which is something that would only happen on television).

Golden Nuggets

When Sophia discovers she's finally a landowner—we can all relate to that. It might take us until the age of 87 to own property. "Rabbits, I'm gonna raise me some rabbits as big as your head."

At other times in the series, Sophia is married to Sal when she sails to America.

Blanche running a home of wayward ex-cons is a better idea than the actual spinoff, *The Golden Palace*.

Everyone in St. Olaf can be traced back to the same brother and sister. I can't believe it took seven seasons to get to that joke. Don't forget that the St. Olaffians were one of the seven lost tribes of Israel.

Sophia calls Uncle Nunzio's goat a pet. I have to say, the repeated jokes about Sophia's crazy Sicilian relatives and their sexual proclivities are still gold.

Since the whole episode is a "Picture it, Sicily," also note that Sophia's father single-handedly invented the ransom note.

At first, Sophia's secret didn't seem like such a big deal, but I get that it'd be something an elderly person of that era would keep quiet. But why does she keep the photo?

7-5 "Where's Charlie?"

Written by: Gail Parent and Jim Vallely
Aired: October 19, 1991
Director: Lex Passaris
Guest Cast: Miles Webber (Harold Gould), Stevie (Tim Thomerson)
Summary: Rose thinks her dead husband is contacting her from the dead.
Rating: ❤❤❤

"Remember Shady Pines?"—Dorothy
"Yeah, it wasn't so bad."—Sophia
"I heard they sold it to some Germans."—Dorothy

This episode is clearly inspired by the movie *Bull Durham,* with Blanche trying to mentor the baseball player. Sophia even mentions the movie, which makes the reference pretty obvious. Part of Blanche's tutelage is having Stevie wear lingerie under his baseball uniform.

The A story though is that Rose receives a ring from Miles, and in clear panic about the intensity of their relationship, starts to believe she's seeing signs from Charlie, from the great beyond. Capitalizing on Rose's insanity, Sophia pretends to be possessed by Charlie, all for her own amusement.

In a C plot, there's more communication with The Great Beyond when Dorothy starts to write a letter to her deceased father. She shows some real issues with her parents' neglectfulness, but decides against it, and instead thanks her mother for a good life. Simplistic, but well done.

Blanche's plot concludes when Stevie chooses her over a baseball gig, but also decides to keep wearing women's clothing which Blanche had initially advised him to do. Except Stevie wants to wear women's clothing out—and that proves too much for her.

Golden Nuggets

When Stevie shows up at the house in the dress, and Dorothy says, "this is too funny," Bea Arthur really was in stitches.

Blanche makes a decent point when she says Dorothy's just jealous that she has a sex life, and all she has is her mother.

Rue McClanahan hit that softball on the first try.

Betty White looked at Tim Thomerson in the dress before filming and said, “You’re the ugliest woman I’ve ever seen.”

Apparently, Charlie and Rose had worked out that after one of them died, the cantaloupe on one side of the fruit salad will be their message. It got me thinking about whether people have worked out words and phrases to give psychics proof that their loved ones are sending them messages.

7-6 "Mother Load"

Written by: Don Seigel and Jerry Perzigian
Aired: October 26, 1991
Director: Lex Passaris
Guest Cast: Stan Zbornak (Herb Edelman), Jerry Kennedy (Peter Graves), Millicent Kennedy (Meg Wyllie), Dr. Halperin (Steve Landesberg)
Summary: Stan tricks Dorothy into going to therapy to try and get her back.
Rating: ❤❤❤❤

"I said it before, and I'll say it again. Sluts just heal quicker."—Sophia

This episode is strong. The A plot has Stan going to therapy to deal with his relationship ending, and he invites Dorothy to go with him. She reluctantly goes, only to realize he's trying to win her back. There's a depth to the Stan/therapy scenes that pulls together his whole character arc for the series. And Peter Graves does a solid job playing the psychiatrist who's smart, but slightly dysfunctional—kind of like Stan and Dorothy. Well done.

For the B plot, Blanche dates a minor celebrity—a local news anchorman, Jerry Kennedy. He seems perfectly fine, and Blanche returns from their evening together more than pleased, but finds his mother at the door scolding her. This culminates in an awkward, but hilarious meeting at Blanche's house where she goes toe-to-toe with the mother. The A and B stories both deal, rather efficiently, with a man's dysfunctional mother issues.

While all that madness ensues, Rose is planning a roast for Jerry, and being herself, can't seem to find anything to make fun of even though everything he says is clearly *roastable*.

Golden Nuggets

The therapy scene between Dorothy, Stan and Sophia is therapeutic.

Blanche returns from her evening with Jerry and gives way too many metaphors for a passionate evening at a motel. Like Dorothy says, you might need to bathe after listening.

I love the levels of quirkiness in a tale of the most famous psychotherapists: The Freud Brothers, Sigmund and Roy, authors of, *If I have all the cheese I want, why am I still unhappy?*

"In the old days, if you had a problem, you fought, you drank, you got a little on the side. You dealt with it."

This is the fourth character played by Meg Wyllie.

Maybe all our issues stem from our childhood hang-ups with our parents.

7-7 "Dateline: Miami"

Written by: Marc Cherry and Jamie Wooten
Aired: November 2, 1991
Director: Peter D. Beyt
Guest Cast: John (Pat Harrington, Jr.), Bob (Fred Willard), Arnie (Lenny Wolpe), Myron (Jesse Dabson), Young Dorothy (Lyn Greene), Young Stan (Richard Tanner), Pregnant Woman (Margaret Reed), Woman (May Quigley), Policeman (Stan Roth), Waiter (Nick Ullett)
Summary: The women recall different, and sometimes weird dates they've had, while Dorothy goes out on a Saturday night.
Rating: ❤❤❤❤

"If you need something to keep you occupied tonight Rose,
why don't you take out a good book and see
if you can find Waldo."—Dorothy
"I've never liked her."—Rose

This is a wraparound episode, with three vignettes about dating disasters.

The first is of Rose going on a date with a jerk, with red flags all over the place, but she doesn't seem convinced until policemen take him away for being a freeway flasher. The red flags included a pregnant woman showing up to ask why he hasn't called, and a male waiter that clearly had a relationship with him. She confesses that she gave him one more date—you think this is ridiculous, but I have friends this gullible.

The second vignette is my favorite. Blanche brings home a date who turns out to be a virgin that left the priesthood. As she attempts to seduce him, Rose gives the boot to his friend, the creep attempting to seduce her. He's pretending to be a widower at this point, but his wife is actually alive and on a fat farm. When the priest and the creep leave, Blanche attempts to get a kiss from Rose.

The third story is set in the 1950s where Sophia tries to persuade a young man to go out with Dorothy. Instead, Dorothy tells Sophia that she's pregnant and going to marry Stan. She reassures Sophia that she's still going to finish school to become a teacher.

Golden Nuggets

Blanche trying to hook up with the virgin priest by taking out a box of sex props, after saying “Boy this brings out the artist in me,” is hilarious.

Blanche, willing to use Rose for her New Year’s kiss, is a nice nod to some sexual fluidity on Blanche’s part. A selfish nod, but a nod nonetheless.

Sophia’s story shows Dorothy confessing her pregnancy, with Stan saying that he “doesn’t know how this happened.” Sophia responds, “Maybe you drank out of the same cup?”

This episode reveals a surprising side of Dorothy—she’s having a quick few-hour fling and openly disclosing it to the Girls. She’s evolved since Season One.

7-8 "The Monkey Show" (Part 1)

Written by: Mitchell Hurwitz and Marc Sotkin
Aired: November 9, 1991
Director: Lex Passaris
Guest Cast: Gloria Petrillo (Dena Dietrich), Stan Zbornak (Herb Edelman), Angelo (Bill Dana), Dr. Halperin (Steve Landesberg), Carol Weston (Dinah Manoff), Stage Manager (Ed Hooks), Cop #1 (Jonathan Schmock), Cop #2 (Matthew Saks), Davey Cricket (Don Siegel), Bryan Norcross (Himself), Man (Richard Reicheg)
Summary: As Dorothy tries to end her relationship with Stan, her sister Gloria comes to visit and ruins everything.
Rating: ❤❤❤❤

"Good news Dorothy. I'm off the monkey."—Stan

Another great one with a strong opening: Sophia alerts Dorothy to the hurricane by telling her of her friend Ida waking up with a leg cramp, a better harbinger of bad weather than any weather app. Sophia also lets her know that her sister is coming to visit and has lost all of her money, which makes Dorothy—having always been jealous of Gloria—absolutely gleeful.

Meanwhile, with this drama unfolding, Stan is still seeing his therapist and has transferred his love for Dorothy to a fake, stuffed monkey the size of a traffic cone. And God bless Herb Edelman, he does seem emotionally connected to the monkey that he's carrying around. Once at therapy, Stan's psychiatrist has him and Dorothy bid farewell to each other, which Dorothy has no problem with. She even comes home to celebrate, not realizing that's insensitive to the Girls whose husbands have died.

In the B plot, Rose is planning a telethon to save a lighthouse, and has to cast the talent along with Blanche. Blanche, predictably, is nixing all the women auditioning—even ones who are clearly talented.

It's no surprise that I love this two-parter since it has Stan and Angelo, plus Stan and Gloria getting caught in bed together. I think that's the fourth time people get busted in bed together on this show. No one locks the door when they have sex in this house, which is a huge oversight! But this might be the worst kind—an ex-husband with his sister-in-law (ick!).

Golden Nuggets

The ending is a shocker, but the therapy scene with the monkey is stellar.

There actually was another Gabor sister, Magda. So, Dorothy would technically be Magda in Sophia's metaphor.

Some insights into Rose's kink level emerge when she says she broke off her passionate affair with a man who played Goofy, because he took off the Goofy head. Also, she needs a separate biology course if she thinks a man's sex can grow back.

Gloria had previously been played by Doris Belack.

This episode was part of a high-concept NBC night, where the hurricane theme ran across three shows during the night, because they all took place in Miami: *The Golden Girls*, *Nurses*, and *Empty Nest*.

We've already learned this season that Stan transferred his feelings for his mother to Dorothy and Sophia. Now he's transferring them to a monkey, and then to Dorothy's sister. This is one needy guy. Might I suggest a pet?

7-9 "The Monkey Show" (Part 2)

Written by: Mitchell Hurwitz and Marc Sotkin
Aired: November 9, 1991
Director: Lex Passaris
Guest Cast: Gloria Petrillo (Dena Dietrich), Stan Zbornak (Herb Edelman), Angelo (Bill Dana), Dr. Halperin (Steve Landesberg), Carol Weston (Dinah Manoff), Stage Manager (Ed Hooks), Cop #1 (Jonathan Schmock), Cop #2 (Matthew Saks), Davey Cricket (Don Siegel), Bryan Norcross (Himself), Man (Richard Reicheg)
Summary: As Dorothy deals with the fallout of Stan and Gloria sleeping together, the women prepare to head to a shelter to flee from a hurricane.
Rating: ❤❤❤❤

"In some primitive societies, they leave their elderly out in a field for large birds to feed on. Where do we draw the line?"—Dorothy

I do despise the beginning of this episode because it has someone fainting and believing everything was a dream, which has just never happened to anyone I know in real life. But I forgive the episode because it's still an entertaining one with lots of great moments.

Dorothy invites Dr. Halperin over to help her process things—which again, not exactly realistic—and he shows up with Harry Weston's daughter, Carol, who he's dating. He's also shared info about his patients with her, including Stan and Dorothy. Dorothy finds out that Sophia set Gloria up with Stan and she's rightfully pissed. I mean, that's some dysfunctional madness. Back at the telethon, Rose is having trouble filling the eight-hour time slot, but the lighthouse gets destroyed by the hurricane and the studio gets turned into a shelter.

Meanwhile, Dorothy tries to evacuate only to find Stan and Gloria in bed again, this time trying to get the cops to help her shoot them. I don't blame her. Justifiable homicide, I say! Sophia flees to her brother Angelo's for guidance, and he simply explains that you can't give a man to one sister, like he's a stick or a doll. Angelo explains it better, trust me.

Back at the studio, Blanche hoards candy so that they can resell it to the evacuees, and Dorothy decides she still wants Stan in her life. She makes up with Sophia, then Gloria, and then Gloria and Angelo all concur that yes, Stan is a yutz.

Golden Nuggets

I like the Sophia and Angelo scene when he says, "Then the boy will marry you!"

Stan and Gloria having sex in Dorothy's bed is some epic sick stuff. I mean Stan has some money, stay out of your ex's bed!

There's an old Minnesotan farm song called, "I never thought I'd grow a hair there."

How to deal with emergencies in the Italian army? Scream for help!

By the end of the series, I was surprised that the character who was always insulting Stan had quickly turned around to set him up with her favorite child. It's a major blind spot for sure, and lacking in basic decency, but it made me wonder which one of the writers had a mother who hated them.

7-10 "Ro$e Love$ Mile$"

Written by: Don Seigel, Jerry Perzigian, Richard Vaczy, and Tracy Gamble
Aired: November 16, 1991
Director: Lex Passaris
Guest Cast: Miles Webber (Harold Gould), Angelo (Bill Dana), Mort (John P. Connolly), Barry (Harvey Vernon), Maître d' (Joe Mays), Waiter (David Pressman), Guido (Phil Leeds)
Summary: Rose becomes so frustrated with Miles' cheapness that she decides to go out with Blanche's rich Texan friends. Meanwhile, Blanche loses control while babysitting Sophia.
Rating: ♥♥♥

"You called missing persons in Sicily? You got it wrong. You call them to lose somebody." —Angelo

This episode has equal time devoted to each of the A/B stories, with Rose having trouble with Miles and Sophia sneaking off to Sicily while Dorothy's off on a cruise. Getty is adorable and rascally when she closes the door and says, "fasten your seatbelt, slut puppy," when she surreptitiously rifles through Dorothy's drawer and finds "the list," and when she travels to Italy, only to return like an innocent little gypsy claiming that she returned from a short walk. She's so cute.

Miles and Rose are also quite lovable, as Rose sort-of cheats on him just to get taken to a fancy restaurant as he's become even cheaper than usual. Miles busts her and confesses that his doctor recently told him that he's in good health and that he has to tighten his budget.

Golden Nuggets

I like when Guido responds to Sophia's confession with an "eh."

Dorothy says she gambled on the cruise, but we know that Dorothy has a gambling problem, so this seems like a continuity error.

Blanche loves a tight man, to a distracting degree.

"Frickin frugal" is a Scandinavian term.

Dorothy's off on another romantic venture this episode, and it sounds like it could be the same guy from "Dateline: Miami."

One of the biggest laughs the show ever received from the live audience came from Uncle Angelo's line about shaving his back for nothing.

The old-age budget: Miles has a point to be stressed about living to 100, having a girlfriend, and paying for meals. A man his age might have budgeted to 75 or so, and the thought of living passed 85 would be terrifying.

7-11 "Room 7"

Written by: Tracy Gamble and Richard Vaczy
Aired: November 23, 1991
Director: Peter D. Beyt
Guest Cast: Sal Petrillo (Sid Melton), William (Roy Brocksmith), Man (Gibby Brand), Sheriff (Don Stark)
Summary: Blanche takes the Girls back to Atlanta to stop the demolition of her grandmother's home.
Rating: ❤❤❤

"How long do you think you can stay handcuffed?"—Dorothy
"My personal best is 32 hours. But of course, then I had someone to play with."—Blanche

I always like episodes that show Blanche's softer side, and in this one we get to see her innocent side, listening to wind-chimes outside her grannie's window.

We do have to suffer through one of those "This is Heaven" scenes, where a character almost dies and ends up in some kind of pseudo-heaven. Sophia has a clear-as-day trip to the afterlife where her deceased husband gives her a message for Dorothy, but also tells her that God isn't ready for her yet. Dorothy thinks it's a hallucination until Sophia reveals that Sal used her nickname "spumoni face."

As corny as I find the "heaven" stuff, Sophia's response—like mooning a chain gang, and wanting to eat possum—is genuinely good stuff. The A story is about Blanche going to Atlanta, to stop her grandmother's home from being knocked down. There, she confesses to Dorothy that she talks to her grannie when she visits, and proceeds to handcuff herself to the radiator. Dorothy tries to talk sense into her, but she won't listen. Eventually, Blanche emerges with wind-chimes and says her grannie told her to go; she falls asleep that night listening to them.

Golden Nuggets

I love when they throw Rose out of the car for singing. Sometimes, Rose deserves it.

Blanche's 32-hour handcuffing record is impressive and requires follow-up questions (like many of Blanche's stories).

When Blanche recalls the young boys singing, “I see London, I see France, I see Blanche’s underpants...” Do you laugh, cry, or both?

This is Sid Melton’s final episode.

While filming, Rue McClanahan was accidentally handcuffed to that radiator when the keys to unlock her broke.

I enjoy the nuance in the spiritual subtext. Blanche feels her grandmother’s presence in that room, and through those wind-chimes. It’s all a hunch. And I think it’s the lack of specificity that makes Dorothy more accepting of her experience.

7-12 "From Here to the Pharmacy"

Written by: Gail Parent and Jim Vallely
Aired: December 7, 1991
Director: Lex Passaris
Guest Cast: Bill (Bruce Kirby), Security Guard (Ed Call), Woman (Sergia Simone)
Summary: A soldier returning from the Gulf War, wants to rekindle his romance with Blanche.
Rating: ♥♥♥

"Old age? You don't leave fingerprints anymore.
Hopi Indians are walking around saying,
'How does she do it?'"—Dorothy

This is a bit of a snoozer, and they do a similar joke in a later episode, where Rose can't remember an old boyfriend. Anyway, a soldier that Blanche slept with comes home and reaches out, and although she doesn't remember him, she does spend the night with him again. But ultimately, she realizes she doesn't want to be exclusive with him and calls it off—which is Blanche for "this guy's a little boring."

The redeeming part of the episode is the B plot, where Sophia thinks that Dorothy's trying to kill her because she found out there's $35,000 in Sophia's will that she's been hoarding. This becomes a point of serious contention because both Gloria and Phil had been sending Sophia checks all these years, while Dorothy made financial sacrifices. As a lesson to Sophia, Dorothy financially cuts her off, but only for a brief time before deciding that she likes taking care of her mother.

Golden Nuggets

One of my favorite running jokes is Dorothy putting the tea aside, saying it's for her mother. But I have to throw in that I love when she sips the coffee and says if she hadn't had to save so much money, she wouldn't be living with a slut and a moron.

Apparently, Blanche gets really old-fashioned after a one-night stand. Especially when they give her a hat.

Rose had to fight a cow named Henrietta in court for her Charlie's estate, in front of Henrietta's peers.

Sal never saw Sophia naked.

By this point—although the jokes are strong—the plots seem a little repetitive. We just learned that Miles is struggling with his finances, and now we discover that Sophia is worried about what to leave her kids when she dies. And the Blanche's commitment phobia we've seen a few times. But still, more than a few laugh lines.

7-13 "The Pope's Ring"

Written by: Kevin Abbott
Aired: December 14, 1991
Director: Lex Passaris
Guest Cast: Miles Webber (Harold Gould), Priest (Steven Gilborn), Detective (Fred McCarren), The Pope (Eugene Greytack)
Summary: When Sophia finds out the Pope is in town, she tries to find a way for him to bless her sick friend, Agnes.
Rating: ♥♥♥

"I paid with nature's credit card."—Blanche
"You never leave home without it."—Dorothy

This episode combines a lot of ideas that the *Golden Girls*' fans have already embraced. Sophia's superstitious Catholicism practice where she would steal the Pope's ring for magical powers, there's Blanche's toxic dating advice, as well as the Girls competing, this time, Blanche and Dorothy competing for who gives Rose the best birthday gift. Dorothy gets her an original Mickey Mouse Club sweatshirt, while Blanche literally gives Rose the gift of being suspicious of her boyfriend—a detective to follow Miles around.

Miles comes over to spend time with Rose and she confesses that there's a detective spying on them, causing him to storm off. Meanwhile, Sophia returns from visiting the Pope and quickly divulges to Dorothy that she stole his ring after his security team whisked him away.

Soon after, Rose discovers that Miles is having a secret, surgical procedure. Sophia comes in to say that she can't find the ring, but Dorothy figures out that she's lying and gives it back to the Pope's handler. Sophia's disappointed and goes to the hospital to visit her sick friend, while giving Dorothy the guilt treatment.

When Rose visits Miles, she learns that he's had his eyes done to look younger. The episode ends with the Pope dropping by the hospital, and Rose returns home to say that he answered her prayers and blessed Agnes!

Golden Nuggets

When Sophia tries to turn water into wine with the Pope's ring, I giggled.

Miles feeling frisky on the lanai just seems so disrespectful. The lanai is sacrosanct.

Charlie and Rose making out in St. Olaf's most romantic trysting place, "Mt. Pushover." Now that's a good one.

Blanche never tells the story, but it involved a men's club, a vine rope, and a large bottle of Absorbine Jr.

There should be a type of women's detective class where you learn—with the best of intentions—how to find out if a man has a violent history, is married, etc. Blanche is on to something.

7-14 "Old Boyfriends"

Written by: Jamie Wooten and Marc Cherry
Aired: January 4, 1992
Director: Peter D. Beyt
Guest Cast: Thor (Ken Berry), Sarah (Betty Garrett), Marvin (Louis Guss)
Summary: Rose can't remember an old boyfriend that comes to visit.
Rating: ♥♥♥♥

"I've got man trouble and I need help from someone with experience. I hear you're a tramp, Rose."—Sophia

This episode begins with Blanche and Sophia going through the Personal Ads to find Sophia a date. Meanwhile, Rose can't recollect a former boyfriend, Thor Anderson, that's coming to town. Then, when Sophia's date, Marvin, comes to the door, he brings his sister. But Sophia can't be picky, so she lets the sister come along.

Rose confesses perhaps the biggest secret of the show—she had 56 boyfriends in high school, which is why it's difficult to remember Thor. This incenses Blanche, as Dorothy names Rose the grand poobah of sluts. Sophia enters with her own man trouble, exclaiming that when she tries to make out with Marvin, his sister Sarah interrupts.

Thor dines with Rose and Blanche, telling them that she was his first kiss, prompting Rose to remember that she dated Thor to make Charlie jealous. Sophia tries to kiss Marvin when he reveals that Sarah's really his wife, and she's dying, so they created the ad to find him a wife. Uh-oh. The bigger shock is that Sophia's considering it.

Later on, Rose invites Thor over to let him know that she never loved him. He kisses her farewell, and she finally remembers the kiss, but Thor is and was a terrible kisser. She doesn't tell him that though. I don't think the kiss looked that bad. Sophia and Dorothy go to Sarah and Marvin's, and although Sophia tries to go along, she sees the love they have for each other and backs out of the plan. Each confesses they were doing it for each other.

Golden Nuggets
The kitchen table scene where Rose is declared a slut, and Blanche gets offended, is a standout.

Rose mentions meeting Charlie her senior year, but in another episode has said that she met him when she was seven years old.

There's a lot of slut-talk here: What constitutes a slut, Blanche being upset that's she not considered *the* slut, what constitutes a boyfriend, and whether you can have a lot of boyfriends without going all the way.

Rose wasn't allowed to date until her senior year. But boy did she make up for it.

Ken Berry co-starred with Betty White and Rue McClanahan on *Mama's Family*.

I've accepted worst dates than Marvin and his sister. When Sophia says, "It doesn't look like he'll kill me," I thought, I have the exact same vetting style.

7-15 "Goodbye, Mr. Gordon"

Written by: Gail Parent and Jim Vallely
Aired: January 11, 1992
Director: Lex Passaris
Guest Cast: Malcolm Gordon (James T. Callahan), Chuck (Jack Bannon), Ron (Phil Proctor), Pat (Jana Arnold), Kent (Kent Zbornak)
Summary: Dorothy's high school teacher returns and plagiarizes her work.
Rating: ❤❤❤

"When you're 17, a cow can seem dangerous and forbidden."—Rose

like that the final season of the show still had the women's characters evolving, while maintaining the histories we'd come to know so well. An ongoing issue we've been dealing with has been Dorothy's self-esteem, especially with men. Her high school teacher, Mr. Gordon, reconnects with her and sort-of pursues her romantically. But he also asks her to edit an article he's writing, so we get the sense he's using her. Sophia sees this unfolding and warns her, but Dorothy doesn't realize it until Mr. Gordon shows her the article and hasn't added her name. It's painstakingly obviously that he's duplicated her work and taken the credit. She drops him.

The more I think about Mr. Gordon, the more I wonder what a sad con this is, because he works in pretty quickly that he needs help on this assignment. Did he remember that Dorothy used to worship him and think, oh, can she help me? Did he travel all the way to Florida for this? Has he done this before? The whole thing is really sketchy.

The episode is fun though. There's a fantastic B story where Rose invites Blanche and Dorothy to be guests on the show where she's become an associate producer. She had pitched "women who live together" not realizing it would be a show about lesbians. In reality, she outs her friends who aren't gay, which would cause quite a stir back then. The women are furious, but it ends up fueling Blanche's potential sex life, because as Sophia said previously, "sluts just heal quicker." Apparently, women are calling her for dates, and men want to prove their manhood to her.

Golden Nuggets

Blanche and Dorothy fielding awkward questions on live TV is the centerpiece of this episode.

Blanche uses the fact that men think she's a lesbian to pick up men at the grocery store. What a lifehack.

Blanche's fling with her calculus professor got her a full scholarship at MIT.

James Callahan, playing Mr. Gordon, was eight years younger than Bea Arthur.

I'm truly tired of jokes where Sophia calls Dorothy ugly. I'm convinced this was part of the reason for Bea Arthur ending the show.

7-16 "The Commitments"

Written by: Tracy Gamble and Richard Vaczy
Aired: January 25, 1992
Director: Lex Passaris
Guest Cast: Jerry (Ken Howard), Don (Terry Kiser), Bellboy (Biff Yeager)
Summary: Blanche worries that she's losing her sex appeal.
Rating: ❤❤❤

"Sounds to me like you put out before dinner again."—Rose

This is where the Girls get to be silly, especially around men. Blanche becomes unnerved when Jerry—the guy she dates as a favor to Dorothy—won't put the moves on her. Meanwhile, Dorothy hops right into bed with a guy playing George in Beatlemania. I don't know why Sophia dislikes him so much. Dorothy has dated far worse, and I like this deranged musician's energy. She causes him to break off from the band, becoming the Yoko of Beatlemania. Then when she hears his horrible music, she bolts and deserts him. Not cool, Dorothy. If you're going to be Yoko, see it through!

Blanche's date attempts being a modern man at first, splitting the bill and not holding doors for her. She explains that she doesn't want to be treated equally—she wants to be treated better. Amen. But then Jerry dates her and doesn't touch her, which freaks her out and she takes him to a sleazy motel to seduce him. But that freaks *him* out. Turns out, Jerry's old-fashioned and believes in waiting, even for a first kiss. He kisses Blanche at the very end though, causing her to exclaim that she feels like a lady. Strange she never sees him again.

Golden Nuggets

Dorothy coming out singing, "She Loves You" with her fake Beatle is just the best.

Blanche telling Jerry he dodged a bullet right after that is kind-of accurate.

Dorothy acts sex-crazed, while Blanche waits the whole episode for a kiss. It's an interesting switch, and I'm not sure if it was intentional, but Dorothy even gets to say Blanche's line, "I'm stunned."

Yoko Zbornak is the best name for a groupie that I've ever heard.

A man refused to sleep with Rose the time she was radioactive.

In the third Warren Beatty joke of the series, Sophia claims Warren Beatty passed up the chance to sleep with her. I guess she's the one woman, huh? Warren, your loss. But my theory is that one of the writers slept with Warren Beatty because that's one too many jokes at his expense (this is also a joke).

7-17 "Questions and Answers"

Written by: Don Seigel and Jerry Perzigian
Aired: February 8, 1992
Director: Lex Passaris
Guest Cast: Alex Trebek (Himself), Johnny Gilbert (Himself), Merv Griffin (Himself), Charley Dietz (David Leisure), Coordinator (Derek McGrath), Mr. Hubbard (Bill Erwin), Mrs. Hubbard (Camila Ashland), Professor Bradley (Raymond Forchion)
Summary: Dorothy auditions for her favorite game show, *Jeopardy*, and dreams that she's a contestant.
Rating: ❤

"Isn't this dog amazing? He can find anything!"—Rose
"Anything? A viable Democrat for president, go!"—Sophia

This episode is a big yawn, full of a gimmicks and guest stars, and the theme I hate most—dissing Dorothy. She tries out for *Jeopardy*, passes the written test, and even though she's clearly smart enough, doesn't get chosen. Apparently, America wouldn't root for her due to Dorothy acting like an insufferable snob. This was an experience that had happened to one of the writers, Jerry Perzigian. I think it's mean-spirited. And before that, we get a ridiculous dream sequence where Dorothy plays against Rose, whose idiotic final answer wins. The other dream-contestant is Charley from *Empty Nest,* and there's an appearance from Merv Griffin.

The B story has Rose befriending a sweet, elderly couple at the hospital she does volunteer work, where they take a liking to Jake, the dog that Blanche and Dorothy gave her to cheer up. Rose keeps saying the dog reminds her of Rusty, a dog she once had, and the tale bores everyone to tears. Then it becomes not-so-pleasant when the wife of the elderly couple dies and Rose gives Jake to her husband.

Golden Nuggets

When Dorothy proves that she's memorized the St. Olaf yearbook in order to get through the *Jeopardy* trials, you know how serious she is.

No sex stories in this episode, which partially accounts for the low rating.

I like the story of Rusty the dachshund, who rescued Rose's pets from a burning house and went back to get the TV.

We learn from Sophia that Dorothy was a bragger in grade school. Perhaps Dorothy was overcompensating because her mother was so mean to her.

Alex Trebek's friendship with Betty White is what he believed got him the guest spot.

Dorothy says to Merv Griffin: "You are the most beloved man in American. You are bright, you are charming, you are the anti-Trump." It's almost like that's a fact.

7-18 "Ebbtide VI: The Wrath of Stan"

Written by: Marc Sotkin
Aired: February 15, 1992
Director: Lex Passaris
Guest Cast: Stan Zbornak (Herb Edelman), Angelo (Bill Dana), Peterson (Lane Davies), Tracy (Jackie Swanson), Judge (Art Metrano), Police Officer (David Doty), Court Reporter (Cynthia Lea Clark)
Summary: Dorothy and Stan are accused of being slumlords.
Rating: ❤❤❤

"Don't spend all your time in prison hating me, Dorothy. Learn a trade."—Rose

I like this episode, because of a certain amount of silliness that existed in the seventh season. You have to dismiss some of the ridiculousness, like Rose forgetting that Angelo's landlords are Stan and Dorothy, and that the city of Miami would be that concerned with roaches that they would arrest the landlords. Then you'd have to believe that the judge would punish them by making them stay overnight in one of the apartments. Oh, and Blanche is hooking up with some guy in a van outside. Oh, and Stan doesn't use his regular lawyer, because he likes a cute, blonde one he meets at a bar. So yeah, pretty stupid stuff all-in-all, but I enjoy episodes with Stan and Angelo, and the trial scene cracks me up.

The B story is about Dorothy taking Sophia shoe shopping, which evidently is an ordeal because Sophia drives the shoe salespeople crazy, disliking anything they bring her. The strong visual here is the gag that has since become a meme, where Sophia comes back with a balloon that Blanche pops, leaving her to ponder, "What's old age going to take from me next?"

Golden Nuggets

The trial scene with the prosecutor schmoozing the witnesses works well. First, flirting with Blanche, then telling Sophia she has a wild bod for a woman her age. That's the zinger.

Blanche planning a rendezvous in a laundry truck outside isn't the big surprise. It's that Stan is still so into Dorothy that he tries to get her into bed, while they're in their court-ordered room.

There was a similar plot on *Maude,* where Maude and Walter were accused of being slumlords because of an apartment building they purchased.

Sophia reveals her secret crush to be Luther Vandross.

Sophia helps Dorothy reframe her feelings for Stan by thinking of him as her old shoe. I think that's how the writers wanted to leave their relationship before the finale.

7-19 "Journey to the Center of Attention"

Written by: Jamie Wooten and Marc Cherry
Aired: February 22, 1992
Director: Lex Passaris
Guest Cast: Myrtle (Jane Dulo), Eva (Ann Nelson), Ron (Don Mirault), Frank (Warren Munson), Roger (Kevin Brief), Bartender (Gregory White)
Summary: Blanche becomes jealous when Dorothy becomes popular at The Rusty Anchor.
Rating: ❤❤❤

"Boy, when the mask falls off, it really makes a thud."—Rose

We've seen Dorothy sing throughout the show—she mentions a high-school performance of Oklahoma! in the Henny Penny episode where she sings as Turkey Lurkey. She does a great impersonation of Cher singing "I Got You Babe," and of course, the "Miami, You've Got Style" song. But in this episode, she takes it up a notch. However unrealistic it is on the show, Bea Arthur was a legit Broadway star, so she more-than pulls this off.

The episode opens with Dorothy planning to sit in front of the TV for the night and Blanche dragging her to the Rusty Anchor, where lo and behold, Dorothy becomes a sensation singing the classic, "What'll I Do." Blanche immediately becomes jealous as Dorothy keeps returning *and singing*, loving the male attention. Finally, Blanche resorts to dressing up and singing "I Wanna Be Loved by You" (made famous by Marilyn Monroe) and embarrassing herself. At the end, she confesses how envious she was of Dorothy, and they agree to go to The Rusty Anchor on different nights.

I enjoyed the B story where Sophia plans herself a funeral celebration—inspired by a rowdy Irish wake—so that her friends can celebrate her life. Except Rose forgets to tell her friends that she's not actually dead. Oops.

Golden Nuggets
Dorothy's performance of "What'll I Do" at The Rusty Anchor is touching.

We learn one secret to Blanche's success with men—she walks into bars announcing that she's not wearing a bra or underwear.

Not sure I believe that Sophia's close friends wouldn't have called to find out that Sophia wasn't actually dead.

This was Rue McClanahan's favorite episode.

Best silent performance of the series: The man at the Rusty Anchor who walks away from Dorothy.

Bea Arthur sang "Hard-Hearted Hannah" in Season Two of *Maude*.

It was satisfying to see Dorothy as charming and talented. It feels like the writers are trying to redeem themselves for insulting her, even though the slams against her, I'm sure, were fun to write. Even Sophia gets teary.

7-20 "A Midwinter Night's Dream" (Part 1)

Written by: Kevin Abbott
Aired: February 29, 1992
Director: Lex Passaris
Guest Cast: Miles Webber (Harold Gould), Brent (Hank Brandt), Derek (Marius Weyers), Rabbi (Neal Lerner), Carol Weston (Dinah Manoff), Policeman (Doug Ballard), Tony Segreto (Himself), Barbara Weston (Kristy McNichol), Dreyfuss (Bear the Dog)
Summary: Blanche hosts a full-moon party where hijinks ensues and Sophia tries to reverse a curse put on Dorothy decades ago by a Sicilian witch.
Rating: ❤❤❤❤

"You know what kills me? The year you locked me up in Shady Pines, she roamed around free."—Sophia

There sure aren't a lot of unpredictable episodes of *The Golden Girls*. Sure, there are a lot of surprise scenes and endings, but this two-parter is just a delight that it goes in all kinds of unexpected directions. All the characters are comfortable at a certain level of unpredictability: Sophia's obsessively superstitious *and* would totally trip a rabbi to reverse a spell; Blanche would totally lose her mind, falling for a clearly-sketchy foreigner; Rose would totally consider marrying Miles for a free trip; and Dorothy would totally kiss Miles in a frenzied state of "full-moon madness."

But all that quickly unfolds. Blanche plans a party that's on both a full moon and during a leap year, and invites only men, which, I gotta give it to this woman, she is not subtle. Sophia immediately recalls a curse put on Dorothy by a village witch in Sicily, Lena Pascarelli. Dorothy gave her the cold that eventually killed her, which, not to be in such a Covid-mindset, but just thinking out loud... are we allowed to put Sicilian curses on people who give us Covid?

There are three tasks Sophia must complete to reverse the curse: kiss a fool, help a holy man and reveal the betrayal of a loved one. Meanwhile, Rose wins a free honeymoon and convinces Miles to marry her just to collect it. Then Blanche notices how the men seem to be acting, ignoring her, and aggressively hitting on all the women including Sophia. Carol, their neighbor, comes over to get in on the fun, but leaves because she doesn't enjoy the male attention. Blanche then runs into a British man, Derek, who seems into her and none of the other ladies. The episode ends with Miles and Dorothy in a moment of sheer insanity, kissing on the lanai, and being spotted by Sophia, who mutters, "Hello Judas."

Golden Nuggets

I like Sophia's first two solutions to reverse the curse.

Blanche's necklace has jumpstarted many passionate affairs, but this is the first time she wears it with clothes (maybe that's why she doesn't get lucky).

Newsflash for Dorothy, those Sicilian witches can fly.

A Midsummer Night's Dream is a Shakespearean play consisting of several subplots including a wedding, and the guests, who are manipulated by fairies, causing them to act foolishly.

7-21 "A Midwinter Night's Dream" (Part 2)

Written by: Tom Whedon
Aired: February 29, 1992
Director: Lex Passaris
Guest Cast: Miles Webber (Harold Gould), Brent (Hank Brandt), Derek (Marius Weyers), Rabbi (Neal Lerner), Carol Weston (Dinah Manoff), Policeman (Doug Ballardd), Tony Segreto (Himself), Barbara Weston (Kristy McNichol), Dreyfuss (Bear the Dog)
Summary: Blanche's full-moon party continues, as Dorothy endures the guilt over kissing Miles, and Blanche realizes Derek is a con man who stole her necklace.
Rating: 

"Get a clue, Dorothy. Men would rather pay for cupcakes."—Rose

What works about Part 2 is that it wraps up all the conflict, but adds new, even sillier stuff: Sophia plays off her neighbors' sisterly hatred for each other; Miles and Dorothy fight about their kiss, and Rose makes them reconcile, much to Sophia's dismay; and Blanche gets conned by, but makes up with, a jewel thief, who Rose also makes out with! Dorothy ends it by saying it really was like Shakespeare, with magic and moonlight, and the wrong people falling in love, quoting Puck in *A Midsummer's Night's Dream*:

"If we shadows have offended, / Think but this, and all is mended, / That you have but slumber'd here / While these visions did appear. / And this weak and idle theme, / No more yielding but a dream..."

Golden Nuggets

Rose never quite understands Dorothy's "cupcake" metaphor, but it still gets her angry enough to break the mug.

Blanche has a list of things she won't do with guys she doesn't trust—admittedly, it's a short list.

Rose is the only character that never quite gets to have a wedding during the series (even though Blanche's engagement from the Pilot ends with the groom not showing up). This pseudo-engagement to Miles is the closest she gets.

The women lose a lot of jewelry during this series. Maybe it's because Blanche tells thieves that she has a safe.

At first, I thought, is this the only *Golden Girls* episode where all four women get kissed (Sophia kisses the fool after all)? And then I realized, it's even weirder. You never see Blanche kiss Derek, though you can safely assume there had been kissing in the four hours they spent together. But the proclamation still stands: This is the only episode that represents a night that all the women get kissed.

7-22 "Rose: Portrait of a Woman"

Written by: Robert Spina
Aired: March 7, 1992
Director: Lex Passaris
Guest Cast: Miles Webber (Harold Gould), Randy (Tom Villard), Mr. Tanaka (Keone Young), Harry (Angelo Tiffe), Lillian (Gloria Dorson), Charles (Glen Vernon), Student (Dylan Lawrence), Don (Robert Yacko), Teacher (Carol Spillman)
Summary: Blanche convinces Rose to give Miles a naughty picture of herself for Miles' birthday.
Rating: ♥♥

"Be proud. You're a Petrillo. Which in Italian means, 'Hey, I'm on a break here.'" —Sophia

This episode will remind you of simpler times, when sending sexy pictures was a much bigger deal. Now it's done before the first date! But alas, this is a big deal for Rose. Blanche spots Rose wrapping a golf club for Miles's birthday and persuades her to go get a "boudoir photo." But when he gets ready to unwrap it, his friends show up. Rose leaves mortified, prompting Miles to come and apologize, comparing Betty White's legs to Betty Grable's, and all is forgiven.

I don't love the other half of the episode. Dorothy goes to career day and gets offered an easy, high-paying job from a former student, watching over corporate management-types while they're on retreats. She doesn't find it fulfilling and quits after a few days. This is a whole lot of BS. Someone Dorothy's age would want to pocket some of that salary before going back to teaching. It also aggravates me that the writers never had Dorothy get whatever degree she would need to become a full-time teacher. That would've been nice.

Golden Nuggets

There's a scene that rolls during the credits of Sophia doing boudoir photos that is absolutely priceless.

The flannel nightgown that gets Miles hot is quite the sight. Also, the story of them reenacting Godzilla just demonstrates that Rose is not Blanche.

Gunter Hanchop, St. Olaf's leading shepherd and notary, spoke of his solitary existence with the sheep. Rose gave him scotch and made him realize how mean sheep are when they're drunk. But not like cows.

Dorothy was nicknamed Attila the Sub when she was a substitute teacher in Brooklyn.

It occurred to me that all the executives in Dorothy's class are men, because in 1992, there weren't a lot of women in top-management positions.

The writers really loved the "Joe Mama" jokes and I think they're terrible—honestly, a big part of why I gave this episode two hearts.

7-23 "Home Again, Rose" (Part 1)

Written by: Gail Parent
Aired: April 25, 1992
Director: Peter D. Beyt
Guest Cast: Janet (Jessica Lundy), Larry (Lou Wagner), Pete (Rudolph Willrich), Man (Paul Solomon), Man #1 (Mario Roccuzzo), Man #2 (Kevin Cooney), Man #3 (David Cromwell), Sarah (Robin Faye Bookland), Dr. Thompson (Linden Chiles), Nurse (Audree Chapman)
Summary: The Girls crash a high school reunion, where Rose has a heart attack.
Rating: ❤❤❤

"I lost my first husband in a tar pit."—Dorothy

Blanche comes up with a scheme to crash a high school reunion, because Rose wasn't feeling well and missed hers. The Girls arrive and steal IDs off the table. Blanche gets Susan Armstrong, a popular, but hated girl; Rose picks Kim Fung Toy, a Korean foreign-exchange student; Sophia picks Mrs. Gonzalez, a Spanish teacher; and Dorothy picks Cindy Lou Peeples, a well-liked student. The Girls start to leave as they announce that Dorothy—as Cindy Lou Peeples—is Prom Queen, but they all get busted. Just then Rose, who's been complaining about not feeling well the whole time, collapses of a heart attack.

When they get to the hospital, Blanche makes a pact with God that if Rose recovers, she'll stop having sex. And she's not kidding. She immediately turns down a pass from the doctor! When they visit Rose, they start talking about making life changes. Sophia might study to become a lawyer, Dorothy wants to go out more, and Rose is thinking of having her head frozen, and wants the Girls to have their heads frozen too.

Blanche's daughter Janet, the one that hates her, comes to visit. Blanche reveals to her that she has found religion, to which even her granddaughter says, "I miss sexy grandma." The Girls show up at the hospital and are told that Rose went into cardiac arrest.

Golden Nuggets

I like the different personas the Girls take on at the reunion.

Rose says that in St. Olaf they don't believe in psychiatrists, but we know they had at least two famous psychotherapists: The Freud Brothers, Sigmund and Roy.

Blanche's sex life is so notorious that even her daughter thinks her good mood is due to a visit from "Uncle Whoever."

Rose's great-grandfather once removed his neighbor's appendix when poker stakes got too high.

I love when Sophia says she wants to go to law school and Dorothy says, "You'll be 96 when you get out," to which she responds, "I'll be 96 anyway." What a refreshing outlook. It reminds me of how Kim Kardashian passed the baby bar exam, even when people were giving her flack for it. Always channel your inner Kardashian or your inner Sophia.

7-24 "Home Again, Rose" (Part 2)

Written by: Jim Vallely
Aired: May 2, 1992
Director: Peter D. Beyt
Guest Cast: Kirsten (Lee Garlington), Janet (Jessica Lundy), Dr. Shrewsbury (Paul Collins), Sarah (Robin Faye Bookland), Nurse (Audree Chapman)
Summary: As Rose prepares for surgery, she makes the Girls promise to freeze their heads after they die.
Rating: ❤❤❤

"My hiney's asleep."—Sophia
"Fine, we'll keep our voices down."—Dorothy

A big part of the series is how the Girls are family. But in the hospital, as Rose goes through surgery, they keep trying to see her and are told that only family can go in. I think this was especially relevant to the gay fanbase, who at the time were not allowed inside the hospital rooms of their partners. So, the episode acts as an allegory for the stupidity of rigidly defining a family on any specific terms. If there's someone outside a hospital room that wants to comfort their friend, lover or partner, who is anyone to stop them?

The famous visual gag of the episode is Rose's hospital dream, with Blanche, Rose and Dorothy waking up as just heads because of Rose's pre-surgery wish. In the dream, they discuss how they died and Sophia walks in with a full body, quipping that she tipped the guy and was paired with a young body.

Apparently, even Rose's daughter Kirsten at first dismisses the Girls' relationship, until they tell her that if Rose needs physical therapy, then they'll all pitch in and help her, because that's what family does. In that moment, Kirsten realizes the depth of their friendship and allows them into Rose's hospital room.

Golden Nuggets

The women in the hospital singing the Rheingold beer commercial.

Even in Rose's death dream, Blanche manages to get lucky, as her final words are in a bathtub saying, "Thank you baby, glub, glub, glub."

Dorothy's summary of St. Olaffians. They fight over whether it's macaroni and cheese, or cheese and macaroni; they gave cows the right to vote; and they once burned a magician at the stake for pulling a rabbit out of a hat.

Bea Arthur was claustrophobic, so they had to be creative with the frozen head scene, putting all the actresses in office chairs and wheeling them to the table.

If there's any lasting definition of family, it's the person who'll take out a mortgage to take care of you when you're sick.

7-25 "One Flew Out of the Cuckoo's Nest" (Part 1)

Written by: Don Seigel and Jerry Perzigian
Aired: May 9, 1992
Director: Lex Passaris
Guest Cast: Lucas (Leslie Nielsen), Stan Zbornak (Herb Edelman), Reverend (Earl Boen)
Summary: Blanche fixes up her Uncle Lucas with Dorothy to keep him busy while she's on a date; but it all backfires when they end up falling in love.
Rating: ❤❤❤

"I'll scare us up a mess a something"—Sophia

I definitely like the finale, but it's not my absolute favorite episode. But IMDb gives this episode the highest ranking out of all the episodes, so that's worth noting. I do love that Dorothy, after all the insults about her love life, gets a good, handsome guy like Lucas. And I just pretend that the spinoff, *The Golden Palace,* never happened and they all just stayed in that house with Dorothy visiting frequently.

Blanche cons Dorothy into keeping her uncle company because she wants to hang out with a guy that she met in the produce section. She tells him that he wants to talk to her about being a teacher. At first, they seem bored with each other, but when they figure out that they were tricked by Blanche, they decide to pull a prank and act like they have fallen head-over-heels in love. And so, Lucas proposes to drive Blanche even crazier. But alas, joke's on them—they really do like each other. So, the episode ends with a real proposal.

Golden Nuggets

Blanche's father supposedly sold Hollingsworth Manor in an earlier season when he wanted to be a country singer.

Dorothy spills the beans way too quickly to Lucas that Blanche is probably shacked up in a motel. I'd like to think Blanche would be at a hotel.

Mr. Snuffles, Rose's piglet, alienated by the other pigs, runs away to Chicago and surrenders herself to the Oscar Mayer people.

The idea for Lucas and Dorothy to pretend they're getting married came from Paul Witt and Susan Harris, who did something similar to Tony Thomas during the *Soap* days. They had flown to Italy and pretended to be engaged and Tony, instead of surprised, basically told them that clearly they were into each other and everyone working on the show knew they liked each other. Shortly after, they got together and got married.

7-26 "One Flew Out of the Cuckoo's Nest" (Part 2)

Written by: Mitchell Hurwitz
Aired: May 9, 1992
Director: Lex Passaris
Guest Cast: Lucas (Leslie Nielsen), Stan Zbornak (Herb Edelman), Reverend (Earl Boen)
Summary: The Girls prepare for Dorothy's wedding to Lucas.
Rating: ❤❤❤

"You're a furry little gnome and we feed you too much."—Dorothy

The wedding plans continue and what works well in this episode is that they don't change too many fundamental things. Although Dorothy gets married and moves away, the other three decide to stay together, which was the right choice (again, ignore the spinoff). I hate when shows have finales where the characters have to move out of the country, or sell the house, or change everything about what you like. I prefer them to stay frozen in time.

Although Rose had considered living with her daughter, and Sophia was pondering living with Lucas and Dorothy, they both decide against it. Good choice. Then, on the way to the wedding, Stan kidnaps Dorothy in a limo. But in a nice way. He's hurt that she didn't invite him to the wedding. He says he's not actually kidnapping her, but bringing her to the church in style, as a gift. Then he compares himself to the lone hair on his head, saying she's the big, crazy bald skull. That's the least romantic metaphor I've ever heard, and yet, it works for the Zbornaks. Dorothy explains that things were going so well with Lucas that she didn't want to deal with him. They tell each other "I love you" and she pulls the lone hair out of his head. I love how the writers resolved Stan and Dorothy.

The wedding ceremony is funny, yet charming and beautiful. We hear the characters' inner monologues as Dorothy walks down the aisle, and each inner thought is funnier than the last. Blanche's thoughts are kind of pervy, Rose is singing "The Farmer in the Dell," and Lucas and Dorothy are communicating telepathically. And Sophia thinks she's about to sneeze, but it turns out she's crying. That's a sweet little nugget. Stan hesitates when they ask if anyone has cause for objection, and Herb Edelman does some really good acting with just one expression of regret. All-in-all, a perfect wedding scene.

The scenes at the house get super-schmaltzy. Sophia tells Dorothy that she's going to stay with the Girls and goes on about how it's been her great privilege being her friend. But it turns into a laugh when she *almost* gives Dorothy cash. When the four women finally have to say goodbye, it's clear that the actresses are coming from a real place. This has been confirmed by the actresses and everyone that worked on this episode. Though Bea had been the one to decide to end it, she was teary and full of sadness.

I guess why I don't love it enough to give it four hearts is that in reality, Dorothy is just moving, but the Girls are crying as if she's leaving them for good. And Dorothy's speech is what you'd say to a group of friends that you're not going to see that often. But this is her mother living in that house, and she's moving to Georgia to live with Blanche's uncle. They should see each other quite frequently! So, although the emotions are real for the actresses ending a wonderful show, it does ring a little bit false to me. When it does get me emotional, it's because I know these characters are running off to do that horrific spinoff and I'm thinking, "Just stay in Blanche's house!" And of course, now I get emotional because the actresses are gone.

Golden Nuggets

I love the wedding scene and I normally hate sitcom wedding scenes. The inner monologues are the best.

The sex between Dorothy and Lucas is so good that they named it!

Dorothy's the first main character to appear in the pilot and is the first main character to leave in the finale.

Bea Arthur hated the wedding dress! I concur. What was that costume designer thinking? And yet, Rose and Blanche's dresses are lovely and Sophia in that little pink number is just plain adorable.

Soft criticism, but where are all the Petrillo and Zbornak relatives? No Angelo? Boo.

During the final scene, when Dorothy exits a second and final time, with the Girls looking around for Dorothy to see if she'd come back, the emotions were so high that the embrace between Estelle, Betty and Rue was real.

I know a big point of the show was that the Girls could find happiness without settling down with a man, but it's also nice to show the audience that one of them can end up in a romantic, respectful relationship. Lucas seems to get Dorothy and I only wish that we had a few more episodes of his character.

If You Only Watch One Episode

"I'm a very lucky woman. Not only do I have a lot of friends in the community, but I have a lot of good friends at home. Friends who care about me and care about each other. I count my blessings every day because I have the kind of friends who stand by you through the bad and the good. When you're lucky enough to find that kind of friendship, I guess you just wanna pass it on."—Sophia

When you're a superfan of a television show, advising someone on the best episode is always a challenge. It's a loaded question for sure. And it comes with the bias of who my favorite character is (Sophia). But obviously I have one in mind that works for the superfan and the new viewer—Flu Attack (Season 1, Episode 21). It's the one where Blanche, Dorothy and Rose all come down with the flu right before attending a charity dinner. For me, it's a perfect episode that showcases all four women exhibiting their quintessential qualities.

At first the Girls are discussing the charity dinner and Sophia pins a dress on Dorothy, who slouches to hide her height, just as she did when she was a little girl. Then Blanche laments over how she's sorting through so many dating options. But then Rose enters and reveals she's not feeling well and is seeking aspirin, leading to Dorothy's inquiries as to what kind of aspirin she needs which still makes me laugh. And I have seen this episode *a lot*. But we all have that hypochondriac friend who has six types of every medication, and we also know people who barely take anything when they're sick, like they're almost feral. Either way, the next scene reveals that Rose infected Blanche and Dorothy, and we get another trademark of a great *Golden Girls* episode—a visual of the three women in a row, in coordinated outfits (this time, their sick robes—blue, yellow, and pink).

When you pick the episode apart, it has all the components that I look for. That first component is that the A and B stories, like in all the best episodes, combine at the end in a clever way. In "Flu Attack", the Girls being sick is entertaining enough, but the question of who's going to be awarded the " Best Friend of the Friends of Good Health Award" leaves us wondering who will get it. It doesn't occur to the three of them, or to us, that it could be Sophia. So, when she wins, it's delightful. Her speech at the end is an example of why Estelle Getty was such a fresh discovery to audiences when the show started. Like, where the heck was this actress all these years?

Another component of this fantastic episode is the Girls arguing with each other, and not just about one thing. They're at each other's throats about being sick, each thinking they deserve an award, and they throw plenty of insults at each other. Usually, sitcoms take a little longer to pull off such animosity between their leads, but *The Golden Girls'* writers had developed each and every character's ability to cut the other ones down so well that their disses are so well earned. Some of the acts of cruelty are silent—as when Dorothy drinks all of the orange juice after Rose asks if there's any left—but Rose has some good digs at Dorothy, like when she says her nose looks like a banana.

Other trademarks of a perfect episode are a "Picture it, Sicily" story from Sophia, a "Back in St. Olaf" from Rose, and sexual innuendo from Blanche. We get the ear-salve-turned-to-pesto tale from Sophia, and though Rose's story gets cut off about her cousin getting his sideburns caught in a hay baler, we do find out her mother used to make her gingerbread cookies when they were sick. But the moment that really shines is when Blanche questions Dorothy about whether she stole the heating pad, and if not, "what other electrical appliance" is she using under that blanket.

Blanche's vanity emerges quite a few times as she glances in a mirror, remarking that even while sick, she does remain devastatingly attractive. Dorothy reaches levels of uber-grouchiness as she cannot tolerate Blanche wanting to watch her soap opera. And neither of them can handle Rose's cheery disposition that includes wanting to play games. Through all of this, Sophia's trying to get a date for the event like a teenager, and when she finally gets one, the others slam the door in her face. The Girls fight, they compete over who's going to win an award, and then in the surprise twist of Sophia winning, they come together in an authentic moment of friendship.

But it's the overarching theme of this episode that I love the most, that the Girls are more than just active members of society, but are in the prime of their life. This is obvious when they learn one of them is winning the "Best Friend of the Friends of Good Health Award" and can't decide who'll get it, because they all do so much charity work. And they're not just competitive about the award, they're competitive about their dates. Even Sophia shows off her young date to all the women in the audience, 75 and older.

But it's Sophia's winning speech that takes the cake as it's on-point, touching, and adorable without being overly sentimental or lame. It really gives the episode the moment of tenderness and heart it needed on top of all the laughs. They're family and lucky to have found each other. Like I've said before, this show was a bit of a squad goal.

After You Watch

After you've gone through 180 episodes of *The Golden Girls*, I hope you love it as much as I did. I hope you see why it's viewed as timeless, and why it won so many awards, and received so many accolades. For the fans that re-watched, I hope that like me, you've gained even more of an appreciation of the show. I find that the acting is still strong, the jokes still land, and most of the plotlines are relevant. Yes, if this show was redone (and I'm not sure I would want that), watching the Blanche character navigate dating apps in her 50s would be a hoot and I imagine that Dorothy would have to deal with anti-vaxxers and Flat Earthers in the Miami school system. Rose inevitably would be caught up in a number of internet scams and Sophia would probably be living an almost-identical life, except I'm sure she'd have a TikTok advice channel that would provide her with a sizable side income.

The show will forever be a comfort-food show—it packs some emotional punches, but the show aired before main characters died for ratings or award-nomination grabs. There's no episode of *The Golden Girls* that's traumatizing or scandalous. In fact, you can keep it on while the kids are around and most of the racier jokes will escape them. They sure as hell escaped me until I was about 35. It will also prepare you for telling off almost anybody, including your friends, family, bad dates, jerks dating your children, doctors, teachers, in-laws, ex-husbands, and even neighbors.

The dreaded *Golden Palace*

You can, I guess, watch *The Golden Girls'* spinoff, *The Golden Palace,* that ran for one season and 24 episodes, from September 1992 to May 1993. I watched a few episodes and there was just none of the magic. Everything seemed dialed down without Bea Arthur, especially since a lot of the jokes came from her, or were directed at her, and her perspective on things was so integral to the show. The premise of the spinoff is that the women invest in a hotel and run it, with the help of the hotel manager, played by Don Cheadle, and the chef, played by Cheech Marin. So already it had a gimmicky vibe. But in reading the plots of the episodes, they all seem like rehashes of earlier *Golden Girls* episodes, or desperate "this only happens on a sitcom" storylines. They did seem to get some notable guest stars, like George Burns, which I'm sure had to do with Betty White and her Hollywood connections. Estelle Getty's character turns up on *Empty Nest* back in Shady Pines retirement home, but there is no mention why she's there without the Girls or Dorothy. Whoever conceived of that disaster should be flogged.

Some of the plotlines included Miles getting remarried (no thanks), and Stan dying, but it turns out, he's really alive and hiding from tax evasion (a double no thanks). Even on the Wikipedia page, they say that a lot of the Girls' defining traits were dialed down: Blanche wasn't as sexual, Rose wasn't as dim, and Sophia wasn't as snarky (triple no thanks).

You can...

Catch the women on other old sitcoms like Bea Arthur on *Maude*, and Betty White on *The Mary Tyler Moore Show* (and a number of television shows), and Rue McClanahan on *Mama's Family* (and also on a number of television shows). But I'd argue for at least three out of four of them, *The Golden Girls* was their best work. Okay, maybe all four, but I don't want to offend someone who prefers them starring in something else.

For the superfan who wants more...

The podcasts:
http://www.outonthelanai.com
Hosts H. Alan Scott and Kerri Doherty know their stuff. They go deep, going over 30 minutes per episode, and know not just the background of the actresses, but every detail about what went into each episode. This is again, for the superfan, the super-obsessed. You know who you are.

https://podcasts.apple.com/us/podcast/dr-cheesecake/id989061459

Host Danielle Soto uses *Golden Girls* episodes to solve life's problems, which true confession: I have done. Her social media pages on Facebook, Instagram, and Twitter are fantastic fan pages.

Websites for reference:

https://www.imdb.com/title/tt0088526/?ref_=nv_sr_srsg_0

Go to IMDB for confirmation on guest stars, air dates, and other technical information of course. But it also has pieces of trivia per episode, as well as more detailed goofs that usually involve staging mistakes like wardrobe mishaps, or a part of the set that appears and disappears. You can also search the entire careers of each actress here, as well as each guest star. IMDB is the go-to for the TV-obsessed, and the superfan.

https://www.imdb.com/title/tt0088526/?ref_=nv_sr_srsg_0

https://www.imdb.com/search/title/?series=tt0088526&view=simple&count=250&sort=user_rating,desc&ref_=tt_eps_rhs_sm (The episodes ranked by IMDB voters)

https://www.buzzfeed.com/nelsonr5/the-golden-girls-the-definitive-ranking-of-every-9q8y

Websites to fan out with:

If you thought journalism was dead, look no further than Refinery 29's deep dive into the # of lovers each of the Golden Girls had. I didn't have time to fact-check this, but let's just say, it looks like well-done research. Bless these people for creating some real news.

https://www.refinery29.com/en-us/2015/08/93152/golden-girls-how-many-dates

You can't watch the show without wanting a town history of St. Olaf. This has a pretty solid list of things like the cuisine, the language, and the strange holidays and inhabitants of everybody's favorite strange, idiotic, and often twisted small town.

https://goldengirls.fandom.com/wiki/St._Olaf

Visit YouTube.com for video compilations of the Girls like:

All of Sophia's Sicily stories:
https://www.youtube.com/watch?v=1KB9PCevkLU
Top 10 Musical Moments:
https://www.youtube.com/watch?v=KkQqvMAd3L4
Blanche's sexiest moments:
https://www.youtube.com/watch?v=efrpPRxvk4Q
Dorothy's savage moments:
https://www.youtube.com/watch?v=Ms1uYc28pD4
Rose telling every St. Olaf story:
https://www.youtube.com/watch?v=Q1Z3E4d02xk&t=136s
The Wiki Fan site
https://goldengirls.fandom.com/wiki/The_Golden_Girls_Wiki

The books:

*Golden Girls Forev*er by Jim Colucci (an unauthorized look behind the lanai)
If I Knew Then, What I Know Now... So What? by Estelle Getty and Steve Delsohn
My First Five Husbands... and the Ones Who Got Away by Rue McClanahan
If You Ask Me and of Course You Won't by Betty White
Betty & Friends: My Life at the Zoo by Betty White
Here We Go Again: My Life in Television by Betty White
Betty White in Person by Betty White (written in 1987, during the second season of *The Golden Girls)*

My favorite episodes by Season (rated with four hearts):

Season One:
Rose the Prude, episode 3
The Competition, episode 7
Heart Attack, episode 10
That Was No Lady, episode 14
In a Bed of Roses, episode 15
Flu Attack, episode 21

Season Two:
Ladies of the Evening, episode 2

Take Him, He's Mine, episode 3
It's a Miserable Life, episode 4
Twas the Nightmare Before Christmas, episode 11
The Sisters, episode 12
The Actor, episode 14
Diamond in the Rough, episode 22

Season Three:
Old Friends, episode 1
The Housekeeper, episode 4
Nothing to Fear but Fear Itself, episode 5
The Artist, episode 13
Dorothy's New Friend, episode 15
My Brother, My Father, episode 17
Larceny and Old Lace, episode 21
Mixed Blessings, episode 23

Season Four:
Yes, We Have No Havanas, episode 1
The Days and Nights of Sophia Petrillo, episode 2
The One That Got Away, episode 3
Sophia's Wedding, episodes 6 & 7
The Auction, episode 11
You Gotta Have Hope, episode 17
Till Death Do Us Valley, episode 19
Foreign Exchange, episode 24

Season Five:
Sick & Tired, episodes 1 & 2
Not Another Monday, episode 7
The Mangiacavallo Curse Makes a Lousy Wedding Present, episode 23

Season Six:
Once, in St. Olaf, episode 2
How Do You Solve a Problem Like Sophia, episode 8
Girls Just Wanna Have Fun... Before They Die, episode 10
Melodrama, episode 19
Witness, episode 21
Henny Penny... Straight, No Chaser, episode 26

Season Seven:

The Case of the Libertine Belle, episode 2
Mother Load, episode 6
The Monkey Show, episodes 8 & 9
Old Boyfriends, episode 14
A Midwinter's Night's Dream, episodes 20 & 21

*You should note that these are my personal preferences, and a lot of fan favorites might be missing from this list.

About the Author

Marissa DeAngelis holds a BA in journalism from the University of Maryland with a minor in film and comparative literature. She lived and worked in New York City as a copywriter for over a decade and moved to Los Angeles in 2020 to continue her writing pursuits. While living in New York, she performed standup comedy and would like to get back on stage in Los Angeles. She considers herself a cinephile and would love to write a novel about old Hollywood one day. If she were a Golden Girl, she would be Sophia.

Other Riverdale Avenue Books Binge Watcher's Guides You Might Like

The Binge Watcher's Guide to Doctor Who:
A History of the Doctor Who and the First Female Doctor
By Mackenzie Flohr

The Binge Watcher's Guide to the Films of Harry Potter
An Unauthorized Guide
By Cecilia Tan

The Binge Watcher's Guide to The Handmaid's Tale
An Unofficial Companion
By Jamie K. Schmidt

The Binge Watcher's Guide to Black Mirror:
An Unofficial Companion
By Marc W. Polite

The Binge Watcher's Guide to The Twilight Zone:
An Unofficial Journey
By Jason Trussell

The Binge Watcher's Guide to Riverdale
By Melissa Ford Luken

The Binge Watcher's Guide to Supernatural:
An Unofficial Companion
By Jessica Mason

www.ingramcontent.com/pod-product-compliance
Lightning Source LLC
LaVergne TN
LVHW010555100826
845148LV00014B/2725

9781626016156